IN THE SHADOW OF THE GENERALS

For Deirdre

In the Shadow of the Generals
Foreign Policy Making in Argentina, Brazil and Chile

MARTIN MULLINS
University of Limerick, Ireland

LONDON AND NEW YORK

First published 2006 by Ashgate Publishing

Reissued 2018 by Routledge
2 Park Square, Milton Park, Abingdon, Oxon, OX14 4RN
605 Third Avenue, New York, NY 10017

First issued in paperback 2021

Routledge is an imprint of the Taylor & Francis Group, an informa business

© Martin Mullins 2006

Martin Mullins has asserted his moral right under the Copyright, Designs and Patents Act, 1988, to be identified as the author of this work.

All rights reserved. No part of this book may be reprinted or reproduced or utilised in any form or by any electronic, mechanical, or other means, now known or hereafter invented, including photocopying and recording, or in any information storage or retrieval system, without permission in writing from the publishers.

A Library of Congress record exists under LC control number: 2006929152

Notice:
Product or corporate names may be trademarks or registered trademarks, and are used only for identification and explanation without intent to infringe.

Publisher's Note
The publisher has gone to great lengths to ensure the quality of this reprint but points out that some imperfections in the original copies may be apparent.

Disclaimer
The publisher has made every effort to trace copyright holders and welcomes correspondence from those they have been unable to contact.

ISBN 13: 978-1-138-35609-2 (pbk)
ISBN 13: 978-0-815-38968-2 (hbk)
ISBN 13: 978-1-351-15580-9 (ebk)

DOI: 10.4324/9781351155809

Contents

List of Maps		*vi*
Preface		*vii*
1	Introduction	1
2	Theoretical Considerations: The Need for Inclusive Approaches	19
3	Argentine Foreign Policy	47
4	Brazilian Foreign Policy	73
5	Chilean Foreign Policy	101
6	Conclusions	127
Bibliography		*135*
Index		*163*

List of Maps

Map of South America   viii
Map of Argentina   46
Map of Brazil   72
Map of Chile   100

Preface

This is a propitious time for a study of the foreign relations of the Southern Cone. States across South America are becoming increasingly strident in their dealings with the United States and the wider world. Changes in the global political economy have afforded Argentina, Brazil and Chile more autonomy and as a consequence hemispheric relations are now in a time of flux. The political presence of Hugo Chavez, the impending Venezuelan entry into Mercosur and the election of Evo Morales in Bolivia are liable to complicate matters further. Power relations around the world are changing and Brazil is now an important player in global diplomacy. The existence of Mercosur lends weight to Brazil in trade talks and increases the profile of Argentina. The two countries have put aside their historic rivalry and have built a strong relationship, particularly in the area of external relations. This book examines the prospects for a hemispheric free trade agreement and the probable future course of the Mercosur project.

This work also addresses theoretical concerns in the discipline of International Relations. The task of explaining foreign policy formation in the Southern Cone calls for an inclusive methodology. The region's history, relations between civilian powers and the military and the imperative of development are all important drivers of foreign policy in the Southern Cone. Interpretive techniques are required to gain an understanding of both the continuities and discontinuities in the area of foreign policy. The case of Argentina, in particular, demonstrates the limits of those approaches that focus exclusively on the relative power and capabilities of nation states. The aim of this work is to bring local circumstances into view and demonstrate the salience of national political cultures to the discipline of international relations.

Map of South America

Chapter 1

Introduction

The subject of this book is the foreign policies of Brazil, Argentina and Chile. The relative importance of the various drivers of foreign policy formation in the three countries will be considered. This work addresses the historical evolution of foreign policy in the Southern Cone and examines the impact of the dictatorships of the 1980s on this area of policy. The impact of identity politics and evolving historical narrative constitutes an important element of this study. The aim is to provide the reader with an understanding of the political and cultural factors that have shaped foreign policy formation in Brasilia, Buenos Aires and Santiago.

For over a century these three countries have jockeyed for position in the Southern Cone of Latin America. The relative power and influence of the three ABC countries (Argentina, Brazil and Chile) has changed dramatically over time and today it is Brazil that represents the dominant force. This, in itself, has profound implications for international relations in the region as Brazil seeks to assert itself across the wider continent and project its influence globally. The study of foreign policy in the Southern Cone is of interest in and of itself, however, it also serves to illuminate many of the key issues facing global polity today. Firstly, relations with the hemisphere's hegemonic power, the United States, have long been a central concern of policy planners in the region, as has the related matter of US interventionism. Secondly, the study also illustrates the political dynamics of an emerging regional trade bloc, namely Mercosur. The key question facing the nations of the Southern Cone is whether the Mercosur agreement will be superseded and absorbed by a wider regional arrangement.[1] Thirdly, the book examines the implications of the emergence of a nascent regional power, in this case Brazil. Fourthly, this work examines the dynamics of international relations at the periphery of world system.

A key unit of analysis in this work will be Mercosur. Established in 1991, it is the most important economic grouping in Latin America. The organization is made up of Argentina, Brazil, Paraguay and Uruguay. In 1996, Chile was granted associate status, this allowed Santiago to pursue bilateral trade negotiations with third parties whilst maintaining a formal link with the regional trade bloc.[2] Throughout much of the 1990s, Mercosur demonstrated itself to be a dynamic trading area with intra-regional rising from just 9% of total trade in 1990 to 25% in 1998. During the late

---

1   Mario E. Carranza, 'Can Mercosur Survive? Domestic and International Constraints on Mercosur', *Latin American Politics & Society* 45:3 (2003): 67–103.

2   Bolivia, Colombia, Ecuador, Peru and Venezuela are also associate members of Mercosur.

1990s, the grouping experienced a series of crises as relations cooled between the two principals, Argentina and Brazil. However, post 2000, the prognosis for the pact is more positive. Mercosur is no longer faced with a sceptical Argentine government, which under ex-president Menem in the 1990s, had favoured good relations with the United States over those with its Mercosur partners. For Brazil, the Mercosur project lies at the heart of its foreign policy. The trade bloc represents both a method of projecting itself more effectively in the wider world and of resisting US domination in the Southern Cone of Latin America. The smaller countries of the region are facing a dilemma as to whether or not to fall in behind Brazil and Argentina in creating a viable alternative to a hemispheric free-trade area led by the United States. The success or failure of Mercosur will to a large extent determine the future shape of international relations in the region and so determine the foreign relations of Argentina, Brazil and Chile over the longer term.

Foreign policy formation in less powerful nations receives little attention.[3] From the realist perspective, power is the primary determinant in the area of international relations and so the focus is directed onto the locations where power is concentrated. The dominant theme of such literature is the foreign policy of the United States. Other large players also attract attention; the European Union represents a formidable force in economic diplomacy around the world and is able to challenge the United States in this area. In the case of Latin America, the power exerted by the United States has obscured the dynamics of inter-state policies in the region. This is beginning to change; the increasing global profile of Brazil, the seeming durability of the Mercosur project and the emergence of a more strident leadership across the continent is generating interest in foreign policy making in Latin America.

The United States has been a powerful force in Latin America. Certainly, US policy has been a constraining factor on the practice of foreign relations in the region. As a result, autonomy in Latin America is often perceived as something lacking and as a goal to be achieved. However, whilst constraints do exist on the practice of external relations, this does not diminish either the necessity of affording attention to foreign policy making in the Southern Cone or the fascinating nature of such an inquiry. Constraints exist on all actors in the social realm. Absolute freedom of action in the area of international relations does not exist.[4] Even a power as dominant as the US finds itself restricted in the actions it can take. It operates in an international system, which although lacking any over-arching authority, still places restrictions on the hegemonic power. These restrictions may take the form of certain norms and procedures that have to be followed in the international system. Just as individuals must act within a certain culture so it is with nation states. Relative power is an enormously important consideration but there are other factors that need to be examined. The political culture of the country also has an impact. This will limit

---

3 Naeem Inayatullah & David Blaney, 'Knowing Encounters Beyond Parochialism in International Relations' in Yosef Lapid & Friedrich Kratochwil (eds), *The Return of Culture and Identity in IR Theory* (Boulder, 1996), p. 68.

4 John Gerard Ruggie, *Constructing the World Polity* (London; New York, 1988).

the alternatives available to political leaders. This political culture has its basis in the distant past as well as in more recent events. Economic motives are increasingly prominent in the conduct of international relations. Behaviour on the world stage will have economic repercussions and it is frequently difficult to disentangle economic motives from so-called harder politics. The ongoing struggle for resources around the world demonstrates the strategic value of such commodities as oil and water. International relations takes place in a complex environment made up of material and metaphysical elements where the actors involved respond according to the subjective and objective assessments of the situation.

In the case of the countries of the Southern Cone, all these elements combine to make up the context of the region's international relations. There are constraints; the United States is a powerful force in hemispheric politics. However, there is also a degree of autonomy. These conditions have given rise to a variant of the realist school, peripheral realism (*realismo periférico*). This school of thought accepts the existence of asymmetrical power relations in the hemisphere and the region's marginal position in the international system. This realism of the periphery, with its focus on autonomy constitutes important phenomena in the region.

Relations with the United States

There is a long history of disputes between the countries of the Southern Cone and the United States. These have tended to revolve around the familiar theme of unilateral intervention on the part of the United States. It is the case, that much of the history of hemispheric relations closely reflects the concerns of the world community post-September 11, 2001. The nations of the region have long sought to restrict the ability of the United States to intervene in the politics of its Latin American neighbours. Much of the recent debate in the region on the war in Iraq has tended to focus on this issue of unilateral versus multilateral action. For the United States alone to identify dangerous states and deem it necessary to instigate a policy of regime change is of course not without precedent in Latin America. The willingness of both Chile and Mexico to defy the United States in crucial Security Council votes on the issue of Iraq demonstrates both the centrality of these issues to Latin American nations *and* the limits of US hegemony in the region.

The complex relationship between Latin America and the United States dates back to the early part of the nineteenth century. The Munroe doctrine of 1823 made it clear that the United States saw the Americas as a separate system in world politics, and that it would endeavour to resist outside interference. It became apparent in the nineteenth and early twentieth centuries that the United States also reserved the right to intervene where it thought necessary in the domestic affairs of those countries to its south. The Roosevelt Corollary of 1904 explicitly recognized this right or duty to intervene. We have seen a number of such interventions over the past century. In terms of overt interference such actions have been concentrated in Central America and the Caribbean, but across Latin America the presence of the United States is also keenly felt.

The bipolarity of the Cold War years added a certain urgency to Washington's dealings with Latin America, as foreign relations came to be seen though the prism of the ideological battle with the Soviet Union. Internal conflicts within Latin American countries were perceived in the same way.[5] During this period, we see a number of cases of the US in conflict with left wing governments and revolutionary insurgencies. The end of the Cold War has created a new environment in the Americas. The collapse of the Soviet Union lessened the imperative to intervene on the part on the United States and afforded the countries of the region greater autonomy in their dealings with the wider world. In the mid-1990s, the potential existed for a more realistic and constructive relationship between the US and Latin America.[6] Recent events and the advent of the so-called 'War on Terror' have further distracted the attention of the US away from the region. The focus on terror has also changed the nature of the United States' engagement with the region with an increased focus on security matters and military cooperation.

There is a curious paradox at the heart of Latin American international relations. Political leaders are fearful both of too much and too little attention from the United States, too much attention can restrict their room for manoeuvre but too little attention also has its drawbacks. Since the end of the Cold War the declining strategic importance of the region and increasing security concerns in the Middle East had led to fears that the region will be left to its own devices. Hirst (2003) argues that the region no longer figures in US strategic thinking. In economic terms we also see a decline in the importance of Latin America.[7] The relative importance of the Latin America countries as trading nations has fallen in terms of the value, this despite a rise in the volumes of that trade.[8] In the combination of a declining strategic importance, a low economic profile and the continuing political and financial instability, there is a perceived risk of the marginalization and even *Africanization* of the region.

The Wider World

As the United States has focused its attention elsewhere, relations with the European Union have, for the counties of the Southern Cone, taken on a greater importance. In economic terms, the EU represents an important trading partner, so important in fact that trade flows between Mercosur and the EU exceed those of the United States

---

5   Gabriel Gaspar Tapia, 'Desafíos y Dilemas de Seguridad en América Latina en la post Guerra Fría', *Estudios Internacionales* 141 (2003): p. 42.

6   Jorge G. Castañeda, 'The Forgotten Relationship' in Foreign Affairs 83:3 (2003).

7   Mónica Hirst, 'Los claroscuros de la seguridad regional en las Américas', Nuevo Sociedad, 185 (2003): 83–101.

8   William I. Robinson, 'Global Crisis and Latin America', Bulletin of Latin American Research 23:2 (2004): 135–153.

and the Mercosur.⁹ In investment terms too, the EU has been an important source of capital to the Mercosur region with substantial investment being made principally in the banking and telecommunications sectors. On the European side, Mercosur represents an example of 'South–South' regionalism that the EU has long tried to encourage. The EU has an established preference for dealing with other regional organizations in trade talks as was demonstrated in its initial reluctance to negotiate a trade deal separately with Chile. The Spanish and the Portuguese both have a long-standing cultural and political connection with the countries of the region. Spain, in particular, has tried to position itself as a bridge between the wider European Union and Latin America.¹⁰ Both parties, but particularly the Mercosur countries, gain some leverage through this engagement. In their dealings with the US on a proposed Free-trade Area of the Americas (FTAA), the EU represents an important counterweight in the negotiations. In political terms, for many in the Southern Cone, the EU represents more than a mere trading partner – it also represents a model for regional integration. The EU's pattern of cooperation with its social component and supranational institutions is seen as an alternative to the North American Free-trade Agreement between the US, Canada and Mexico with its lack of a social policy and absence of transfers of wealth. The political dimension of Mercosur creates an affinity between the South American and European integration processes, and differentiates it from NAFTA.¹¹

Asia also represents an important trading partner for Argentina, Brazil and Chile. In general terms, we see a four way split in terms of the destination of trade, the US, the EU, Asia and intra-regional trade. This split explains the seemingly oxymoronic notion of 'open regionalism' so prominent across the Southern Cone, but particularly so in Chile. In the context of existing trade flows, Brazil, Argentina and Chile are all anxious to keep their various markets open. In recent years, relations with Asian countries have taken on a decidedly political tone. This phenomenon is driven by Brazil as it seeks to build a coalition of middle-ranking powers in order to gain greater leverage in global trade negotiations. Brazil has forged close relations with India and China. In part, this move is also motivated by a belief on the part of the administration of Lula de Silva that South–South trade links provide an important mechanism to pursue trade growth. For Brazil, a hemispheric trade agreement with the US is associated with high costs.¹² In Brazil, the politics of development over the past decades has created sensitive areas in terms of opening up the Brazilian market to foreign competition. The authorities have long been protective of those sectors

---

9   Nicola Philips, 'Integration and Subregionalism in the Americas', *International Affairs* 79:2 (2003): p. 336.

10   Andy Klom, 'Mercosur and Brazil: a European Perspective', *International Affairs* 79:2 (2003): 351–368.

11   Laurence Whitehead, 'The European Union and the Americas' in Victor Bulmer-Thomas, & James Dunkerley (eds), *The United States and Latin America: The New Agenda* (London, 1999), p. 63.

12   Phillips, 'Integration and Subregionalism in the Americas', p. 340.

that have a high technological content and those seen as vulnerable if markets are thrown open to foreign competition.

Mercosur

Intra-regional trade has become an increasingly important feature of trading patterns. Throughout the early and mid 1990s, the percentage of exports from Argentina, Brazil and Chile destined for Latin American markets grew rapidly. In the late 1990s there were some reversals but important patterns of intra-regional trade had been established. There has been some debate as to the long-term implications of these trading relations and whether or not intra-regional trade is primarily made up of products from the less dynamic areas of the local economies. Investment patterns have also begun to change, reflecting the growing importance of economic linkages between the nations of Mercosur and its associate members. The 1990s saw large investments from Chilean companies in Argentine utilities. At the same time investments coming in from North America and Europe are, in part, based on the existence of Mercosur.[13]

The trajectory of the organization has not been straightforward and during the 1990s the organization experienced some setbacks. Structurally, Mercosur has suffered from a number of weaknesses. Historically, the organization has suffered from institutional deficits in that its supranational institutions are relatively weak. This has led to difficulties in resolving disputes between the members. Furthermore, the relationship between the two principal members, Brazil and Argentina has not always been a close one and in times of difficulty, both have resorted to unilateral actions which have damaged the Mercosur project. The most serious of these episodes was the 40% devaluation of the Brazilian currency, the Real, in early 1999. This adjustment was made in the context of severe macroeconomic difficulties experienced by Brazil. The impact in Argentina was very serious as Argentine industry struggled to compete against cheap Brazilian imports. This tendency for unilateral actions has weakened the organization over the years and has continued into the early part of the twenty-first century. On a global level, the countries of Mercosur and Chile have been reluctant to limit their room for manoeuvre in negotiations with third parties. In the case of Brazil, there has been reluctance on the part of the foreign policy establishment, the *Itamaraty*, to restrict its freedom of action in any way.

Many of the trading bloc's difficulties stem from the fact that the rationale behind the Mercosur project has never been clear. The principal question is whether or not Mercosur is intended primarily as a negotiating device in forthcoming talks with the United States on hemispheric free trade and in wider global trade talks. This question relates to a major difficulty for the Mercosur project, namely, the perception of Brazilian dominance within the organization. If Mercosur is such a negotiating device, it is a Brazilian device. Such a perception is not without foundation as there

---

13 Carranza, 'Can Mercosur Survive? Domestic and International Constraints on Mercosur', p. 71.

is a strong tendency within the Brazilian elite to see their country as the regional hegemon. Mercosur can thus be construed as a vehicle for the regional ambitions of Brazil and a method to counter-balance US influence in the region. There are fears that other smaller countries in the Southern Cone may be paying a price for the sake of Brazilian regional and global ambitions and in order to support Brazilian tactics in wider trade negotiations. Certainly, it has long been a stated policy of Brazil to keep the power and influence of the United States in the region down to a minimum. Such a desire is also reflected in the discourse of some political groups in Argentina and Chile. In all three countries there are strong historical tendencies that have striven to resist US hegemony in the region. However, both in Santiago and in Buenos Aires, particularly during Menem's presidency, there has been a keen awareness of the cost of antagonizing the US. In contrast to the vibrant debate in Latin America, in the United States, the Congress and business groups tend to dismiss the sub-regional initiatives and the preference is for Mercosur to be replaced by a hemispheric trade bloc.[14]

The countries of Mercosur and its associate members retain their own distinct foreign policy goals and there are difficulties in achieving consensus. Mercosur is just over a decade old. The EU, which has had a good deal longer to develop common policies and goals, cannot achieve consensus on many issues. Mistrust and suspicion were the order of the day as the members of the European Union attempted to deal with the Iraq crisis in 2003. It remains true that 'European Project' means different things to different member states and that there are those who fear a Franco–German agenda for European integration. So it is that in the Southern Cone many question Brazilian motives and are wary of Brazilian leadership in the region's wider relations.

World War Two was the glue that bound Europe together and formed the backdrop to the Treaty of Rome. In terms of inter-state violence South America has been relatively peaceful over the last century. However, the shared trauma of dictatorship has cemented relations between the region's civilian governments. There have been rivalries between the countries of the region and considerable tensions have existed in the past between Argentina and Chile. In December 1978 the two countries were at the point of war over a territorial dispute in Tierra del Fuego and only an intervention by the Pope prevented full-blown hostilities breaking out. Problems remain between Chile and her northern neighbours, Peru and Bolivia. In the case of Brazil and Argentina there was also a long-standing rivalry between the two countries. Across the Southern Cone during much of the 1970s and 1980s the respective armed forces were in control. In all cases, defence policy and to some extent diplomatic policy was predicated on intra-regional rivalries. During these years a geopolitical paradigm dominated the thinking of military planners. The situation has improved greatly over the past two decades. The democratization of the region has led to a move away from the traditional agenda of regional politics dominated by border disputes and local

---

14 Philips, 'Integration and Subregionalism in the Americas', p. 338.

rivalries. Hirst (1998) refers to the dovish vocations of the new democracies.[15] The determination to avoid a repeat of the human rights abuses of the 1970s and 1980s has united a generation of politicians from Argentina, Brazil and Chile. The politics of democracy and human rights has been an effective glue in binding the region's nations together. Furthermore, the shared experience of military intervention has led to an appreciation of the commonalities between the nations and has lessened the hold of particularist tendencies, especially in Argentina and Chile.

The Transition to Democracy

A process of democratization took place across the Southern Cone in the 1980s and the early 1990s. The nature of the changes in Brazil, Argentina and Chile was not homogenous. An appreciation of these different trajectories on the road to full democratization is a key element in understanding foreign policy formation in the region. The manner in which the transition to democracy occurred determined, to a large extent, the configuration of power within the new civilian regimes. This, in turn, has fed into the process of foreign policy decision making. One key element was the extent to which the military retained their influence post-dictatorship. The more influence components of the old regime had over the civilian authorities, the more continuity in policy terms.

In the case of Argentina, the institutional rupture was sudden and definitive and during the 1980s Argentina went through a profound transformation. The abject failures of the military junta in the Falklands/Malvinas War, the nightmare of the 'dirty war' and severe economic problems all led to a re-evaluation of Argentina's position in the world. This process was accelerated to some extent by the complete withdrawal of the military from Argentine politics. Such were the debacles of the 1970s and 1980s that the military no longer enjoyed any influence and a number of institutional changes, following the return of democracy, weakened their role within the Argentine state. In this new environment the Argentine governments that followed were anxious to normalize relations with its neighbours.

The changes in Brazil were more gradual. The country's foreign policy has been marked by a degree of continuity despite the regime change. This continuity is explained by the continued influence of social and political forces that either garnered and/or maintained their power during the years of military rule.

In Chile, the armed forces retained influence. Of the countries being discussed, it is here that the traditional agenda of regional rivalries and border disputes has tended to linger on. Tensions remain between Chile and its two northern neighbours, Bolivia and Peru. Chile maintains that there is no outstanding dispute with Bolivia but the government in La Paz has been garnering support for a reopening of the issue of Bolivian access to the sea. In the case of Peru the dispute centred on the

---

15 Monica Hirst, 'Security Policies, Democratisation, and Regional Integration in the Southern Cone' in Jorge Domínguez (ed.), *International Security and Democracy: Latin America and the Caribbean in the Post-Cold War Era* (Pittsburgh, 1998).

city of Arica has yet to be resolved to the satisfaction of both sides. In each case the issue of illegal immigration from both Peru and Bolivia has added to the difficulties. These continuing problems in the northern desert are a legacy of the War of the Pacific (1871–73), a conflict that continues to poison relations between Chile and her neighbours. On these issues, the 'historical agenda' retains its dominance. In contrast, Chile's relations with Argentina have shown rapid improvements and issues relating to frontier disputes have been settled by civilian governments.

Contemporary Brazil–Argentine relations have almost completely overcome the 'historical agenda' and long-standing rivalries have faded into the background. Cooperation between the two countries extends into the most sensitive areas of national security. A series of confidence building measures dates back to the 1980s. Subsequently, we have seen nuclear facilities opened up to inspection and an agreement signed on non-proliferation. Closer political links have allowed the armed forces of the two countries to cooperate extensively. In the area of security, Chile has been much slower in entering into cooperative arrangements with Brazil and Argentina, due, in part, to a sceptical military. The case of Chile, post-Pinochet, is interesting because it demonstrates the impact that domestic political structures can have on the conduct of foreign relations. The continuing existence of authoritarian enclaves at the heart of the Chilean state has had a tangible effect on foreign policy. These enclaves ensured traditional geopolitical thinking continued to have an impact on policy through the 1990s. Escudé and Fontana (1998) argue that in the area of national security even the analysis of the Chilean Centre-Left have become heavily militarized.[16] This contrasts with the citizen-centric policies of Argentina and is explained by the power exerted by the Chilean military throughout much of the 1990s.

Historical Narratives and National Identity

The distinct historical experiences of Brazil, Argentina and Chile have impacted upon their engagement with one another. Here we are discussing not only the different nature of the transitions to democracy but also the longer historical processes that have fed the national identities of these three countries. In the field of International Relations there has been much debate as to how salient a factor national culture is in terms of foreign policy.[17] Realists, and neorealists in particular, have tended to decry the proposition that such subjective factors constitute an important variable in the international affairs opting instead to focus on power as the major determinant. For his part, Gilpin argues that perception plays a key role in determining how the costs and benefits of a particular course of action are analysed.

---

16 Carlos Escudé & Andrés Fontana, 'Argentina's Security Policies Their Rationale and Regional Context' in Jorge I. Domínguez (ed.), *International Security and Democracy: Latin America and the Caribbean in the Post-Cold War Era* (Pittsburgh, 1998).

17 Lapid in Yosef Lapid & Fredrich Kratochwil, (eds) *The Return of Culture and Identity in IR Theory* (Boulder, 1996).

Foremost among the determinants of these perceptions is the historical experience of the society. What in particular, have been the consequences for the country from past attempts of its own and others to change the international system, and what lessons has the nation learned about war, aggression and appeasement.[18]

In Brazil, Argentina and Chile there are strong national narratives based on the past, particularly the nineteenth century. Academics and practitioners in the area of international relations agree that history has played an important role in determining policy.[19] In all three cases we can detect exceptionist tendencies in the national culture. That is to say, we find present political belief systems that emphasize the particular characteristics of that nation and its citizens. The relationship between the nature of exceptionalism and relative power is difficult to disentangle. Certainly in terms of co-temporality, one finds unexpected combinations. Argentina's exceptionalist tendencies, emphasizing the influence of the country internationally, co-existed with a sharp decline in the country's relative power. This relationship between changing power relations, national narratives and foreign policy is a fascinating area. Such was the profundity of the crisis in Argentine identity in the 1980s that it did have an impact on the conduct on international relations and a sharp break in policy occurred in the 1990s.

The foreign policy debate in Argentina after the return to democracy demonstrates the manner by which material circumstances can interface with long-standing beliefs about the characteristics of a nation and ideas about their place in the world. Menem's foreign policy of the early 1990s was based on a realization that Argentina's conduct on the world stage was out of step with the power relations in the hemisphere. The conclusion was that Argentina needed to ally itself more closely with the United States. Argentina's political culture had previously been hostile to any acceptance of US hegemony in the region. Theoretically, this shift was informed by the debates in Argentina surrounding the nature of autonomy in the international system and profound questions as to the purpose of foreign policy. A strong tendency emerged in Argentine political and academic circles that questioned the notion that national autonomy was a function of Argentina's ability to resist the will of the hegemon, the United States. A less strident notion of autonomy was developed wherein there was an acceptance of the limitations of autonomy in any system where power relations were uneven and social norms existed. The idea that the welfare of the citizens should form the basis of diplomacy also gained currency at this time. Di Tella (ex-foreign minister) argued that Argentina should avoid conflict with the great powers

---

18 Robert Gilpin, *War and Change in World Politics* (Cambridge, 1981), p. 146.

19 Jose Miguel Insulsa, Ensayos *Sobre Política Exterior de Chile* (Santiago, 1998); Figari, *Pasado, Presente y Futuro de la Política Exterior Argentina* (Buenos Aires, 1993); Clodoaldo Hugueney, 'Brazilian Foreign Policy at the Beginning of the Twenty-First Century' in Álvaro De Vasconcelos & Helio Jaguaribe (eds), *The European Union, Mercosul and the New World Order* (London, 2003).

in order to maximize the welfare of the Argentine people.[20] Following this logic, in a unipolar world it was imperative to maintain good relations with the United States. This position was informed by the politics of development. Indeed development was a centrepiece of politics across the region and foreign policy was often subordinated to the achievement of economic development.

Economic Foreign Policy

In the case of Chile trade considerations were the key drivers of foreign policy. Indeed such was the focus on trade that the government of Aylwin was criticized for devoting excessive attention to this area.[21] Post-Pinochet, in macro-economic terms the country did not suffer the same trauma as Argentina. In fact the country's economy during the 1990s was seen as the success story of the region. As a result, there was no wholesale re-examination of Chilean politics and institutions in the short term. All this is not to say that Chilean political culture was in stasis during this period. Important changes were taking place, many in response to the excesses of the Pinochet regime. These changes are best seen in the context of a gradual agreed (*pactado*) transition and the extreme reticence on the part of successive *Concertación* governments to address the issue of the past. This was in stark contrast to the confessional atmosphere pertaining in Argentina. This said, at a profound level, the Argentine and Chilean authorities in the 1990s shared a philosophy whereby ideologically driven politics were jettisoned in favour of pragmatism. In both cases this pragmatism was underwritten by the imperative of development.

With the Chilean military still maintaining that it had performed an historic duty in ruling the country for 16 years and handing back power to the civilian authorities, the belief amongst the armed forces was that they had nothing to apologize for. Powerful right-wing parties in the Congress who were anxious to protect the legacy of General Pinochet supported the armed forces in this belief. Thus, in the decade after the hand-over of power, the military and their supporters retained a good deal of influence in Chilean political life. As a result, there was some continuity in the country's foreign policy. It remained dominated by a desire to open and maintain markets for Chilean exports. However, there were also some changes in Chilean foreign policy after 1990. The fact that a civilian government replaced Pinochet's regime changed the atmosphere in which Chilean diplomacy took place. On taking power Alywin was warmly welcomed around the world, particularly in Europe where the previous regime had been extremely unpopular among the European Left. All this was in stark contrast to the isolation of the 1970s and 1980s. However, the Aylwin and Frei governments continued to concentrate on economic diplomacy and did little to raise Chile's profile on the international stage. In other words, they

---

20 Escudé & Fontana, 'Argentina's Security Policies. Their Rationale and Regional Context', p. 54.

21 Jorge Heine, 'Timidez o pragmatismo? La política exterior de Chile en 1990' (Santiago, 1990).

did little to re-institute a Chilean activist stance that existed prior to the coup of 1973. It is fair to say that their options were limited and the world had changed. The Cold War was over and in the early 1990s there seemed little chance of developing alternatives to the dominant paradigm of liberal economics and export led growth. In the case of Chile, with the country showing strong growth, there was no perceived need to develop an alternative and the priority remained to open up markets to Chilean exports.

Of the three countries in this study, Brazil demonstrates the highest degree of continuity in the area of foreign policy between the authoritarian period and the democracy which followed. As is the case with Chile, the explanation lies in part with the nature of institutional framework after democratization. Firstly, the reputation of the armed forces remained relatively intact and they retained some authority following democratization. Secondly, the *Itamaraty*, the elite within the Brazilian civil service charged with the management of the country's foreign relations, retained their control over foreign policy throughout both the years of military rule and during the civilian administrations that followed. The major ideological currents underpinning Brazilian foreign policy remained constant. Brazil has seen itself as the dominant power in the Southern Cone, and the desire to build up strategic industries has been strong enough to resist pressures from the outside for wholesale reform. Hostility to United States' interference, specifically in South America, has been consistent. The economic weight of Brazil in the region has afforded the country a higher degree of autonomy than its neighbours. In particular, Washington has long been aware that any hemispheric free-trade deal is worthless without Brazilian involvement. Brazil may have moved away from its import substitution model of development but the ambitions that informed that model are still present amongst the Brazilian elite. Insertion into the world economy is attractive to Brazil only if it helps to achieve the goal of creating a modern diversified economy.

In examining the foreign policies of Argentina, Brazil and Chile after the dictatorships a number of wider issues arise. Primary amongst these are the changes that have taken place in global trade over the decades. From the time of the coup in Chile (1973) to the Treaty of Asuncion in 1991, the nature of the world economy has been transformed. Not only had the economy changed but the world political map had also been profoundly changed. By the early 1990s the countries of the Southern Cone were faced with a new set of realities. The United States was the world's undisputed hegemonic power and regional blocs were now part of the world's political geography. In ideological terms, liberal market economics and free trade were in the ascendancy. In terms of the capital available to feed the process of development, short term and more mobile funds are now dominant. The imperative to attract such funding drives much of the politics of the Southern Cone. Mercosur is no different in this regard and so policy sets must be put in place in order to encourage inward investment.

In all three countries economic development is a key driver of foreign policy. During the so-called 'lost decade' of the 1980s, a heavy price was paid by large segments of the population. Robinson (2004) cites the example of Argentina in the period 1980–2001.[22] During this period, unemployment rose from 200,000 to 5 million, the number in poverty rose from 1 million to 14 million, illiteracy from 2% to 12% and functional illiteracy rose from 5% to 32%. In Chile, the policies of the Pinochet regimes impacted disproportionately on working class groups. The military governments resulted in a sharp rise in poverty levels.[23] In the 1990s the civilian administration across the Southern Cone put a high priority on development as a way forward in tackling social problems. The chosen path of development in each case would prove to be an important determinant of foreign policy. The Chilean reliance on export-led growth led to differences of emphasis when compared to Brazil and Argentina who continued to rely, to a greater extent, on their much larger internal markets.

Regional Identity?

Regionalism has a long history in Latin America and important questions surround this element of the Mercosur regional project. Mercosur has been described as the most successful ever example of Latin American regionalism. It has also been distinguished from previous attempts at integration in the region. On this occasion the project was not driven by dependency theory and based upon a policy of import substitution, rather there was an implicit acceptance of the need to integrate the region into the world economy. This said, for many the importance of Mercosur lies beyond mercantile considerations. For Cardoso in 2001, Mercosur represented his country's destiny and not a mere free-trade agreement.[24] Similar sentiments are to be found among elements of the political elite in both Argentina and Chile, though in the case of the Chilean political elite there is perhaps less consensus on Chile's future role in the Mercosur project. The issue of Mercosur's external tariff is important (it is much higher than that of Chile) but there are more fundamental issues at stake. These issues relate to the future role of Chile in the international system, and go to the heart of debates around Chilean national identity and they are far from being settled. In Chile, as elsewhere in the continent, 'exceptionalism' is an important component of national identity. There are elements of that Chilean 'exceptionalism' that complicate the scenario with regard to Chile's participation in regional projects. This is in part due to the country's history and the manner in which its past has been interpreted. Chile's geographical position also plays a part. Though less relevant in these times of global travel and high-tech communication, its position behind the formidable Andes and beneath the harsh deserts of the Atacama has lead to a sense of isolation from the rest of the continent. The Chileans came to see themselves as

---

22 Robinson, 'Global Crisis and Latin America'.

23 B. Bosworth, R. Dornbusch, and R. Laban, *The Chilean Economy, Policy Lesson and Challenges* (Washington, DC, 1994), p. 9.

24 Amaury de Souza, 'The European Union Mercosur and New World Order' in Álvaro De Vasconcelos & Helio Jaguaribe (eds), *The European Union, Mercosul and the New World Order* (London, 2003), p. 201.

an oasis of calm in a turbulent region. The local saying, '*Una buena casa en un mal barrio*' ('a good house in a bad neighbourhood') expressed the sentiment. Such a philosophy has tended to lead the Chileans to eschew regional agreements for fear of being tarred with the same brush as their neighbours. The discourse surrounding Chilean attempts to negotiate an entry into the NAFTA during the early to mid-1990s were marked by this desire to see themselves as distinct from the rest of the continent. In 2003 Chile finally signed a Free-trade Agreement with Washington.

In Brazil and in post-Menem Argentina there is now less reticence about the Mercosur project and more sympathy for a Latin-Americanist viewpoint. Certainly, aspects of the relationship between Brazil and Argentina in the security area would tend to suggest that this project is more that just a temporary agreement on the way to full integration into the world economy. Mercosur and attempts to promote regional cooperation are not just economic projects. There is also an element of so-called 'hard' politics, in that, in coming together the countries of the region do increase their influence across the globe. The distinction between hard and soft power or high and low politics is problematic, this is particularly the case in Latin America with the stress on development and the reliance on trade in order to achieve that development. It is this focus on development that is both an important driver of the Mercosur initiative and potentially its undoing. The question that arises is whether or not Mercosur, as a political project, can withstand the development potential of a hemispheric free-trade agreement.

Regional arrangements in South America will take on a more permanent nature if there is a strong sense of solidarity in the region and if participants see their futures as closely tied to that of their neighbours. This is only partly a function of trade. Identity is also an important consideration in the region's international relations. Latin American solidarity has a long history dating back to Bolivar. The manner of the initial break with their Spanish colonial masters closely tied the Argentine and Chilean nations. Those that liberated Chile crossed the border from Argentina under the leadership of an Argentine General, José de San Martin. In this regard Brazil had a distinct experience, playing host to the exiled Portuguese court. This said, here too there developed a strong appreciation of a shared identity with its neighbours. There is much that can be shared in terms of history and culture among the peoples of the region and the notion of *Latino* has a great resonance from the Rio Grande to Punta Arenas. However, as David Miller (1995) suggests identities are not only formed from what is on the *inside* but also by what is perceived to lie outside the borders.[25] In this regard relations with the United States are crucial. Their great northern neighbour has both a centrifugal and centripetal effect on regional arrangements in Latin America. Good relations with Washington can be perceived to offer a great deal to peripheral nations. Certainly bad relations with the US can be very costly. During the 1990s both Santiago and Buenos Aires sought to foster close relations with the United States with a view to improving their economic prospects. In pursuing this course they eschewed closer ties with their neighbours.

---

25 David Miller, *On Nationality* (Oxford, 1995).

In centripetal terms, Latin American is often defined in terms of its difference to the United States. The manner in which these differences are constructed varies widely. It can be constituted by a simple preference for so-called *Latino* values and can coexist with an admiration of the North American way of life. On the other hand it can be informed by a deep-rooted hostility to the United States born out of history, ideology or both. In the case of the more hostile, their position draws much of its energy from the reaction to repeated US intervention in Latin American affairs. In all three countries there is a long history of a nascent hostility to the US and this has fed into their respective foreign policies. According to Soares de Lima, cited in Da Motta (2002), the United States constitutes a pole of revulsion in Brazilian foreign policy.[26] Much of the effort expended on the Mercosur project is driven by a desire to limit US influence in South America. The case of Argentina is instructive in that it shows both the centripetal and the centrifugal forces at work. For many decades up until the 1990s Argentina had one of the most consistently anti-US positions at the UN. Measured by their voting record, Argentina was more radical than either Libya or Iraq and was exceeded only by that of Cuba. Carlos Menem presided over a profound shift in Argentine policy. During the 1990s his government courted the US at every possible opportunity. Such was the change that in 1991 Argentina was one of the very few Latin American countries that voted in favour of a US-inspired resolution on human rights in Cuba. Such a pro US stance combined with Argentina admittance as an Associate Member to NATO, raised the hackles of its neighbours and tended to weaken the drive towards regional solidarity. Menem's policy also attracted a good deal of criticism at home. Chile's position with regard to the United States has been both more consistent and somewhat circumspect. Its reliance on exports into the North American market has tended to ensure a more conservative orientation in its relations with Washington.

Some Preliminary Conclusions

Post-2000, with the advent of centre-left governments in Argentina and Brazil combined with a more strident centre-left government in Chile, the region's relations with Washington are thrown into sharp relief. In terms of good hemispheric relations the combination of leftist governments, an overtly interventionist Republican administration and the Chavez government in Venezuela, this is not the most propitious time. The insurgency in Colombia adds to the problems, with the Brazilian government anxious to avoid large scale US military intervention in a neighbouring country. With the departure of Menem, Argentina has become closer to Brazil and more distant from the United States and the determination of Lula and Kirchner to develop ties with Chavez in Venezuela has complicated the picture. As we see the

---

26 Soares de Lima, cited in Pedro Da Motta Veiga, 'Brasil a inicios del nuevo milenio: Herencias y Desafíos de la Transición' in Roberto Bouzas (ed.), *Realidades Nacionales Comparadas* (Buenos Aires, 2002), p. 73.

development of a Brasilia-Buenos Aires axis, the Chilean leadership is making more positive statements about closer involvement in the Mercosur project.

To sum up, there are a number of forces at play that determine the international relations of Argentina, Brazil and Chile. These forces cannot be isolated from one another and it is the interplay of these policy drivers that determine the nature of foreign policy. Firstly, there is the issue of the relative power of the three countries in question. In economic terms Brazil accounts for some two-thirds of the Mercosur GDP. It is the dominant force in the region and within the Mercosur bloc. Secondly, Mercosur has been perceived in various ways through time and there have been differences of emphasis in each of the member countries and in Chile. Within Brazil, Mercosur is perceived as a vehicle to maximize the country's power. The Brazilians have been unwilling to allow their leadership of the bloc to be challenged for fear that any dilution of their influence would result in limited autonomy. In Argentina, the representation of Mercosur has varied according to priorities of the political leadership. During Menem's tenure in office it was simply one of two tracks being pursued and would not be allowed to interfere in the more important project of building close relations with the United States. More recently under Kirchner's administration, relations with Brazil have taken on a more strategic importance.

Thirdly, there is the overarching issue of relations with the United States. Here the issues of trade and non-intervention dominate as they have done for many decades. Fourthly, we have the impact of a changing international environment. On emerging from the 'lost decade' of the 1980s the countries of the Southern Cone were faced with a world where there was only one superpower. In economic terms the import substitution model adopted in the 1970s was no longer seen as viable and so insertion into the global economy was seen as a priority. As a result, across the region, we have seen the economization of foreign policy formation. Fifthly, the process of democratization has been extremely important. It has facilitated the development of a new atmosphere between the main regional protagonists. Geopolitical thinking, with its roots in nineteenth century, heavily influenced the foreign policy of Argentina, Brazil, and Chile. The respective militaries had all been schooled in this tradition hence it was only with their departure that a more positive ambience could be created. During the 1980s and 1990s relations improved across the region with long-standing border disputes settled and military rivalries fading into the background. Democratization has an explanatory power in that the nature of that process determined to some extent whether or not there was continuity or a change in policy between the old regimes and the new. In both Brazil and Chile there was a higher degree of continuity during the transition period to democracy. In Argentina such was the profundity of the institutional rupture that policy was inevitably affected. Sixth, there are the shifting patterns of national and regional identity to be discussed and in particular whether we are witnessing the re-emergence of a political regionalism. Lastly, there is the issue of development. Trade is now a crucial component of foreign policy. The impact of development politics is interesting, it is a key determinant, but development or even economic considerations do not always carry the day. The opposition of Southern Cone countries to the invasion of Iraq is evidence of this. In Latin America as a whole, only Colombia, Nicaragua, El Salvador, the Dominican Republic, Panama and Costa Rica were part of the 'coalition of the willing'. In the case of Chile, their position on the Security Council meant a very public defiance of the dominant power in the hemisphere, the United States.

From the perspective of the discipline of International Relations the question arises as to which paradigm of thought or combination of ideas best explain the realities of foreign policy formation in the countries of the Southern Cone. The case of the Southern Cone demonstrates the benefits of accepting the commensurability of theoretical perspectives in the discipline. Realist models explain the wish of Brazil to compete with the US and the manner in which it pursues greater autonomy in the region. However, at the periphery such is the imperative of development that foreign formulation cannot be separated from domestic political demands. Indeed for Brazil, it is suggested that foreign policy is but an extension of domestic policy. Such throughputs do not comply with classic realist conceptions of foreign policy being a separate field. Nor is it easy to integrate discussion of identity politics and the role of historical narratives into realist models and yet both possess an important explanatory power. Hence, we need to utilize the insights from other traditions in order to create a nuanced picture of the formation of foreign policy in the Southern cone. The nature of the Mercosur project serves to underline this position. It is driven by power politics in that it serves as a vehicle for Brazilian ambitions, the project is also strengthened by Latin American identity politics across the Southern Cone and it is strongly linked to domestic political agendas. In short, the international relations of Argentina, Brazil and Chile can only be explained by reference to competing and distinct forces in a complex social system.

Chapter 2

Theoretical Considerations: The Need for Inclusive Approaches

The discipline of International Relations is primarily focused on the Great Powers. Within the field, the realist/neorealist paradigm continues to be dominant, hence attention is directed towards the power and capabilities of actors in the international system. Both in terms of content and personnel, the United States holds the pre-eminent position in international relations and the priorities of the US are reflected in the output of the discipline. The realist tradition presents us with much that is valuable in examining international relations in general, as well as the inter-state relations of the Southern Cone. There is no doubt that changes in the relative power of Argentina, Brazil and Chile have had a profound effect on intra-regional relations and relations with third parties, in particular with the United States. Over the past half-century the power and influence of Brazil has grown steadily, relative to its Southern Cone neighbours, and this fact explains many of the changing dynamics of international relations in the region, the Western Hemisphere and further afield.

Historically, the three countries have been very sensitive to changes in the balance of power between them. In the last decades of the nineteenth and throughout much of the twentieth century, concerns over the balance of power in the region were a main driver of foreign policy. Relations with countries outside this subsystem were frequently a function of the power relations within the Southern Cone. During much of the twentieth century Brazil sought to gain a privileged relationship with the United States in order to strengthen its claim to regional leadership. Argentina and Chile have had to come to terms with relative declines in power and capability. The reaction of the ruling elites to these changes has been interesting and a lack of convergence between ideology/world view and relative power, particularly in Argentina, merits attention. As Brazil has grown stronger, its relationship with the United States has changed. From the late 1960s, Brazil has become more assertive and more strident in its desire to become a regional power in its own right. Argentina was no longer seen as an impediment to this ambition and indeed from the late 1980s onwards Argentine support in achieving this goal was seen as essential. Increasingly, the United States came to be seen as the major obstacle to the Brazilian goal of regional leadership. The strong support for the Mercosur project within the foreign policy making elite is in large part explained by Brazil's desire to resist US hegemony across the whole hemisphere. The imperative to form alliances in the face of asymmetrical power relations sits well within the realist paradigm. Since the late 1980s, Brazil has sought to gather other countries of the Southern Cone around it in order to counter the power of the United States. With hemispheric free-trade talks on the agenda this has become all the more important.

Over the last decade, for Argentina and Chile the principal question has been whether or not to throw their lot behind the Mercosur project or to seek a privileged relationship with the United States. A realist explanation is again valuable. There are costs and benefits in both scenarios. During Menem's government, the policy options were framed in realist terms and a decision was taken to pursue closer relations with the United States. This was seen as offering the most benefits to Argentina, both in economic and political terms. The debate surrounding this policy is very instructive and has important theoretical implications.

Realism and Beyond

Keohane (1986) lists three basic assumptions of realism and neo-realism. Firstly, the state is the basic unit of analysis. Secondly, states are power maximizers. Thirdly, in international relations we are dealing with rational actors.[1] Vasquez (1990) adds a forth tenet, a sharp distinction between domestic and international politics.[2,3] Power

---

1 Robert Keohane, 'Realism, Neo-Realism and the Study of World Politics' in Robert Keohane (ed.), *Neorealism and its Critics* (New York, 1986).

2 John A. Vasquez, 'Coloring it Morgenthau: New Evidence for a Old Thesis on Quantitive International Politics' in John A. Vasquez (ed.), *Classics of International Relations* (London, 1990), p. 19.

3 Realism is comprised of a rich and varied literature and it is impossible to do justice to this tradition here. Whilst some authors have identified central tenets there are those within the realist school who do not comply with such definitions. Morgenthau is a key figure in the development of realism canon and yet many of his views do not sit easily with more generic definitions of realism. As Keohane point out Morgenthau acknowledges that the assumption of rationality was descriptively not correct. Within Morgenthau's work, there are apparent contradictions on this issue of rationality. Realism was not entirely secure with the empiricism of the Enlightenment, yes it adopted many of its premises, but there was an awareness of a continuing reliance on intuition. Nowhere is this unease reflected better than in the writing of Morgenthau. In *Politics Among Nations* we see Morgenthau at his more 'scientific', political realism believes that politics, like society in general, is governed by objective laws that have their roots in human nature. Just as the discovery of certain laws was crucial in the physical sciences so the discovery of such laws in the human sciences is central to the realist. In *Politics Among Nations*, Morgenthau seems very much at ease with the scientific project. In 'Scientific Man' written some two years earlier, Morgenthau demonstrates himself repeatedly to be uncomfortable with scientific method and here there are echoes of the conservative ideal, a statesman who instinctively *knows*. In this work, politics is an art, not a science, and what is required is not the rationality of the engineer but the wisdom and moral strength of the statesmen. Morgenthau straddles not just the two hundred years or so of post enlightenment philosophy but also finds himself at one with Machiavellian notion of *the Prince*. The wise and morally strong statesman is not a figure imported from the empiricist/positivist discourse. There is also the position of the 'English School', as represented by Martin Wight and Hedley Bull amongst others. Here international politics is seen as a branch of history and hence there

is relative and what matters in the realist paradigm is the distribution of military power.[4] From the neorealist perspective there is a self-conscious attempt to limit the variables under examination. Writing in this vane Waltz points out:

> In defining international-political structures we take states with whatever traditions, habitats, objectives, desires, and forms of government they have. We do not ask whether states are revolutionary or legitimate, authoritarian or democratic, ideological or pragmatic. We abstract every attribute of states except their capabilities.[5]

Though Waltz does attempt to introduce a more scientific methodology, like his predecessors we still see very diverse and at times contradictory ideas sitting uneasily together. Consider these two passages, the first clearly owes much to the scientism of the enlightenment, whilst the second shows an awareness of the constructed nature of the international system: 'A political structure is akin to a field of forces in physics.'[6] Then: 'Structure is a generative notion; and the structure is generated by the interactions of its principle parts.'[7] In order to understand the structure it seems logical that we would have to know something of its component parts, but Waltz cautions us against this. He rightly assumes that any such examination would lead the theorist back to traditional realism's reliance on supposedly less rigorous methods and inevitable allow the entry of subjective factors into any study. We are left with Waltz's systematic approach in which any serious consideration of the system is made problematical by a reluctance to study the nature of the units. We must avert our eyes, try not to stare, as it were, at the individual parts but instead we concentrate on the whole system. Realism in International Relations has tended to operate on the basis of an abstraction from cultural diversity.[8] The reductionism of neorealism also means the temporal plane is ignored, the history of the actors is only seen as relevant in that it might inform us on relative capabilities. The impact of history on the perception of human agents is not addressed.[9] Both space and time are neglected by this paradigm.

---

are fewer attempts to preordain the nature and human actors. Hans J. Morgenthau, *Politics Among Nations. The Struggle for Power and Peace*, New York (London, 1985); Hans J. Morgenthau, *Scientific Man vs Power Politics* (Chicago, 1946); Hedley Bull, *The Anarchical Society. A Study of Order in World Politics* (London, 1977); Martin Wight, *Power Politics* (Harmondsworth, 1979).

    4   David R. Mares, 'Foreign Policy in Argentina, Brazil and Chile: The Burden of the Past, the Hope for the Future', *Latin American Research Review* 29 (1994): p. 112.

    5   Kenneth N. Waltz, 'Political Structures' in Robert Keohane (ed.), *Neorealism and its Critics*, p. 94.

    6   Kenneth. N. Waltz, 'Anarchic Orders and Balances of Power' in Keohane, *Neorealism and its Critics* p. 61.

    7   Ibid., p. 61.

    8   Jahn Beate, *The Cultural Construction of International Relations* (Basingstoke, 2000), p. xi.

    9   Stephen Hobden suggest that historical sociology may be able to offer International Relations a method for a more profound analysis of international politics. Stephen Hobden,

In any attempt to explain international relations among the ABC nations, realist positions are deeply problematic and whilst neorealist abstraction may offer some benefits, it obscures more than it illuminates. The process of abstraction denies us important information and makes any explanation of the foreign policy-making process at best partial. The problems with such approaches can be illustrated by the nature of foreign policy decisions taken in the period following democratization in Argentina, Brazil and Chile. However, Argentina post-1983 provides the starkest example of the shortcoming of realist/neorealist methods. The government of Alfonsín used foreign policy as a tool in managing civilian-military relations.[10] If we take the realist idea of the primacy of the state, and the separation of the domestic and the foreign policy spheres we simply cannot arrive at a full account on the nature of Argentine foreign policy in the 1980s. Across the Southern Cone, foreign policy and the process of democratization are closely related with the former seen as a method of strengthening new democratic institutions.[11] As such, foreign relations were a function of intra-state relations, hence, a highly nuanced method is required, one that can take account of such circumstances. Moreover, Waltzian abstraction is of limited use because we need an appreciation of the history and culture of civilian-military relations to gain a full understanding of the imperative of managing such relations and how these processes ultimately fed into the formation of foreign policy. In all three countries the nature of the transition to democracy, and in particular the status of the military in that process, had a profound effect on the construction of foreign policy. Even to treat the state as a unitary actor is therefore problematic. Instead then of 'averting our eyes' and ignoring the nature of individual units in the international system we need to detect and examine the motives of the various and distinct actors at work within the state.

The realist assumption of rational actors and power maximizers is also difficult to sustain in the Southern Cone. The Menem team was explicitly critical of Argentine foreign policy making since World War Two on the grounds that it was not based on rational principals and was instead fed by the idiosyncratic nature of the Argentine national identity. This was an opinion shared by those outside the political circle of Menem. For Tulchin, the Argentine leadership had been living 'in a world of dreams constructed over the course of a century by a distorted perception of the world around them'. Tulchin goes on to argue: 'The political culture underlying foreign policy was still dangerously detached from a hard, objective analysis of the world around Argentina.'[12] This is at odds from core tenets of the realist paradigm. Both the

---

International Relations and Historical Sociology (London, 1998).

10 Andrew Hurrel, 'Security in Latin America', *International Affairs* 74:3 (1998). Rut Diamint also makes the point that foreign policy was used to manage civilian-military relations across Latin America. Rut Diamint, 'Security Challenges in Latin America', *Bulletin of Latin American Research* 23:1, (2004): pp. 43–62.

11 Paulo Paiva & Ricarda Gazel, 'Mercosur: past, present, and future', *Nova Economía Belo Horizonte* 13:2 (2003): p. 126.

12 Joseph S. Tulchin, 'Continuity and Change in Argentine Foreign Policy' in Heraldo Munoz & Joseph Tulchin (eds), *Latin America in World Politics* (Boulder, 1996), p. 172.

notion of rational actors and of power maximizers do not appear to correspond to the case of Argentina. Realism in the late 1980s in Argentina was a normative position, in effect those around Menem campaigned for the adoption of realist principals in the construction of foreign policy. This is somewhat different to the perspective of the realist school in IR. For this school posits that realist principals *are* the basis of the inter-state relation, for Cavallo and Di Tella realist principals *should have been* the basis of Argentine foreign relations.

In Chile, following the departure of the military from government, a similar type of political discourse emerged. The politicians of the *Concertación* called for a more pragmatic politics, one based on rational thought.[13] Implicit in this drive to impose rationalism in politics was the belief that it has been absent in the past. Chile had scarcely emerged from 16 years of military rule during which a virulent form of nationalism had come to occupy a prominent place in the country's political culture. There is an important difference between realist thought and the type of debate that has occurred in Chile and Argentina over the last two decades or so. The Chilean and Argentine political class has sought to protect itself from what they perceive as dangerous forces in society and have deliberately sought to insulate themselves from these forces. Realist thinkers on the other hand have tended to ontologize the disengaged perspective. Whilst the Chilean and Argentine elite has sought redemption with instrumental reason and social responsibility, realist thinking has attempted to naturalize these positions. It ceased to be a prescriptive movement and now instead claims to tell it like it is. This is a crucial distinction.

The journey to the type of purified realism we see in both Chile and Argentina is worthy of attention. In both cases difficult historical experiences have tended to undermine national self-confidence and resulted in a crisis relating to the place these countries should occupy in the world. There was a retreat to realism as the political classes dominant in the 1990s sought to reorientate foreign policy on more scientific and rational grounds. There are important differences between reactions in Argentina and Chile to the years of military rule. The institutional rupture was more severe in Argentina, the military and their supporters were seriously weakened and had lost their authority by the handover of power in 1983. In Chile, there was a degree of institutional continuity in that the military retained a position of influence in the new configuration of power after 1989. This limited the room for manoeuvre of the new civilian authorities. Their reaction was to adopt a low profile on the international stage and to try and rebuild relations around the world, and move away from the confrontational approach to international politics adopted by the Pinochet regime.

In Brazil, there was a still greater degree of continuity, particularly in the area of foreign policy formation. The military in Brazil were not as tarnished as they had been in either Argentina or Chile and there was less of a reassessment of ideas that drove Brazilian foreign policy. The gravitational forces that tore at the Argentine and Chilean national narratives were much weaker in Brazil. There was then no retreat to

---

13 Jeffrey Puryear, *Thinking Politics: Intellectuals in Democracy in Chile* (Baltimore, Maryland; London, 1994).

rationalism, no imperative to impose the politics of responsibility.[14] Brazil continued to pursue its ambitions of regional leadership. Its continuing economic ascendancy continued to underwrite its strategic goals.

Argentine policy makers during the Menem administration were informed by a particular variant of realism. *Realismo periférico* or peripheral realism is different to mainstream realism in a number of important respects. More attention is paid to the dependent status of Argentina in the political economy of the world and the phenomenon of imperialism is addressed. Those that campaigned for a more realist foreign policy did so on grounds not usually associated with the realist school of thought. Di Tella argued that foreign policy should be for the people and linked it explicitly with the domestic realm of politics. This connection between internal politics and external politics is strong throughout the Southern Cone. In Argentina, Brazil and Chile external relations have long been linked to, even subordinated to developmental goals. A sharp distinction between domestic politics and external politics is simply not sustainable in the context of Latin America. The central function of the state here has been developmental for generations. This does not mean that the security function is any less important than in traditional centres of power, rather that the source of any threat to security is often seen as lying within the country, with the poor. Hence development became a security issue, it is a method of diffusing an internal threat to the regime, a threat that in many cases was more severe than those existing outside the borders. This is not to dispute the value of realist/neorealist insights into inter-state relations are not valuable, they clearly are. Rather it suggests that a more inclusive approach is necessary.

The issue of the complementary approaches has generated much debate within the field of IR. Chakrabarti Pasic argues: 'In the neorealist world, social and cultural factors are relegated to the domestic realm, where they remain irrelevant to the working of international relations.' She goes on to argue for more inclusive orientation that would take into account social and cultural aspects of the state in question. At stake, she believes, is a richer and more relevant set of theories.[15]

The Importance of the Local Level

In order to achieve this goal of greater inclusivity, more attention needs to be given to processes taking place at a local level. The rationale behind this work is to return to the human subject at the heart of any process of political decision making. Any

---

14 In the case of Chile, Wilde contends that the politicians of the Concertación followed Weber in his distinction between the ethics of principled convictions and the ethics of responsibility – they opted for the latter. Alexander Wilde, 'Irruptions of Memory: Expressive Politics in Chile's Transition to Democracy' in *Journal of Latin American Studies* 31:2, (1999), pp. 473–500.

15 Sujata Chakrabarti Pasic, 'Culturing International Relations Theory: A Call for an Extension' in Yosef Lapid & Fredrich Kratochwil (eds) *The Return of Culture and Identity in IR Theory* (Boulder, 1996), pp. 85–86.

such return needs to move beyond straightforward ideas of rational actors and power maximizers. In the first instance we need to afford the subject a place in the world. Hosti encapsulates the self-awareness of many in the realist school.

> No observer in a field so replete with complexities, ethical problems and historical consequences could fail to detect certain biases in his or her analysis. Even the most objective scholar is partly a prisoner of his or her experiences, the values predominant in his or her society, and the myths, traditions and stereotypes that permeate his or her society.[16]

Realism has been struggling with the problem of agency in international relations for over half a century: the two solutions offered have been the objective technocrat and the sexier but equally implausible 'knowing' statesman of Morgenthau. A viable alternative would seek to address the matrix of thought processes that relate to their culture.

Outside the field of IR, the nature of the human agent has been at the centre of many crucial debates. In sociology, literature and philosophy the thoughts, texts, actions of human beings have been examined in a way that transcends any recourse to the notion of the rational actor. International Relations has always been an importer of ideas from other disciplines. But this has not always taken place in a self-conscious manner. Indeed there has been a tendency in IR to seek to inculcate itself from other disciplines. Steve Smith argues that this

> division of international relations from other social sciences seems more a logical consequence of the pervasiveness of realist assumptions than a reflection of some specific feature of its subject matter.[17]

He identifies a noticeable gap between IR and other social sciences and argues for more linkages. This is a view shared by Neufeld who also argues for a more inclusive approach in the field.[18]

The descriptive capacity of realist international relations theory is challenged by the political evolution of the Southern Cone countries. Theoretically as well, there are strong arguments that cast doubt on the major tenets of the realist paradigm. Both the presumption of the rational actor and the power maximizer are highly

---

16 K.J. Holsti, *International Politics. A Framework for Analysis* (Englewood Cliffs, N.J, 1967), p. 19.

17 Steve Smith, 'Paradigm Dominance in International Relations: The Developments of International Relations as a Science', *Millennium Journal of International Studies*, 16:2. (1987): p. 199.

18 Neufeld argues that we need to lose the 'Cartesian anxiety' that unless we find the 'Archimedean point of indubitable knowledge that can serve as the foundation of human reason, then rationality must give way to irrationality, and reliable knowledge to madness'. Mark Neufeld, 'Reflexivity and International Relations' Theory' in Turenne Sjolander, Claire and Cox, Wayne S. (eds), *Beyond Positivism Critical Reflections on International Relations.* (Boulder, 1994), p. 16.

questionable. The epistemological basis of realism is derived from various sources including the field of history, the natural sciences and various forms of positivism.[19] In general, little attention was paid to epistemological issues in realist literature. Realists saw themselves at the head of that tradition of objective thought that stretched back to the Copernican revolution; they were influenced, as were others in the area of social sciences, by Newtonian physics. Here it is useful to think of traditional schools of International Relations as under the sway of the empiricism of the Enlightenment. An important figure in this movement was John Locke, said to have been the founding father of empiricism.[20] The writings of Hume, Comte and Kant also had a considerable influence. The eighteenth and nineteenth centuries are key periods in the thought underpinning thinking in the field of International Relations. For George:

> it was an age when, in the unique technological circumstances a narrowly based interpretation of social reality was transformed into a universal agenda for all theory and practice; when, in the search for a secure secular foundation for understanding the modern world, the discourse of meaning associated with human history and politics was appropriated by the scientific project; when an image of reality centred on a model of the natural sciences was projected into the study of human society by figures such as Hume, Kant, Comte, Dilthy, Marx, Russell and Popper.[21]

It is the universalism of this tradition that is its defining characteristic. The result for mainstream IR is the tendency to ignore both time and space as important variables.[22] Of the two, the geographic dimension often carried less weight.[23] Instead, a homogenous space is developed where similar rules apply to the agents operating within this space, but there is a danger that in seeking to abstract *the local* a great deal that is valuable is lost.

Identified as an alternative philosophical lineage the work of Geertz, Heidegger, Gadamer and Ricouer all stress the local over the universal.[24] In terms of IR, what comes into view is precisely the *national* of the inter-national. Given their experiences

---

19 K.J Hosti, 'Mirror, Mirror on the Wall, which Are the Fairest Theories of All?', *International Studies Quarterly* 33 (1989): p. 255.

20 Bertrand Russell, *History of Western Philosophy* (London, 1946), p. 589.

21 Jim George, 'International Relations and the Search for Thinking Space: Another View of the Third Debate', *International Studies Quarterly* 33 (1989): p. 272.

22 The English School of International Relations is a clear exception here.

23 Indeed, Foucault makes an interesting general observation in this regard, observing geography's general absence in historical analysis. 'A critique could be carried out of this devaluation of space. Did it start with Bergson or before? Space was treated as dead, the fixed, the undialectical, the immobile. Time, on the contrary, was richness, fecundity, life, dialectic.' Michel Foucault, 'Questions on Geography' in Michel Foucault, *Power/Knowledge Selections Interviews and Other Writings 1972–1977* (Hassocks: The Harvester Press, 1980).

24 Clifford Geertz, *Local Knowledge, Further Essays in Interpretative Anthropology* (New York, 1983); Clifford Geertz, *Towards an Interpretative Theory of Culture* (New York, 1973); Martin Heidegger, *Being and Time* (Oxford, 1962); Hans-George Gadamer, *Truth and*

as post-colonial countries any study of the political culture of Argentina, Brazil and Chile needs to take into account the importance of local conditions. Traditionally mainstream international relations has had very little to say about those nations away from the traditional centres of power. In part, the rationale behind this work is to hold local circumstances in view, this in order to explain to the action of agents embedded in their space. Moreover, it is argued that any attempt to explain the actions of a human agent requires that this spatial dimension remain part of our analysis. Ricouer is clear on this point:

> all objectifying knowledge about our position in society, in a social class, in a cultural tradition and in history is preceded by relation of *belonging* upon which we can never entirely reflect. Before any critical distance, we belong to a history, to a class, to a nation, to a culture, to one or several traditions. In accepting this belonging which precedes us and supports us, we accept the very first role of ideology, that which we described as the mediating function of the image of self-representation. Through the mediating functions we also participate in the other functions of ideology, those of dissemination and distortion.[25]

The idea that belonging and self-representation is important in any understanding of the action or thought of an individual is now orthodoxy across a range of disciplines. In sociology, anthropology and psychology both concepts form central elements of the discipline. The fact that this is not the case in International Relations is curious especially given the *national* component of International Relations.[26] The attempt to abstract this key element of global polity is extremely self-limiting for the researcher. In effect it is to ignore the impact of being say French, Chilean or Argentine. Again it is instructive to remember that the debate in Argentina on the country's international relations focused on the need to have less of an *Argentine* content in policy. To have as a starting position, the abstraction of national characteristics is to lose sight of the processes that led to the adoption of a pragmatic outlook during the Menem administration. Furthermore, such an approach does not allow us to detect the re-emergence of nationalism in Argentine policy terms from the second half of the 1990s onwards. Ruggie (1998) also argues for the salience of national characteristics in international politics:

Method (London, 1975); Paul Ricoeur, *Hermeneutics and the Human Sciences*, edited and translated by John B. Thompson (Cambridge, 1981).

25 Paul Ricoeur, *Hermeneutics and the Human Sciences*, p, 245.

26 Beirsteker is forthright in his criticism of the theoretical basis on international relations, he writes, 'Let us not deceive ourselves. "The vast majority of scholarship in international relations (and the social sciences for that matter) proceeds without conscious reflection on its philosophical basis or premises. In professional meetings, lectures, seminars, and the design of curricula, we do not often engage in serious reflection on the philosophical bases or implications of our activity."' Thomas J. Biersteker, 'Critical Reflections on Post-Positivism', *International Relations International Studies Quarterly* 33, (1989): p. 265.

Accordingly, contra neorealism, I suggest that the fact of *American* hegemony was every bit as important as the fact of American *hegemony* in shaping the post world war II international order.[27]

This lack of attention to *lo nacional* allows for the continued existence of rational, power maximizing statesman. Moreover, it permits the realist IR scholar to continued to reside in the universalist tradition of enlightenment thinking. To engage with the local would require a more interpretist approach that took cognizance of cultural and historical factors. Such an approach would throw open the discipline of International Relations. Rather than this representing a descent into epistemological chaos, the inclusion of such approaches would enrich our understanding of the nature of international relations and counter the dangers of an overly abstract approach.

The driving force behind those thinkers who sought to sanitize the realist position was the desire to achieve an objective position. This aspiration to attain objectivity is defined by Nagel as:

> The attempt [is] made to view the world not from a place within it, or from the vantage point of a special kind of life or awareness, but from nowhere in particular and no form of life in particular at all. The object is to discount our pre-reflective outlook that makes things appear as they do, and thereby to reach an understanding of things as they really are.[28]

'Objectivity of whatever kind is not the test of reality. It is just one way of understanding reality.'[29] Nagel further argues that the divisions between objectivity on the one hand and subjectivity on the other may in fact be unsustainable in that both are always present and there are times when one is more suitable to use than the other, but they rarely operate in isolation.

> Often the objective viewpoint will not be suitable as a replacement for the subjective, but will coexist with it, setting a standard with which the subjective is constrained not to cross.[30]

International relations transverses the realms of the objective and the subjective. In terms of relative capabilities and in terms of power the notion of objective analysis is often sustainable. However, in matters relating to identity and nationhood subjective forces are clearly at work.

In questioning the viability of the 'view from nowhere' we can turn to Martin Heidegger for support. The philosophy of Heidegger is a philosophy of

---

27 John Gerard Ruggie, *Constructing the World Polity* (London; New York, 1988), p. 14.

28 Thomas Nagel quoted Charles Taylor, 'Engaged Agency and Background in Heidegger' in Charles Guignon (ed.), *The Cambridge Companion to Heidegger* (Cambridge: Cambridge University Press, 1993), p. 322.

29 Thomas Nagel, *The View from Nowhere* (Oxford, 1986), p. 26.

30 Thomas Nagel, *The View from Nowhere*, p. 153.

embeddedness.³¹ Heidegger offers us an image of the subject or Dasein in a particular time/space surrounded by the implements of that time/space, living a life in which the subject puts these tools to work.³² It is the day to day, which conditions the thinking of the subject; he or she has a set of tools and a world to go to work in. There are tools present but there is also a background. The mind of each subject operates against a certain backdrop. This is the 'lifeworld' and each of us occupies a different "lifeworld". This is important because we come to the world with a particular set of ideas that are determined by the nature of this 'lifeworld'":

> Every interpretation has its fore-having, its foresight, and its fore-conception. If such an interpretation, becomes an explicit task for research, than the totality of 'presuppositions' (which we will call the 'hermeneutical situation') needs to be clarified and made secure beforehand.³³

Taylor sums up Heidegger's task stating that he had: 'to recover an understanding of the agent as engaged, as embedded in a culture, a form of life, a "world" of involvement, ultimately to understand the agent as embodied'³⁴ Heidegger narrows the ground available to those who claim to possess reason in that their ways of being are contingent on the nature of their particular world. In such a situation, it is difficult to privilege one kind of thinking over another. The subject no longer has any need to leave himself, nor indeed the, argument posits, can he even execute such an escape.

---

31 Heidegger has being criticized for focusing on the individual and neglecting to view the condition of the Dasein from a more social perspective. Critics include Heidegger's former student Hannah Arendt who portrays Heidegger as a fox trapped in his own lair. See Arendt's essay 'Heidegger and the Fox' in Hannah Arendt, (ed. Peter Baehr) *The Portable Arendt* (New York, London, 2000). It is true that the way forward for Dasein does lie in a withdrawal from the 'they' in a search for an authenticity of self. However, whilst the Dasein was not going to find any authenticity until he distanced itself from the 'they' of society, that does not mean that Heidegger does not recognize the impact of the 'they' on that society. In fact in his call for the retrieval of a personal space Heidegger implicitly accepts this force. Within 'Being and Time' it is explicitly accepted that, 'Dasein is essentially Being with others' (para 237). To hear the 'call' of conscience Dasein does need to step back and listen. So whilst Heidegger might call for a retreat from the social world he is aware of pubic norms and their impact; 'As thrown, it [Dasien] has been submitted to a "world" and exists factically with others. Proximally and for the most part lost in the "they"' (para 381). For our purposes, we are more interested in the descriptive elements of 'Being and Time' and here Dasein is a social being.

32 The position of Dasein in terms of temporality is discussed by Moran in his 'Introduction to Phenomenology'. Moran argues that the Dasein is both ahead of himself and in the past, thus occupying a broad temporal space. Moran's argument is confirmed by paragraph 385 of 'Being and Time'. See Dermot Moran, *Introduction to Phenomenology* (London; New York, 2000) and Martin Heidegger, *Being and Time*. (Oxford, 1962).

33 Martin Heidegger, *Being and Time*, para. 232.

34 Charles Taylor, 'Engaged Agency and Background in Heidegger', p. 318.

The Past and the Present

Not only is it important to locate the human subjects in terms of geographical location but also in terms of their position historically. Argentina, Brazil and Chile have all experienced profound transitions during the 1980s and 1990s. The nature of these transitions had a direct impact upon the construction of foreign policy.[35] More generally, a transition is marked by a move from one state to another different state of being. In effect, we are discussing a move away from the past into the new and distinct present. The introduction of new political practices and the creation of new institutions signal a break with the past. However, if we consider the nature of human subjects within the new regimes, difficulties arise with regard to any sharp distinction between the past and the present. Certainly, in the case of the individual, it is difficult to argue that the past does not have an impact on the present. For millions of citizens in Chile, the transition has involved a coming to terms with the past.[36] In Argentina, the dirty war has left a powerful and disruptive legacy.[37] In the field of psychology there is a widespread acceptance of the importance of the past in the constitution of the human subject.[38] The important point here is that from the psychological perspective the idea that the past can simply be left behind by either an individual or a society without some ill effects is mistaken. Furthermore, any attempt to seek to exclude the past from the present is presented as counter-productive and even dangerous.[39] Such dangers can feed into the political process. So how is it that the past can threaten the present? The philosophies of Heidegger (1962) and Benjamin (1970) both stress the impact of past on the human subject and society.[40] In anthropology, Geertz (1973) has explored the notion of a "thick present" that includes elements of the past. Given the acceptance of the salience of the past

---

35 Jorge Heine, *Timidez o pragmatismo? La política exterior de Chile en 1990* (Santiago, 1990). Joseph S. Tulchin, 'Continuity and Change in Argentine Foreign Policy' in Heraldo Munoz & Joseph Tulchin (eds), *Latin America in World Politics* (Boulder, 1996); Pedro Da Motta Veiga, 'Brasil a inicios del nuevo milenio: Herencias y Desafíos de la Transición' in Roberto Bouzas (ed.), *Realidades Nacionales Comparadas* (Buenos Aires: Altamira 2002).

36 Jonathan R. Barton & Warwick E. Murray, 'The End of Transition? Chile 1990–2000' in *Bulletin of Latin American Research*, 21:3 (2002), pp. 329–338.

37 Marguerite Feitlowitz, *A Lexicon of Terror. Argentina and the Legacies of Terror* (Oxford: 1998).

38 There is a wide-ranging literature which examines the impact of the past of the politics of the Southern Cone. Alexander Wilde discusses the danger posed to the transition process in Chile by 'irruptions' from the past. In the case of Argentina, Feitlowitz also identifies the past as a source of political conflict. See Wilde, 'Irruptions of Memory: Expressive Politics in Chile's Transition to Democracy' and Feitlowitz, *A Lexicon of Terror. Argentina and the Legacies of Terror.*

39 Sigmund Freud, *Civilisation and Its Discontents*, translated by Joan Riveiere (New York, 1963); Erik H. Erikson, *Childhood and Society* (New York, 1963).

40 Heidegger, *Being and Time*; Walter Benjamin, *Illuminations, Essays and Reflections* (London: 1970).

across these disciplines, it is surely wise to utilize these insights in the analysis of international politics.[41]

There are many potential avenues for discussion here. I propose to concentrate on two primary areas. Firstly, the impact of historical narratives and secondly the impact of subsequent history on such narratives.

Human subjects are historical beings, that is, they cannot be completely isolated from their historical context. Indeed, the linchpin of the past, present and the future lies in the human subject. It is the human subject that writes of the past, reads of the past, and attempts to recreate the past. It is this same subject living in his/her 'present' that dreams of the future. Humankind is the nexus at which the past and the future meet. The explanation for the attraction of the past lies in the need to identify oneself, to discover one's place in this temporal world. As Lowental argues 'I was' is a necessary component of 'I am'.[42] This could be extended to include 'we were' as a component of 'we are'. The desire to place oneself and one's kind on a temporal plane has been a constant in mankind over a long period.[43]

For the individual it is memory that binds today's subject with their past manifestations. In a world where the physical condition of the subject and that which surrounds him or her is in constant flux, the knowledge that memory can be relied upon to provide some continuity lends strength to identities. Individuals change as they pass through time and it is this memory that prevents a shattering of the self into a number of constituent parts located at different times in history. The unity of the individual over time provides the location for personal growth, similarly the unity of the collective also provides a location for development. It is worth noting in this context that the developmental capacity of the nation is a key element of politics in the Southern Cone.

Nationalism

In international relations, the most salient narratives to consider are national narratives. For Giddens, it is useful to make a distinction between two forms of nation building, the classical and the post-colonial. The former takes place in Europe, from the seventeenth century onwards, where mass education systems constructed

---

41 Citing Geertz's work *The Interpretation of Cultures* (London, 1993) Beate Jahn provides an interesting discussion of Geertz's views on the relationship between man and culture. 'This [Geertz's] understanding of culture suggests that there is no such thing as "human nature independent of culture", in fact, because he is dependent on their cultural production, for "undirected by cultural patterns – organised systems of significant symbols, man's behaviour would be virtually ungovernable, a mere chaos of pointless acts and exploding emotions, his experience virtually shapeless". Hence, if there is no culture without man, there is certainly no man without culture. All men are products as well as the producers of culture.', pp. 4–5.

42 David Lowental, *The Past is a Foreign Country* (Cambridge, UK; Cambridge, New York: 1985), p. 41.

43 Lowental dates this from the seventeenth century.

the imagined community. Even here, the creation of a national community rarely went uncontested.[44] Post-colonial nationalist projects took place on the much less fertile territory of disparate cultures, where there was an absence of a sense of a shared history.

There were attempts to instil a feeling of national identity in Latin America. Here as in Europe, there was sufficient motivation for such an undertaking, with many of the international boundaries contested, it was important that a sense of loyalty should be present among the population. Armies had to be raised and resistance had to be offered. However, the divisions between the elites in Latin America and the mass of the people are evident. The depth of contempt for the local population is striking. For Sarmiento, the Argentine people were made up of an inferior Spanish race and a servile indigenous population, and the solution lay in the introduction of a hard working northern European stock. Thus, for this local leader, Argentina's imagined community lay outside the country's boundaries.[45] It seems that the desire here is to be something else, but there is more to it than that. It should be noted that for the likes of Sarmiento, the past as represented by early Hispanic settlers and Indians was seen as largely negative and the future as potentially brighter and whiter. This pattern is repeated across Latin America.

As Francois Perus draws out, the relationship between a man like Sarmiento and the Argentine *gaucho* is ambiguous. Whilst identifying them as part of the barbarism that holds back the progress of the nation, he also is ascetically attracted to the life of such men.[46] This conflict is a constant in the Argentine psyche, the desire to be cosmopolitan and a longing for the simplicity of the *gaucho* life. In Latin American society we have this curious paradox of a rich *comprador* elite anxious to move the country on, overcoming and overhauling the old ways and yet, at the same time, identifying with those at the frontier.

National narratives then are complex and multifaceted phenomena. At times they are contradictory. The Gramscian idea of national narratives being laid down by successive generations of ruling groups is worthy of consideration. The geological metaphor is employed to describe the process as layer after layer of narrative build up over the decades and the centuries. The various components of such a process need not comply with any internal logic and are on occasions at odds with one another. The interesting quality they possess is the ability to outlive the social phenomenon that supported their creation. This means that power relations can change in such a way that national narratives can come to appear incongruous over time. Though this may be the case, they still retain their hold over people and continue to have an

---

44 Anthony Giddens, *Sociology* (Cambridge: Polity Press, 1993), p. 342.

45 Leopoldo Zea, *The Latin American Mind* (Norman, Okla, 1963), pp. 83–86.

46 Francoise Perus, 'Modernity, Postmodernity and Novelistic Form in Latin America' in Amaryll Chanady (ed.), *Latin America and the Construction of Difference* (Minneapolis: 1994), p. 50.

impact.[47] This tension between narrative and changing realities is an important part of the picture in Latin American foreign relations. Argentina provides us with the best example of how a disjunction between the content of national narratives and actual power relations can impact upon foreign policy. By the late 1980s, this disjunction had been identified by members of the Menem administration. They argued that policy decisions had for too long borne no relation to the actual position of Argentina in the world.[48] National narratives and power relations are not necessarily concurrent. Many of the foundational narratives of Argentina arose in the late nineteenth and early twentieth centuries. This was a time of great promise for Argentina and the country saw itself as having a trajectory likely to result in Argentina achieving great power status. Thus, exceptionalism was a very strong component of Argentine nationalism. Since World War Two Argentina has experienced a steep decline in power relative to both its near neighbour Brazil and to the United States. However, this decline was not reflected in the Argentine mentality and this, for some, led the country to pursue foreign policy sets that were seen by many as no longer appropriate.

National identity is more than simply a reflection of power relations in the world. Cultural traits feed into the nation's identity and this in turn can also impact upon the international relations of a country. For Morse (1995) identity is a collective awareness of an historic vocation.[49] Again using the example of Argentina, the country's elites have perceived themselves as European and this too impacted upon their outlook in the wider world.[50]

There are those elements of identity that lend themselves to attachment to a particular group, but there are also those elements that give rise to feelings of ambivalence or even hostility. Historically, the relationship between the nations of the Southern Cone and the United States has been a difficult one. This, in part, is due to perceived cultural differences. It has been bolstered by a continent-wide *hispanismo*, one component of which is the identification of the 'Anglo-Saxon' north of the continent as being a shallow materialistic place lacking the cultural depth of the southern part of the continent. In all three ABC countries there are long traditions of hostility and suspicion directed at the United States.[51] The origins of this sentiment are cultural, political and historical. It is difficult to be precise about the extent that such feelings shape hemispheric relations but psychologically it is

---

47 Enrico Augelli & Craig Murphy, *America's Quest for Supremacy and the Third World. An Essay in Gramscian Analysis* (London, 1988).

48 See Chapter 3 for the full discussion of the impact of this disjunction.

49 Richard M. Morse, 'The Multiverse of Latin America Identity 1920–1970' in Leslie Bethell (ed.), *The Cambridge History of Latin America* Vol. X (Cambridge, 1995), p. 1.

50 Ezequiel Gallo Argentina: *Society and Politics, 1880–1916* in Leslie Bethell, *The Cambridge history of Latin America* Vol. V (Cambridge 1986), p. 409; Carlos Escudé & Andrés Cisneros, Historia de las Relaciones Exteriores Argentinas, http://www.argentina-rree.com/historia.htmp, 8/8/-015.

51 Soares de Lima, cited in Da Motta, 'Brasil a inicios del nuevo milenio: Herencias y Desafíos de la Transición', p. 73; Frederick B. Pike, *Chile and the United States* (New York, 1983), p. 26; Tulchin, 'Continuity and Change', p. 68.

implausible that such widely held views would not have an impact on actors from the Southern Cone countries. Such narratives can also have an indirect impact on actors in the field of International Relations in that they also reside within the general populace. International agreements need to be sold to public opinion and their political leanings may make it more difficult to strike a deal with diplomats from another country. Widely held beliefs within a country may also encourage politicians to court public opinion. The Mercosur project in Argentina is seen as playing well to a sizable proportion of the electorate who are anti-American in outlook.[52]

There is also the impact of wider regional identities to consider. One of the key debates in across the Southern Cone is on the future of the Mercosur project. This debate is, at least in part, informed by whether or not it will be possible to build upon a sense of Latin American identity. At the outset, the Mercosur project was distinguished from earlier efforts at regional integration on the grounds that it was economically driven and trade and investment flows figured at the centre of the public discourse surrounding the project. Increasingly, the economic rationale for the project has looked somewhat shaky and the political drivers of the regional project have become more prominent. Realist analysis of power relations in the hemisphere can partly explain the motivation of the principal actors. However, in this instance, *latinamericanismo* does play a part. When Lula da Silva speaks of the destiny of Brazil lying with Mercosur he is using the type of linguistic register that feeds identity politics.

History and Narrative

If history is not to be a list or a collection of annals then we must admit the presence of narrative. Once we allow narrative its rightful place in the main body of history then we have begun to close the gap between history and fiction, Hamilton writes:

> To begin with the final demythologized view of the world is to neglect its explanatory origins and so to fail to understand it. And here lies 'the master key' of Vico's science: the discovery of the mythological or *poetic* sources of civilization.[53]

Vico came to recognize the danger inherent in the enlightenment's drive for objective truth and the danger of placing oneself outside history. In juxtaposing Vico's poetics and the demand for truth in history we are straddling one of the great dilemmas of the modern age. As in the area of international relations, there has in the study of history, been a strong desire to achieve a positivistic purity but also a simultaneous demand for meaning, and so, inevitably, narrative input.

---

52 Tulchin, 'Continuity and Change', p. 175.
53 Paul Hamilton, *Historicism* (London, 1996), p. 35.

But the real question is whether or not there is a human history. The epistemological version is the most prudent, but it is also the most disappointing, in accordance with the rules of the cognitive genre, anthropology describes savage narratives and their rules without pretending to establish any continuity between them and the rules of its own mode of discourse. In its Levi-Strausian version it may introduce a functional, or in other words 'structural' identity between myth and explanation, but it does so at the cost of abandoning any attempt to find an intelligent transition between the two. Identity but no history.[54]

For Lyotard, both epistemological and structural variants offer two very partial explanations of history. The former offers us events but little meaning the latter offers us a functional bridge between ascribed meaning and 'events' but it suffers from a similar difficulty as the former in that it plays down the 'events' or myths. For both then the event/myth carries so little power of its own that it is either rendered meaningless or it is so lacking in meaning that it lends itself to functionalist explanations, that is, available to be given an arbitrary meaning. We must opt for a new path allowing both the real of epistemology and the myth used by the functionalists to come together within a broader theoretical framework. There is at once a need to accept the gravitational pull the real exerts in the imagery and the tangible effects the imaginary can have on the real.[55] Hayden White sums up the argument:

> The history, then, belongs to the category of what might be called the 'discourse of the real', as against 'the discourse of the imaginary' or the 'discourse of desire'...we can comprehend the appeal of the historical discourse by recognising the extent to which it makes the real desirable, makes the real into an object of desire, and does so by its imposition, upon the events that are represented as real, of the formal coherency that stories possess.[56]

There is a close and symbiotic relationship between history and fiction. Moreover, narrative plays an important role in the creation of history. However, more structuralist explanations, which suggest events are merely expropriated, tend to underplay the effect of events.[57]

The historical artefact at the heart of International Relations is the nation. The discipline of International Relations has in the main insisted on viewing this entity from a rationalist perspective and it has also attributed rationality to those who that act on behalf of this entity. And yet, it must be apparent that the nature of this artefact does not lend itself to such an exclusive approach. The nation is a product of history expressed in narrative form, although not fictional it relies upon fiction for its strength and durability.

---

54 Jean-Francois Lyotard, *Lyotard Reader*, Andrew Benjamin (ed.) (Oxford, 1989), p. 321.

55 Malcolm Bowie, *Lacan* (Cambridge, 1991), pp. 94–99.

56 Hayden White, 'The Value of Narrativity in the Representation of Reality' in Susana Onega & Jose Angel Garcia Landa (eds), *Narratology* (New York; London, 1996), p. 281.

57 Baudrillard suggests that the age of history is also that of the novel. Jean Baudrillard, *The Illusion of the End* (translated by Chris Turner) (Cambridge, 1994), p. 47.

The politics of nationhood has over the generations imported the discourse of various disciplines. Most striking is the merging of the discourse relating to the individual and that surrounding the nation. Nations are ascribed characteristics, they sometimes need to forgive and other times need to be forgiven and frequently have a destiny or a mission. Like an individual they have a history, the relationship between the past and future generations is often very intimate. As Benjamin recognizes past generations can make claims on those living in the present.[58] Given these complexities the temptation has been to use abstractions to account for the dynamics of international relations. The danger in such an approach is that we lose sight of the reality of international politics. Rationality plays a role, but we can have no doubts that other forces are at work.

The Multifaceted Nature of Power

Realism tends to focus on relative capabilities. There are many components that can feed into power; this is particularly the case when we consider soft power. This variant of power uses persuasion and example as its major tools. If plentiful enough, soft power can sometimes ensure that military measures or 'hard' power, do not become necessary. Both the realist and the Gramscian School suggest that centres of power can impose a set of certain practices on the world. The flow of ideas corresponds to the contours of power in the world and in a given society. The distinction here between these two approaches is that while the realist school would tend to focus on the power relations, Gramscian theory accepts the importance of relative power but adds emphasis to ideological hegemony. This hegemony is achieved through a variety of mechanisms, the important point here is that these mechanisms do not lend themselves to realist approaches. Any assessment of the effectiveness of ideas and their acceptance by populations demands interpretive techniques. To be successful, the wielding of power is dependent upon influence as well as coercion. This is one of the key insights of the Gramscian School and is true both of domestic and international politics.[59]

Foucault, whilst accepting many of the insights of the Marxist critique of society, argues that power also lies in practice. He further argues that in practice both unintended consequences are commonplace and that resistance is an important component of the social system. Foucauldian analysis then stresses discontinuities in practices that develop through time and resists the Marxist tendency to explain social

---

58 Benjamin argues that the claims of the past cannot be settled cheaply. Walter Benjamin, *Illuminations, Essays and Reflections*, p. 256.

59 This issue of soft power is gaining prominence in debates on the manner the United States has responded to the attacks of September 11, 2001. By pursuing such an aggressive stance critics of the Bush administration point to the damage the US is doing to its reputation abroad, particularly in the Arab world. Essentially we are discussing the so-called 'battle for hearts and minds'. In order to undertake such an enterprise there is a need to understand the nature of those hearts and minds.

interaction as purely a relation of class. Foucault shares the Gramscian concern with the spread of ideas, but he also argues that the practice, ideas or technologies come to have a power in themselves. These technologies come to shape the manner in which human actors see the world and they tend to determine the future patterns of relations. The crucial distinction here pertains to the relationship between authorship, agency and power. For Foucault, while human agents are influenced by existing practice/ ideology, it is also the case that the successive production of practice/ideology may have unexpected consequences.

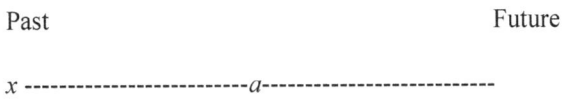

Figure 2.1 Practice/ideology and the human subject

It is not that power relations at *a* are irrelevant, rather past practice/ideology shape future patterns of practice/ideology and outcomes are not determined solely by power. Hence practice (that which passes along the *x* axis), or what Foucault frequently referred to as technology comes centre stage and merits in and of itself specific attention. For Foucault, the ability to co-opt the subject in the exercise of power is crucial:

> He who is subjected to a field of visibility, and who knows it, assumes responsibility for the constraints of power; he makes them play spontaneously upon himself; he inscribes in himself the power relation in which he simultaneously plays both roles; he becomes the principle of his own subjection.[60]

The individual is persuaded to manage his own behaviour. In the context of post-colonial countries such insights are valuable. These ideas can be extended into the sphere of international relations in a number of ways. Firstly, national boundaries provide, and this is particularly true today, no protection against ideas. Thus, ideas transverse the world of sovereign states and impact upon human subjects. Secondly, just as the individual is asked to exercise control over the wider self, so it is that elites are co-opted to discipline the wider body politic. On a metaphysical level national boundaries are somewhat blurred. Historically, the use of domestic elites to discipline the domestic political scene has been an important part of the post-colonial experience. It is not enough simply to view the nation state as a self contained unit operating in the space of inter-state competition.

As both Gramsci and Foucault indicate culture is an important part of the overall picture. This view is shared by Walker (1998):

---

60 Michel Foucault, *Discipline and Punish: the Birth of the Prison* (Harmondsworth, 1979), p. 402.

Far from being largely irrelevant to considerations of power, as so many analysts have supposed, cultural processes have always been central to the way power is constructed, legitimised and transferred.[61]

International politics is not *just* nations competing against one another for maximum material benefit. Certain lands, relationships and beliefs carry a value far beyond their 'book value'. Other lands and people may generate a fear disproportionate to their actual capability. Long-standing fear and hostility may have an impact on any bargaining process. Some cultures themselves may be stronger than others in that they provide a greater reservoir of traditional values so creating a greater resistance towards change. The international system is not always a free market where one object can always be traded for another for the mutual benefit of the traders. There is a cultural topography to be constantly borne in mind. The attachment to certain objects may be stronger in some cultures than in others.

In the Latin American context, the dispute between Chile and Bolivia on the question of access to the Pacific has taken on importance beyond the issues immediately at stake. Similarly, the Malvinas' question for Argentina has very strong political connotations. Such disputes take on a significance beyond that which is immediately at stake. The honour of the nation and the sacrifices of previous generations enter the equation and once they do so objectivity is no longer what drives the process. There are many such disputes in the world, in fact it is the lack of objectivity which is seen as the main problem in attempting to resolve such disputes. In Northern Ireland, the Balkans and the Middle East disparate cultures drive the conflict. These are some of the key struggles shaping global polity and yet realist analysts struggle to account for the actions of human agents in such conflicts.

The Impact of Violence, Fragmentation of Narrative

If national identity and those narratives that sustain them have an impact on the environment in which foreign policy is framed, we can assume that changes in such identities and narratives will also affect policy. Political events in Latin America over the 1970s and 1980s did result in some profound changes in identities and narratives. Across the Southern Cone the military authorities not only set themselves the task of changing regimes but also of changing the relationship between state and society.[62] Brazil, Argentina and Chile lived through a period of profound political change, however it was Argentina where the discontinuities in political culture were at their most profound. The trauma of political violence and economic turmoil led to a widespread reappraisal of the Argentine political culture. In particular whether

---

61 R.B.J. Walker, *Explorations in Peace and Justice: New Perspectives on World Order* (Boulder, 1988), p. 35.

62 Manuel Antonio Garreton, 'Political Democratisation in Latin America and the Crisis of the Paradigm' in James Manor (ed.), *Rethinking Third World Politics* (London; New York, 1991), p. 105.

or not *lo argentino* had served the country well. This sense of national identity had informed the 'dirty war' and had pushed the country in the direction of conflict with the UK over the Falklands/Malvinas. The purpose of the 'dirty war' was precisely to win the battle over which cultural construct would become real in Argentina. For the Argentine military the stakes were high. According to General Diaz Bessone, subversion meant, 'the changing of values, the changing of a national culture'. He added, 'culture is not just sculpture and painting. No, no. Culture is everything'.[63] The battle the military had to wage was for the heart of the nation; at stake was the meaning of being Argentinean. The abject failure of the military was damaging to both themselves as an institution and the national narratives that were employed by the military during their tenure in office. Furthermore, the military here as elsewhere in Latin America, was intimately connected to the idea of the nation. The fact that the Argentine military left office so discredited devalued the notion of *lo Argentino*. This, in turn, had a number of consequences, one of which was the wholesale re-examination of the impact of Argentine political culture on the country's citizens. A debate over the nature of traditional Argentine foreign policy positions was part of this process. In Chile the situation was similar in that again there was an intense battle fought over the meaning of being a *national*.

Those around Menem were determined to open a new chapter in Argentine politics and, in particular, they were anxious to establish a new pattern of international relations for the country. It was the long shadow cast by the generals that allowed for these changes to take place. *Lo argentino* was no longer a point of resistance to such changes as it had been undermined by the events of the previous decades. In Chile the military regime cast a shadow over the civilian administrations of the 1990s, and the effect, though less dramatic, was similar. Again national narratives became less important, in part, because they were discredited. In Chile, history had become a problem to be managed and ceased to be a source of strength. During the 1990s it became clear that a large percentage of the Chilean people had difficulty relating to the country's history and that this was having a pernicious effect on the political culture of the country.[64] These changes in attitudes toward the nation are critically important.

The main canon of work on national identity appears to explicitly accept the imaginary status of the nation.[65] Marxist and Constructivist insights into the function of nationalist rhetoric are also valuable. Elite groups have had an interest in the promotion of nationalist histories. However, the manner in which engagement takes

---

63 Antonius Robben, 'The Fear of Indifference: Combatants' Anxieties about Political Identity of Civilians during Argentina's Dirty War' in Kees Koonings & Dirk Kruijt (eds), *Societies of Fear. The Legacy of Civil War, Violence and Terror in Latin America* (London, 1999), p. 126.

64 United Nations, *Desarrollo Humano. Las Paradojas de la Modernización* (New York, 1998).

65 E.J. Hobsbawn, *Nations and Nationalism Since 1870* (Cambridge, 1990); Anthony D. Smith, *The Nation Invented, Imagined, and Reconstructed* (Reno, 1991) and Wilbur Zelinsky, *The Shifting Symbolic Foundations of American Nationalism* (Chapel Hill, 1988).

place is more knowing that these theoretical positions can account for. The gain for the human subject is a layer of identity. In engaging with their nationalist discourse and in relating to components of both individual and collective identities many people are deciding to engage.[66] The engagement then is not one of a dispassionate observer. For the individual human subject this relationship is characterized by its fecundity and its fragility, hence the passion that surrounds this type of discourse. This is the key to understanding the impact of state violence on national identity. The element of volition makes the construct vulnerable, because that which is identified with must remain attractive. In Chile, the violence of the military and the subsequent failure to deal with this episode rendered *lo chileno* less attractive.[67]

The period from 1973 is one of great dislocation in Chilean society. The aim of the military was 'in part' to depoliticize Chilean society. In terms of the public realm this was largely achieved. The savagery of this period is striking; mutilation, rape and electric shock were all widely practised.[68] These events in themselves profoundly damaged Chilean society. Arendt, in her *On Violence* writes of the social atomization born of state terror.[69,70] Throughout this period we also see the *treasures* of the nation, in particular national narratives become marked or stained. In the first instance, the use of the armed forces in the repression of the Left was damaging to their reputation. In September 1973 the bearers of a proud military tradition marched out the gates of their barracks to seize control of the streets; the army that fought so proudly on the Moro at Arica had now acted with such ferocity in the national stadium.[71] Past military glories would now come to be associated with the mutilation of Victor Jara.[72]

---

66 In her discussion on Lacan and the nature of the ego Anika Lemaire accepts the power of collective identities, 'Civil status, profession, titles, membership of social, political or cultural circles are so many forms assumed by the Ego and all demonstrate the symbolic's dominance over man', Anika Lemair, *Jacques Lacan* (London, 1977), p. 180.

67 See United Nations, *Desarrollo Humano. Nosotros los Chilenos Un Desafió Cultural* (New York 2002).

68 These abuses are now widely documented. Peter Kornbluh's *The Pinochet File* lists the practices of the Chilean secret police, the DINA, and the locations used to keep prisoners. Peter Kornbluh, *The Pinochet File. A Declassified Dossier on Atrocity and Accountability* (New York, 2003).

69 Hannah Arendt, *On Violence* (New York, 1969), p. 55.

70 Again on this matter, Boothby writes: 'political terror induces a pervasive atmosphere of paranoia. By means of this paranoia, the larger social bonds of relation are undermined', Richard Boothby, *Death and Desire, Psychoanalytic Theory in Lacan's Return to Freud* (New York, 1991), p.182.

71 On the damage done to image of the military and change in civilian-military relations see pages 67–68 of United Nations Development Programme, *Desarrollo Humano. Nosotros los Chilenos*, pp. 67–68. The Battle at the Moro in Arica was a key Chilean victory during the War of the Pacific.

72 Victor Jara was a famous Chilean musician. According to witnesses his wrists were broken before he was killed. Mark Ensalaco, *Chile Bajo Pinochet* (Madrid, 2002), p. 74.

Across Latin America, there is a strong connection between nationhood and the armed forces. According to the military folklore, the armed forces are not just part of the nation, they created it.[73] The fact that the Pinochet regime associated itself with the past and made use of the iconography of Chilean history was to destabilize the country's historical narratives. History spiritually fed the military, providing them with succour in their arduous task. Their 'just cause was the defence of salvation of the nation and in name of its permanent values'.[74] According to Gonzalo Rojas Sánchez love of country and its history are necessary characteristics of the military and that each member of the armed forces should be proud of the role the armed forces played in the history of the country. September 11, 1973 was just one such episode, another decisive affirmation of nationhood.[75] For Orrego Vicuña in his contribution to publication *Seguridad Nacional* in 1976, three years into the dictatorship, the importance both of national destiny and history was clear.[76] The historian Verónica Valdivia Ortiz de Zárate, emphasizes the important role of history in terms of justifying the actions of the military junta. History was used as a means of differentiating the military rulers from the Allende government with the former represented as the guardians of continuity and the latter as those who had violated the traditional norms of the country.[77] For Gazmuri, The Molina Doctrine, which holds that the Chilean military has a duty to preserve Chilean values, has as its origins on the battlefields of the 19th century.[78] Hence a relationship developed between that glorious past of the military and the Chile of the 1970s and 1980s. In

---

73 See David R. Mares, *Violent Peace, Militarised Interstate Bargaining in Latin America* (New York, 2001).

74 See Elizabeth Lira and Brian Loveman and their discussion as to how the actions of the military were actually represented as an act of national reconciliation. Lira & Loveman, *Las ardientes cenizas de olvido* (Santiago, 2000), pp. 441–442.

75 Rojas Sánchez in Rojas Sánchez and Fontaine Talavera, 'Debate Sobre La Posición de las FF.AA Frente al Gobierno Militar', *Estudios Públicos*, 91 (2003), pp. 301–310. It is worth noting that Rojas Sanchez is an historian whose views are perceived as close to many in the Chilean military.

76 Francisco Orrego Vicuña, 'Trayectoria y orientaciones de la política exterior de Chile', *Seguridad Nacional.* Santiago 2 (1976): pp. 73–82.

77 'En síntesis, es cierto que tras la intervención hubo una aspiración de recuperar valores y respeto a tradiciones que se consideraban parte de la idiosincrasia nacional, contra los cuales el gobierno de Allende habría atentado. Este anhelo se relacionaba con las denominadas "virtudes militares" como la "fuerza de la tradición", es decir, con el origen de la patria, el cómo se constituyó; de ahí el énfasis en el pasado histórico y el aporte que estadistas, héroes, mártires y líderes han hecho a su materialización.' Verónica Valdivia Ortiz de Zárate, 'Estatismo y Neoliberalismo: Un Contrapunto Militar Chile 1973–1979'. Historia (Santiago) 34 (2001): pp. 167–226.

78 'I personally believe this doctrine was established in the late nineteenth century and based on the national mythical tradition that Chile has always been victorious and has consolidated its nationality on the battlefields.' Cristián Gazmuri, 'The Armed Forces in Democratic Chile' in Angell and Pollack (eds), *The Legacy of Dictatorship: Political, Economic and Social Change in Pinochet's Chile* (Liverpool, 1993), p. 133.

this way the past both underwrote Chilean identity, and was inextricably linked to a terrifying present. The result in Chile was a crisis related to the meaning of being Chilean and the nation's place in the wider world. Foreign policy came to be marked by conformity, a desire for acceptance and a lack of overall direction in foreign affairs.[79]

In both Argentina and Chile the trauma left a political legacy. It shaped the internal politics of both countries for the following decade. It would be strange indeed if the area of foreign relations were somehow immune to such profound social forces. By insisting on compartmentalizing the *domestic* and the *international*, mainstream approaches in International Relations severely limit their descriptive capacity. Crises do have an effect on political systems; history shows this to be the case. Bauman argues,

> Bouts of such insecurity are in no sense novel; neither are the typical responses to them. Both are known to appear throughout history in the aftermath of wars, violent revolutions, collapse of empire, as concomitants of social departures too vast or too fast to be assimilated by the extant policing agencies.[80]

The period of military rule in Argentina and Chile represented just such a social departure. It was not that the military rule in and of itself was without precedent, it was rather the unique and profound impact this period of military rule had on national politics in these countries. History has had an effect on historical narratives and this has destabilized political identities. Thus, any attempt to isolate a social science from the past is abstracting a key causal element. Bryant writes:

> The 'past' is thus never really 'past' but continually constructive of the 'present', as a cumulative and selectively reproducible ensemble of practices and ideas that 'channel' and impart directionally to ongoing human agency. The present, in other words, is what the past – as received and creatively interpreted by the present – has made it.[81]

The relationship between past and present is such that each impacts on one another. Geertz's idea of a 'thick present' may be useful also.[82] There are circumstances when this engagement is more intense than in others. Furthermore, the nature of any engagement can vary across space. In Chile during the 1990s we see flight from

---

79 Jorge Heine, 'Timidez o pragmatismo? La política exterior de Chile en 1990' (Santiago: 1990). Fermandios argues: 'Its [Chile's] correct decision not to look for nor to feign the search for leadership does however run the risk of resulting in wanting for a foreign policy, and of impoverishing the space a country like Chile should occupy.' Joaquin Fermandios,'De una Inserción a Otra: Política Exterior de Chile, 1966–1990', *Estudios Internacionales*, 24: 96 (1991): p. 454.

80 Zymunt Bauman, *Life in Fragments. Essays in Post modern Morality* (Oxford, 1995), p. 185.

81 Bryant quoted in Stephen Hobden, *International Relations and Historical Sociology* (London, 1998), p. 24.

82 Clifford Geertz, *Towards an Interpretative Theory of Culture* (New York, 1973).

history and this in part determines the ultra-cautious nature of Chilean politics in that decade, which is true both in the domestic and the international sphere. In Argentina the situation was different in that we see a rejection of past policies and a sudden rupture in practice and this clearly fed into the country's international relations. This divergence can be explained in large part by the distinct nature of the transition to democracy in the two countries. In Chile, the military retained a degree of institutional power and in Argentina, the armed forces left office completely discredited. In Argentina there was widespread agreement that the military has failed the country, in Chile there was no such agreement and the country remained a 'country of enemies' unable to come to a consensus, hence the paralysis.[83] The forces at play in Argentina post-1983 were such that profound changes in policy direction were possible.

In Brazil the armed forces left office with their reputation largely intact. There was less soul searching than took place in Argentina and Chile and the historical narratives were not disrupted in the same way as they had been in Argentina and Chile. As in the case of Chile, the military retained a powerful position under the new civilian government installed in 1985. Two other factors mitigated against any major change in the direction of the Brazilian foreign policy. The position of the *Itamaraty*, as the guardian of Brazil's external relations, remained largely unchallenged for decades. Secondly, the political culture of Brazil was much less democratic than its neighbours. Historically, power in Brazil has been more concentrated and elite groups have managed policy without much recourse to the mass of the Brazilian people. The absence of embedded democratic practices and the fact that the Brazilian military preserved, at least nominally, some of the institutions of democracy, meant that the cultural rupture brought about by military rule was not as severe as was the case in Argentina and Chile. Political activity continued under the military regime with the military authorities tending to react to opposition's gains by curbing the political space available to them by the passing of ad hoc repressive measures.[84] The conflict in Brazil was less defined and the military authorities were less ambitious in terms of managing the political culture of the country. Military rule here was a more limited project than elsewhere in the Southern Cone. This is partly explained by the much smaller size of the leftist resistance. All this is not to say that history and identity were not important in the construction of foreign policy but rather that institutional and political continuity has allowed such inputs to remain less visible. In Brazil, the lack of an intense struggle over the wider cultural sphere meant that identity was less of an issue. 'Brazilianess', never became politicized in the same way as 'Chileaness' and 'Argentineaness'.

The contestation of history and identity that took place in Argentina and Chile brought such inputs into sharp relief. The crises in each country allowed us to view the role that history and identity played in policy terms. Such inputs were but a part

---

83 Constable and Valenzuela, *A Nation of Enemies* (New York, 1991).

84 Kess Koonings, 'Shadows of Violence and Political Transition in Brazil: From Military Rule to Democratic Governance' in Koonings & Kruijt, *Societies of Fear The Legacy of Civil War* (London 1999), p. 208.

of a larger group of determining factors in the area of foreign policy, but identity politics is a part of the overall picture and cannot be ignored:

National culture plays a role in foreign policy and Morgenthau recognizes the importance of political culture. Moreover, despite the diversity of the groups that make up a society they share a common culture:

> They partake of the same language, the same customs, the same historic recollections, the same fundamental social and political philosophy, the same national symbols. They read the same newspapers, listen to the same radio programs, observe the same holidays and worship the same heroes. Above all, they compare their own nation with other nations and realise how much more they have in common with each other than with members of the other nations...Their intellectual convictions and moral valuations derive from that membership.[85]

This book attempts to capture some of those effects, which derive from political culture, identity and history. Rather that abstracting the individual characteristics of the units that make up the international system the goal is instead to understand and account for the impact of their individual properties. This is but one way of 'doing' International Relations, but it does yield an understanding of the complex dynamics in International Politics. In the case of the nations of the Southern Cone, an understanding of internal political dynamics is invaluable as they are so closely related to foreign policy. This is accepted by those at the institutional coalface. From their distinct political perspectives, ex-foreign ministers José Miguel Insulsa in Chile and Di Tella in Argentina, both accept the saliency of the domestic policies in the area of foreign relations.[86]

Foreign policy is also closely related to notions of destiny and national identity. Over the past two decades in Argentina there has been much discussion as to whether or not this *should* be the case, but very little discussion from the region as to whether it *is* the case. There is ample evidence that such phenomena play an influential role. The problem for the discipline of International Relations is how to relate to cultural, identity and narrative forms. International Relations has available to it a rich philosophical heritage with which to work. The primary issue that arises is how compatible such approaches are with the long established realist tradition. Part of the answers lies in recovery of more nuanced approaches that exist towards culture and identity that exist already within the realist canon. An acceptance of the validity of multiple approaches to the problems of studying international politics

---

85 Hans J. Morgenthau, *Politics Among Nations* (New York, 1993), p. 335.

86 Insulsa, closely linked the country's foreign policy to the domestic political scene; 'foreign policy is a projection of the internal policies of a government ... foreign policy is necessarily related to internal politics'. Jose Miguel Insulsa, *Ensayos sobre política exterior de Chile* (Santiago, 1998), p. 33. Di Tella linked the domestic politics to foreign policy; see Anabella Busso & Alfredo Bruno Bologna, *La Política Exterior Argentina a Partir del Gobierno de Menem: Una Presentación* in CERIR (ed.), *La Política Exterior Argentina a Partir del Gobierno de Menem* (Rosario, 1994), p. 27.

would constitute a step forward. There are instances when the interpretive tradition offers more apt basis for describing political processes. There are also benefits in more systemic or scientific approaches to international relations. Human agents on occasion act on rationalist principals with the goal of maximizing power. This is the Machiavellian moment, but it is only a moment. Human beings are complex creatures and explaining their actions required a multiplicity of approaches and this is accepted across a range of disciplines where understanding human agency is a central task.

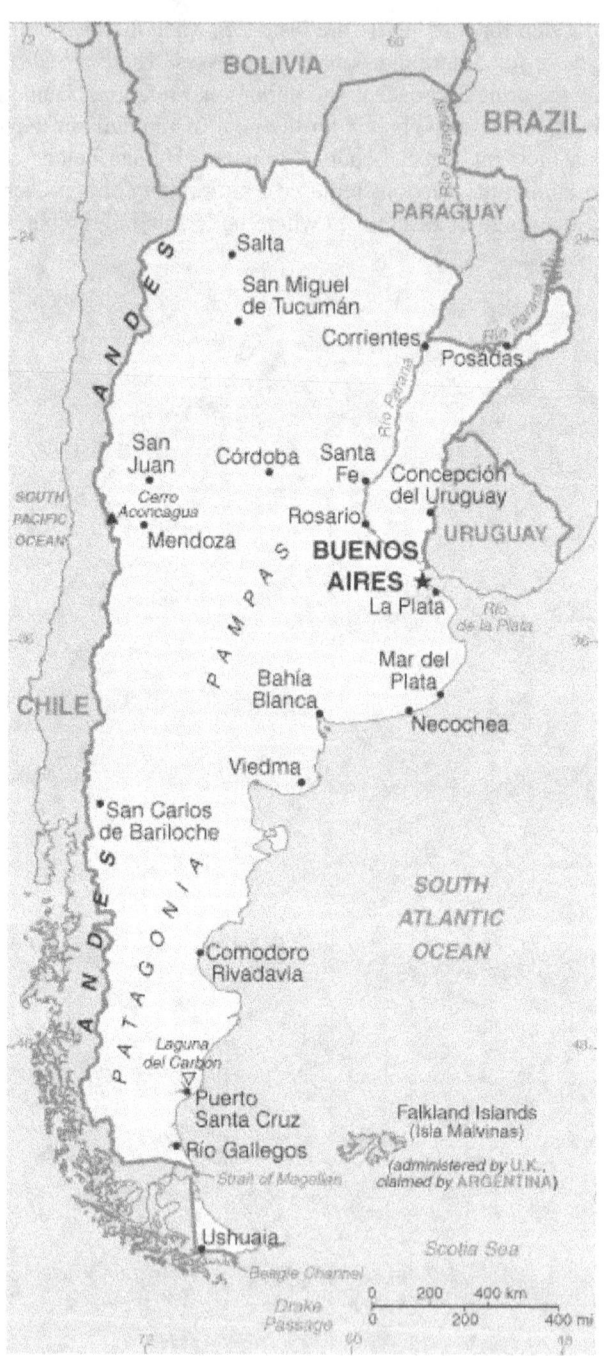

Map of Argentina

Chapter 3

Argentine Foreign Policy

Introduction

Argentina lies in the Southern Cone of Latin America, it borders on Brazil to the North, Paraguay and Bolivia to the northwest and to the west it shares some 5,150 km with Chile. Next to Brazil, it is the second largest country in South America and the territory encompasses the cold harsh landscape of Tierra del Fuego in the South and the sub-tropical provinces in the North East. The heart of the country is *la pampa*, the vast area of grassland in the centre of the country. This formed the basis of the country's economic success in the late nineteenth century, providing home to cattle ranches and other agricultural activities. The population of the country as of July 2005 was over 39 million people.

In recent decades the country has undergone a series of profound crises. Military dictatorship, chronic debt, hyperinflation and defeat in the War in the South Atlantic have disorientated the country and this has affected the governance of Argentina. Since 1983, public policy has gone through a series of profound changes as the various administrations have sought to find a way out of the country's deep economic and political malaise.

There are a number of features that mark out Argentine foreign policy from those of Brazil and Chile. In the first instance, there have been considerable discontinuities in the country's foreign policy. Secondly, there has been a more intense internal debate on the nature and suitability to those policies. Argentine positions within world polity have oscillated between extremes and this, it is argued, damaged the developmental prospects of the country. The importance of Argentina's engagement in world affairs has always been amplified by a tradition of activism in world affairs and its desire to achieve a level of prestige has been somewhat out of line with its relative power. In foreign policy terms, Argentina also shares some common features with its neighbours. There has been the imperative to achieve economic development. This ambition has been a source of much frustration in Argentina as, in regional terms, the country has seen its relative economic performance slip back. The increasing asymmetry, in terms of relative power, between Argentina and Brazil is a serious impediment to good regional relations between the two. Like its neighbours, the government in Buenos Aires has had to wrestle with the issue of regional integration. Since 1991, Argentina has been a member of the Mercosur group, but its levels of commitment have varied through time. Again, like its neighbours, relations with the United States are a key element of foreign policy. Argentina has oscillated between two distinct poles of attraction, one has been that of regional solidarity and the other, closer ties with the United States.

In recent decades Argentina has shared with its neighbours the experience of living under military rule and of a long process of democratization. These processes, here as elsewhere have, in part, shaped the foreign policy decisions of Argentina. Of the countries included in this study, the impact of the transition was strongest here. The combination of massive brutality and abject failure forced the departure of the military, this constituted a sudden institutional rupture. In the aftermath of this trauma Argentina has struggled to redefine itself.

The construction of Argentine identity has been a fascinating process. Like all such constructions, this identity has come to be based partly on the condition of the country and partly on myth. Here, as elsewhere, it is an ongoing process. There are features of Argentine identity that have had a major impact on the country's foreign policy. In Chile and Brazil we see the tendency to create a particularlist historical vision to feed an exceptionalist identity. This is also true of Argentina, but in its case the exceptionalist tendencies have been, if anything, stronger and more out of line with the real capabilities of the nation.

In seeking to describe and explain Argentine foreign policy, there is a need to examine numerous factors that have fed the process. Again, as with Chile and Brazil, we are looking at a configuration of forces that give rise to that policy. These social forces cannot be viewed in isolation and are often closely related and impact on one another. Through time the nature of this configuration changes and one of more elements come to the fore. The need to accept the use of multiple theoretical perspectives is again apparent. Domestic politics, history, identity, economics and relative power all play a role in determining the nature of Argentine foreign policy.

Historical Antecedents

In Argentina, as elsewhere in Spanish America, the initial break from Spain was precipitated by the invasion of Spain by Napoleon's armies in 1808. The war which followed caused administrative dislocation and severely weakened Spanish colonial rule across the Americas. The process of gaining independence from the Spanish crown was strongly linked to that of Chile with San Martin de los Andes leading the liberation forces in both countries. Subsequently, the history of the two countries diverges sharply and their experiences of domestic politics were very distinct. The principal difference between the two countries was that Chile managed to achieve a functioning state before Argentina. By the second half of the nineteenth century, this was to have serious implications for inter-state relations in the region, as despite her smaller size and population Chile had become a formidable military power. During the first half of the nineteenth century Argentina was extremely unstable with ongoing violent conflicts between centralist and federalist forces. It was the time of the *caudillo* or the strong man. Juan Miguel de Rosas was a dominant figure during these decades, ruling the province of Buenos Aires from 1829 until 1852. Away from Buenos Aires, Rosa's enemies united briefly in a desire to form a nation and under the influence of key national figures including Domingo Faustino Sarmiento and Juan Bautista Alberti they began the process of state building in those areas outside the control of the Rosas. The newly formed Argentine Federation continued to function without Buenos Aires and under President Urquiza the Federation was recognized by Britain as the legitimate authority in Argentina. After a series of bloody battles in which the Confederation sought to subdue Buenos Aires by force, it was the leadership in Buenos Aires under Mitre who eventually took the initiative to form a national government. In 1862 Mitre became the first president of the Argentine Republic.

The first national census of 1869 demonstrated that the country remained very underdeveloped. The country was vast (though the borders in the South remained undefined) and the population was less than two million.[1] The standard of living for these inhabitants was extremely low with 78.6% of the population living in *ranchos*, buildings of mud and straw. The rate of illiteracy at this time stood at 77.9%.[2] This was the time of the *gaucho*, the mythological Argentine cowboy operating in the semi-wilderness. As in the Chilean case, there was violence on the Indian frontier and overcoming Amerindian resistance remained a key concern of the government of the time.

From 1860 onwards, there were moves towards a unitary state and over the next two decades the country began to take shape. A key moment in this process was the settlement with Chile over possession of what is now southern Argentina. Chile had through the century gained a good deal of influence in this area and by 1870 was claiming the whole of Patagonia south of the Rio Negro. The War of the Pacific represented an opportunity to settle this issue with its neighbour. Whilst Chile was engaged in a war on its northern borders with both Peru and Bolivia, Argentina was able to take advantage of the situation and with its relative power greatly enhanced by the conflict in and around the Atacama desert, a settlement was arrived at which saw Argentina take possession of enormous tracts of territory which included all of Patagonia to the east of the Andes. Following the Treaty of 1881, there remained a number of outstanding border issues to be settled along the mountainous frontier between the two countries and in the far south around Tierra del Fuego.

Between 1864 and 1870 Argentina fought alongside Brazil and Uruguay in defeating Paraguay in the War of the Triple Alliance. The war was an unparalleled national tragedy for Paraguay who saw their male population decimated, but for Argentina it removed a potential threat to its borders. The victory was in large part due to Brazilian resources. As Argentina grew in strength, it would be Brazil that would come to be its main rival in the Southern Cone. Chile, though in decline in

---

1   Excluding claims to the Antarctic and possessions in the Atlantic the surface area of the country is just under 2.8 million square kilometres. The country is five times the size of France.

2   Ezequiel Gallo Argentina, 'Society and Politics, 1880–1916' in Leslie Bethell' *The Cambridge history of Latin America* Vol. 5 (Cambridge, 1986), p. 359.

relative terms, also constituted an important part of the geopolitical system in the Southern Cone of Latin America. Chile would seek close ties with Brazil in order to offset the threat posed by Argentina and similarly the two larger nations would on occasion court the Chileans in order to achieve a more favourable balance of power. Thus, the ABC countries, as they would come to be known, constituted an important strategic sub-system in the Americas. A fruitless intervention by Argentina, Brazil and Chile at the invitation of Washington in a dispute between the United States and Mexico resulted in a short-lived coming together of the ABC countries. El Tratado de ABC was signed in May of 1915.[3] The arrangement was short lived, it was pulled asunder by domestic dissent and inter-state quarrels surrounding the First World War.[4] The reaction at the time to the ABC initiative is instructive; it set alarm bells ringing elsewhere in Latin America and also in the United States.

From the 1880s Argentina entered a time of good fortune. The country enjoyed decades of political stability and economic growth.[5] The period between 1880 and 1910 is referred to as Argentina's 'golden age'. By the beginning of the twentieth century observers saw a great future for the country. With its natural resources and economic vigour and growing role in world trade, the country seemed destined to rival the United States.[6] Argentina's economic ascendancy reached its zenith in 1939 when it accounted for 33% of all Latin American trade, 80% of its foreign exchange and gold reserves and its national income was 25% greater than that of Brazil.[7] Immigration flows into the country were very strong. In 1914, three quarters of the working class in the country were foreign born.[8] In the course of three decades the country was transformed, and nowhere was this transformation more evident than in and around the city of Buenos Aires. The immigrants fed both the growing economy and their presence provoked a form of strident nationalism. With the immigrants came political ideas from southern Europe, with the doctrine of anarcho-syndicalism which spawned widespread strikes around the turn of the century being particularly strong. The waves of immigration gave rise to a virulent and defensive nationalism which sought to insulate the Argentine nation from foreign influence and discover a true form of *argentinidad*. This nationalism, which took a strong hold in Argentina, would have long-lasting repercussions both in terms of internal and external politics.

The combination of intense nationalism and an extended period of economic success led to a sense of, if not national grandeur, then impending national grandeur.

---

3   Carlos Escudé & Andrés Cisneros, *Historia de las Relaciones Exteriores Argentinas*, http://www.argentina-rree.com/historia.htmp. /7/7-039. The ABC Treaty of 1915 was never ratified by the legislatures in either Argentina or Chile. In both cases the treaty encountered considerable internal opposition.

4   Ibid., p. /7/7-057.

5   Gallo, 'Argentina: Society and Politics, 1880–1916', p. 362.

6   Daniel K. Lewis, *The History of Argentina* (New York, 2001).

7   David R. Mares, *Violent Peace, Militarised Interstate Bargaining in Latin America* (New York, 2001), p. 127.

8   Gallo, *Argentina: Society and Politics, 1880–1916*.

Argentine nationalism took on similar traits to that of the manifest destiny of the United States. The notion of *grandeza nacional* became an important goal in foreign policy formation.[9] At the start of the twentieth century Argentina was the wealthiest country in South America. By the time of the First World War, per capital income was comparable to that of the Low Countries and Germany and exceeded that of Spain, Italy, Sweden and Switzerland.[10] Argentina was becoming wealthy and this underpinned its confidence in world affairs.

In the early years of the twentieth century two key figures, with influence over the longer trajectory of Argentine foreign policy can be identified, Luis María Drago and Hipólito Yrigoyen. Drago gave his name to the Drago Doctrine, which espoused the principal of non-intervention and was driven by a desire to stop armed interventions by European powers and the US in pursuit of commercial interests. The limitations of the Monroe doctrine were plainly exposed in 1902 by the muted US reaction to a bombardment of Venezuela by Britain, Germany and the Italians. Furthermore, even if it was the case that the US would resist European intervention, it was not willing to renounce its own right to intervene. For his part, Yrigoyen espoused the ideals of neutrality, pacifism and the moral basis of international relations. This line of reasoning and in particular his determination to pursue an independent foreign policy line gave rise to the epithet of *Yrigoyenismo*.

The coming of the twentieth century saw the rise of the United States. Throughout the Americas the United States was gradually displacing Britain as the main economic force in the region. However, the case of Argentina was somewhat different. European markets remained by far the major destination for Argentine products. The power and influence of the United States in Argentina was lessened by the similarities in production patterns, which made it relatively unimportant as an export market. There is another important point here, namely the hostile reaction of sections of the Argentine elite to restrictions placed on Argentine exports to the US market. Argentina in the first decades of the twentieth century found itself in a position where a hegemonic power was developing in the North of the Western Hemisphere whilst at the same time the Argentine elites remained distinctly European in outlook and the vast bulk of its trade was destined for European markets. This situation represents an interesting disjunction between patterns of hard power and soft power. In cultural terms, Argentina remained deeply wedded to the continent of Europe. For Borges, it was a country of exiles. At the same time the United States was a growing power and an increasingly strident actor in foreign policy terms.

During both world wars, Argentina was to maintain a neutral position. This was to further distance the country from the United States. In contrast, Brazil sought to gain favour with the US through siding with the Allies and taking an active part in the war. For the most part, Argentina has not pursued this option of seeking to enhance its international prestige through seeking favour in Washington. Instead the

---

9   Guillermo Miguel Figari, *Pasado, Presente y Futuro de la Política Exterior Argentina* (Buenos Aires, 1993), p. 201.

10 Gallo, *Argentina: Society and Politics*, pp. 393–394.

country has, in the main, chosen to pursue an independent foreign policy line. This position has in more recent time fuelled an intense debate on the nature of Argentine foreign policy and, in particular, the risks attached to this desire to retain a high profile in world affairs.[11]

The costs associated with this independent line in foreign policy are all the more apparent in times of economic difficulty. Argentina enjoyed conspicuous economic success in the late nineteenth and early twentieth century. However, the country's reliance on the export of primary goods into the European market made it vulnerable to dislocations in international trade. The Great Depression saw export earnings dry up and resulted in severe difficulties for the Argentine economy. Subsequently, the country has never lived up to its initial promise of economic success. From seeing itself a rival to the United States and as an economic powerhouse in the Southern Cone, the relative decline of Argentina has been striking. Repeated economic crises have undercut the sense of national destiny and led to a reassessment of Argentina's position in the world. Moreover, from the 1950s onwards there was a realization of the importance of foreign capital, and especially capital from the United States. For Figari (1993) this has led to more pragmatism in Argentine foreign policy.[12] Increasing debt levels placed emphasis on the need to retain good relations with lenders and suppliers of capital. The period after 1930 is best characterized as one of long decline. The Peronist era that followed the war was a time of sharp social divisions. In 1964, there was a military coup, however divisions among the military reflected divisions in society. One general followed another into office and the situation was further destabilized by a left-wing insurgency. Between 1973 and 1976, there was a short return to civilian rule. According to Williamson (1992) what eluded the country was a stated idea that could command general allegiance.[13]

Argentine Identity

The construction of, or the arrival to, a national identity is both a complex and contested area of political thought. In the case of the nations of Latin America there is the additional phenomenon of post-colonialism to be considered. Much of a nation's identity is forged during the nation state's formative years. The particular difficulty in the foundation of states in Latin America was that they were formed before a myth of nationhood was available. The nineteenth century is, for Argentina, the key period in this regard and we can detect a number of competing visions within Argentine society. We can also see tensions in the positions adopted by key national figures during this period. In the thoughts of Sarmiento we see the competing ideals of the strong autonomous figure of the *gaucho* and a strong desire to imitate the

---

11 See Joseph S. Tulchin, 'Continuity and Change in Argentine Foreign Policy' in Heraldo Munoz & Joseph Tulchin (eds), *Latin America in World Politics* (Boulder, 1996).

12 Figari, Pasado, *Presente y Futuro de la Política Exterior Argentina* (New York, 2001), p. 191.

13 Edwin Williamson, *The Penguin History of Latin America* (London, 1992).

Anglo-Saxon model of Britain. Civilization and barbarism are juxtaposed and so are the city and the countryside.[14] In Argentina we also see the co-presence of a strong admiration for things European and a strong feeling of belonging to Latin America. Geographically, there is a split between the highly cosmopolitan city of Buenos Aires and the more provincial interior. Such conflicts are played out in not only the politics of the country but also in the cultural life. The life and work of the great Argentine writer, Borges is suggestive of the divisions that exist in the Argentine psyche. In Argentina, as in other Latin American societies there has been a tendency to emphasize *Latino* values over those of the *Anglos*. The former set of values is seen to represent the traditions of the family and a higher spiritual plane.

Like its neighbours, Argentina developed a strong sense of itself as an exceptional country. The narratives that fed this image of Argentina differ from those of Chile and Brazil. The distinct racial mix of Argentina, being more European, fed a sense of superiority over other Latin American countries. The strong growth that began in the late nineteenth century strengthened the idea of Argentina as an exceptional country and as having a particular destiny. However, 'since World War II, Argentina has suffered a severe identity crisis'.[15] The crisis in Argentina identity is reflected in a variety of sources.[16] The fate of nationalist narratives, which no longer exist in benign circumstances, is a fascinating area. There are a number of examples around the globe, where the foundational myths of a society no longer reflect the material circumstances of the nation. Lyotard writes of the black hole of history, thus Budapest 1956 was the abyss for Marxist historical materialism. The decline of Argentina from the 1940s can be read in a similar fashion. A certain vision of Argentina was destroyed in the second half of the twentieth century.[17] One major question for Argentina over the course of the twentieth century has been whether or not the Argentine vision of itself and its role in the world has served the interests of the country. The answer given depends to a large extent on the nature of nationalism itself and whether one takes an essentialist viewpoint. There is no denying the fact that national identities change through time, but elements of such an identity should remain constant for national identity to have any real meaning. For nineteenth century intellectuals such as Gálvez, the Argentine race was unique and the nation merited sacrifice. Such tendencies retain their influence into the second half of the twentieth century. In 1976 the ex-president Arturo Frondizi could argue that the Argentine nation has been engaged in a titanic struggle to:

> Restore the historical truth, to save [our] tradition, to make evident those national roots of our thought and culture in spite of the distortions and deformations that threaten them.

---

14 Tamara Holzapfel, 'Latin America Literature' in Knippers Black (ed), *Latin America – Its Promise and its Problems* (Boulder 1995).

15 Joseph S. Tulchin, 'Continuity and Change in Argentine Foreign Policy', p. 165.

16 Juan Carlos Chaneton, *Argentina: La Ambigüedad como destino La Identidad del País Que no Fue* (Buenos Aires 1998) and Marguerite Feitlowitz, *A Lexicon of Terror. Argentina and the Legacies of Terror.*

17 Jean-Francois Lyotard, *Political Writings* (Minnesota, 1993), p. 313.

Because of our efforts, never in our national evolution has the guiding threat of Argentine essence [*lo Argentino*] been interrupted.[18]

The utility of discussing the identity politics of Argentina here lies in their close association with the country's foreign policy. Given the fact that Argentine positions in world affairs have been frequently out of line with the realities of the power politics of the day, analysts have sought to explain this by recourse to Argentine identity. Tulchin (1996) in his discussion of the trajectory of Argentine foreign policy detects certain continuities and explicitly links them to Argentine identity:

> the continuities across administrations and even across regime changes indicate profound tendencies within Argentine foreign policy that appear to be part of the nation's collective sense of self, axiomatic element of the nation's political culture.[19]

It is the changing fate of Argentina over the past century or so that have thrown these tendencies into sharp relief. The national narratives have not in general tracked the decline in the relative power of Argentina. In the half century between 1880 and 1930 such were the positive developments in Argentine society that the expression 'God is an Argentinean' was coined. By the 1970s such a statement would generate a rueful smile.

Dictatorship and Democracy

The seizure of government by the military in 1976 was part of an established pattern. In the period between 1930 and 1983, of the 23 presidents, 15 were military officers. The regime that came to power in 1976 was distinct from those in the past. Its attitude to the state involvement in the Argentine economy was one cooler than its predecessors. The Videla regime was also notable for its brutality. The military junta, which took power in 1976, had as a central tenet, the permanent elimination of potential subversion in Argentina. The military set about 'reforming' Argentine society, which included an attack on trade unions and the wages of the working classes. In 1976 real wages fell by 35% and in 1978 real wages did not exceed the levels of the 1960s. The military enjoyed support from agriculture and multinational finance, but the policies pursued by the Finance Minister José Martinez de Hoz were hostile to the working class.[20] The economic policies of the government had three key elements. Firstly, to increase agricultural exports, secondly to improve industrial efficiency through lower tariffs and more competition and thirdly, price stabilization through smaller government deficits and lower aggregate demand.

---

18 Jean H. Delaney, 'Imaging El ser Argentino: Cultural Nationalism and Romantic Concepts of Nationhood in Early Twentieth-Century Argentina', *Journal of Latin American Studies* 34 (2002), p. 635.

19 Tulchin, 'Continuity and Change in Argentine Foreign Policy', p. 167.

20 Williamson, *The Penguin History of Latin America*.

The policy of inflating the value of the peso to control inflation led to a surge in imports and consequently a current account crisis. One of the consequences of military rule was a surge in external debt. In 1979 it stood at US$19 billion, in 1980 it was US$ 27.2 billion and by 1981 it had grown to US$ 35.7 billion. Financial problems plagued this so-called reform process and Martinez de Hoz eventually found himself isolated. With a change of military government came a change in policy and a move away from economic liberalism.[21] The economic and financial policies of the military governments ultimately failed. This is important in the sense that the sacrifices could not be justified in the same way they were in Chile.[22] Pinochet's supporters have long tried to promote the notion that without the reform programme pursued by the military regime the strong growth rate exhibited by the country in the late 1980s and 1990s could not have happened. In the case of Argentina, the policies adopted by the military were widely seen as an abject failure.

Over the longer term it was the human rights record of the Argentine military that would have the most serious repercussions. In the period between 1976 and 1983 the military endeavoured to destroy left-wing opposition in Argentina. Estimates vary of the number of dead and/or disappeared, ranging between 10,000 and 30,000.[23] There were many more thousands tortured during this time of terror. In the years following the departure of the military this would lead to a profound period of reflection in Argentina and lead ultimately to a precipitous decline in the respect enjoyed by the Argentine military and call into question their particular vision of the world. These societal changes would ultimately feed into the foreign policy-making process tending to diminish the standing of the more exceptionalist tendencies.

The event that finally precipitated the departure was a foreign policy decision on the part of the military government. There is some discussion as to the origins of the decision to invade the Falklands/Malvinas in 1981. On the one hand there are those who argue that the invasion was driven by domestic considerations and was designed to distract a restive population from the failures of the economic reform

---

21 With the coming to power of Lt General Roberto Viola in March 1981 the programme of trade liberalization was abandoned and more interventionist economic policy was pursued. Laura Tedesco, *Democracy in Argentina. Hope and Disillusion* (London, 1999), pp. 47–49.

22 This is not to suggest the human rights abuses could be justified on such grounds. The supporters of the Pinochet regime do frequently cite the economic success of Chile in the 1990s as justification for the regime and its policies.

23 In its report Nunca Más ('Never Again'), the National Commission on Disappeared Persons (Comisión Nacional Sobre la Desaparición de Personas, CONADEP), set up by elected President Raúl Alfonsín in December 1983, listed 8,960 victims of 'disappearance'. More recent official figures put the number at about 14,000, but some experts believe it to be even higher, due to unreported cases, especially in rural areas. Tedesco cites a figure of 30,000. Laura Tedesco, *Democracy in Argentina. Hope and Disillusion* (London: 1999), p. 64. The number of cases exceeds the number of 'disappeared' in any of the neighbouring countries ruled by military governments at the time, and dwarfed the number of victims whose bodies were found and identified (1,898). http://www.hrw.org/reports/2001/argentina/argen1201-02.htm#P130_28947.

programme and on the other are those who see this as a foreign policy issue with the invasion triggered by a decline in the relative power of Britain. This said, the nature of the regime was certainly a factor:

> The aggressive proclivities of the Argentine military, unchecked in any form of civilian control, provided the key pressure that led to both the initial grab of the islands and the decision to fight a potentially costly war for their control.[24]

The eventual surrender of the Argentine garrison on the islands led to massive protests and the military were forced from power.

During its tenure, the foreign policy pursued by the military was somewhat ambivalent towards the United States. The military were the most willing of the Cold War warriors and yet they retained strong trade links with the Eastern Bloc and the non-aligned movement. They shared with Washington a strong anti-communist position and yet relations with Washington, even before the war in the South Atlantic were somewhat cool. The reasons behind this initial coolness in relations and their subsequent improvement in 1980s lay as much in Washington as in Buenos Aires. The human rights agenda of the Carter administration caused difficulties in the relationship, but during Reagan's years in the White House the human rights agenda was a poor second to virulent anti-communism and the atmosphere between the two countries improved. This improvement was consolidated by Argentine cooperation in the violent conflicts of Central America during the 1980s. Such cooperation was driven by a shared analysis of the nature of the conflict in Nicaragua and El Salvador rather than by any real desire for close relations with the US.

> The Argentine Military thus aided the Reagan administration in its agenda, but in a way that preserved Argentina's cherished foreign policy autonomy and still avoided making friendship with the United States.[25]

Galtieri proclaimed that Argentina marched in step with the United States but his policy of aiding the US in Central America was at odds with that of the foreign ministry. The military dictatorship proved disruptive to the process of foreign policy making, moreover, the military themselves were often unable to unite around a common foreign policy project.[26]

The military were influenced by geopolitics and a Darwinian vision of interstate relations. This placed an emphasis on relations with its neighbours. Despite the fact that all three regimes shared a common purpose in ideological terms (this extended to cooperation against left-wing guerrillas), relations between them were tense and in 1978 Argentina and Chile were at the point of war over a territorial dispute in the

---

24 John Arquilla & Rasmussen Moyano, 'Origins of the South Atlantic War', *Journal of Latin American Studies* (2001): p. 746.

25 Deborah L. Norden & Roberto Russell, *The United States and Argentina. Changing Relations in a Changing World* (London, 2002), p. 25.

26 Ibid., pp. 58–59.

South. Geopolitics enjoyed a renaissance across the Southern Cone and in Brazil and Chile this perspective was also influential in foreign policy circles.[27]

The nature of the transition to democracy in Argentina was different to that in both Chile and Brazil. The military did not retain prestige and institutional power, the debacle of the Falklands/Malvinas campaign and their failure to make any progress on the economic front meant that the military were largely discredited. This was not an agreed or *pactado* transition to democracy. The crises precipitated by the defeat in the South Atlantic War forced the military from office, and they were not in any position to negotiate any institutional role within the new structures. There was less continuity than in either Brazil or Chile. Historically, the Argentine military had taken an active role in the politics of the country and, if not legitimate, military intervention in Argentina was in the past legitimated by broad sections of public opinion.[28] This had changed by 1983. Despite their loss of prestige, the Argentine military remained a threat to the new democracy and the main policy objective of the Alfonsín government was the consolidation of democracy. In order to counter the power of the military, defence spending was cut back from 5.98% of GDP in 1983 to 3.71 in 1984.[29]

Human rights abuses were an important issue during the Alfonsín presidency. Again, this was not a managed process and there was resistance from the military. In particular there were concerns within the military over whether all levels of the armed forces could be punished for following the orders of their superiors. It was this issue that prompted a military rebellion in 1987. The incident began when a Major Barreiro refused to attend a court and took refuge in a military barracks in Córdoba. Eventually, Alfonsín himself was forced to intervene in person to try and diffuse the situation. In the period between 1987 and 1988 there were three military revolts. Early in the transition process, democracy in Argentine remained weak.

With such key issues outstanding, the civilian government used its foreign policy options in an attempt to defend democracy. Across the Southern Cone the international system was seen as offering some strength to the democratic model.[30] In Argentina, we see 'the overt use of foreign policy as a mean of protecting fragile and newly established democracy'.[31] The move to improve relations with Brazil was part of the process of protecting the newly established institutions. Indeed, the

---

27 Howard T. Pittman, 'Geopolitics and Foreign Policy in Argentina, Brazil and Chile' in Elizabeth G. Ferris & Jennie K. Lincoln (eds), *Latin American Foreign Policies. Global and Regional Dimensions* (Boulder, 1981).

28 Alain Rouquie & Stephen Suffffern, 'The Military in Latin American Politics Since 1930' in Leslie Bethell (ed), *The Cambridge History of Latin America* Vol. VI (Cambridge, 1994), p. 249.

29 Laura Tedesco, *Democracy in Argentina. Hope and Disillusion*, p. 64.

30 Jonothan Hartlyn, 'Democracies in Contemporary South America: Convergences and Diversities', in Joseph S. Tulchin with Allison M. Garland (eds), *Argentina: The Challenges of Modernization* (Wilmington, 1998), p. 92.

31 Andrew Hurrel, 'Security in Latin America', *International Affairs* 74:3 (1998): p. 536.

whole Mercosur project is closely related to the democratization of the Southern Cone. It was not simply attributable to the existence of new regimes. The need to manage internal conflict drove, at least in part, the improvement in relations within the Southern Cone. Both Collor de Mello and Alfonsín had reasons to be fearful. Though the transition was less fraught in the Brazilian case, there remained problems in subordinating the military to the will of the civilian administration.

In terms of what was achieved, improved contacts with regional neighbours generated a number of positive effects in terms of civilian-military relations. It allowed for a new analysis to come to the fore and for the geopolitical ideas, prevalent among the armed forces, to become less relevant. Trade links stressed the need for cooperation and not for eternal competition. Improved relations that stressed economic benefits also tended to change the location of responsibility for relations with neighbouring countries within government. Increasingly, those ministries orientated towards diplomacy, trade and commerce gained a more important role. More profoundly, improved relations meant a change in the environment in which the nation state exists. The world became less hostile, relations with neighbours were no longer construed as a zero-sum game and the rationale for high defence spending started to disappear.

Sotomayor (2004) identifies a need for politicians in a democratization process to ensure against uncertainty as a further driver in improving regional contacts.[32] With the internal political situation so difficult to manage, Argentine politicians chose to at least gain some control over the security environment they occupied. This neutralized the historical agenda of border disputes and arms races so making the internal environment less susceptible to external shocks.

There is one further point that merits discussion here, namely, the effect of the dictatorship on the country's national identity. Strident nationalism provides the ideological sustenance for inter-state rivalries. Nationalism tends to stress difference and emphasize the positive characteristics of a particular nation. Typically, such nationalism also highlights the wrongs of the past. There is the tendency to portray one's own country as the victim of overbearing and aggressive neighbours. One characteristic of profound social changes and historical trauma is the manner in which such notions can be damaged and ultimately fall into disrepute. This is especially the case if the institution, which is the bearer of many national traditions, namely the armed forces, loses their reputation. In Argentina the damage to the military was severe. In the period after the military dictatorship of 1976–1983 there was a feeling of intense disappointment and an acknowledged need for reflection on the nature of

---

32 Sotomayor (2004). Discussing the good relations between Menem and Collor de Mello, Sotomayor argued that their shared fear of anti-democratic forces cemented the relationship: 'the civilian leaders of the two countries made an alliance to appease their rivalry in order to focus on their most important threat, military insubordination'. Arturo C. Sotomayor Valazquez, 'Civil–Military Affairs and Security Institutions in the Southern Cone: The Sources of Argentine–Brazilian Nuclear Cooperation', *Latin American Politics and Society*, 46:4 (2004): p. 42.

Argentine society. It was somehow no longer appropriate to espouse the virtues of *lo argentino*. In a country struggling to overcome the excesses of the 'dirty war', national pride was a difficult emotion to conjure up. History then, has an impact and the shadows of Generals Videla and Galtieri lay over the process of foreign policy making. The response was similar to that of Chile, in that reinsertion into the international community offered hope, indeed the international community offered standards of civilized behaviour that had been absent for a number of years. It was no longer possible to project Argentine values onto the world.

> Thus in the decade or more after 1983, the discussion of the foreign policy came to identify the 'correct policy' with policies that were realistic and appropriate to the world as it was, not as Argentine leaders might wish it to be.[33]

This was a new situation, one that allowed for the formation of new policies. In terms of foreign policy, Argentine historical narratives had two important strands that had shaped decision making over the course of the century. Argentine exceptionalism had mitigated against both close relations with the United States and with its neighbours. The decline in national self-confidence meant that both these polices could be considered as realistic options.

Regional Relations

During the Alfonsín administration closer relations with its neighbours was the preferred option. Argentine–Brazilian relations over the course of the twentieth century were marked by competition and distrust between the two countries. In the first decades of the twentieth century the two powers struggled with each other for strategic advantage. The propensity of Brazil to use its traditionally closer relationship with the United States to gain advantage over its neighbour was a notable aspect of this dynamic until the 1980s. The reconciliation between Brazil and Argentina has been the most profound change in not only Argentine policy but also in the inter-state relations in the Southern Cone. There remains some unease about the preponderance of power on the Brazilian side, 'Nevertheless, the problem of Brazilian power is no longer understood in strategic let alone military terms'.[34] In many respects it is more difficult to account for Argentine motives in this rapprochement. Brazil seeks to be a genuinely global player and this involves constructing a regional arrangement in which Brazil is seen as the leader. The rationale behind Argentina's engagement in this project is more multifaceted. We have already discussed the domestic drivers of regional pacts, but as democratization took hold this type of motivation would become less apparent. Indeed after more than 20 years of improving democracy this

---

33 Tulchin, 'Continuity and Change in Argentine Foreign Policy', p. 166.
34 Hurrel, 'Security in Latin America', p. 534.

line of argument may be less useful today. By the start of the twenty-first century the Argentine military was no longer a significant actor in the country's politics.[35]

Argentina's commitment to the Mercosur project did waiver in the course of the 1990s. As democratic institutions became stronger the emphasis turned more towards economic growth. This led Argentina to adopt a set of policies more akin to Chile, in that the country became open to other trading relationships. In particular, in the period around 1993–1994, a hemispheric trading pact was the preferred alternative for the Argentine government. In 1989, Carlos Menem was elected president, and his economic team were less than convinced about the long-term viability of the Mercosur project. They saw Mercosur as a mere stepping-stone on the way to a wider trade agreement.

> While Brazil's strategic commitment to MERCOSUR remained stable during the bloc's first decade, Argentina's was more ambiguous and internally divided. Despite the economic importance of the process of regional integration, Argentina's foreign policy strategy during the 1990s made the development of improved relations with the United States its first priority.[36]

Initially under Menem, Mercosur was a vehicle for Argentine insertion into the world economy.[37] The dilemma as to the eventual fate of sub-regional pacts such as Mercosur did not really arise as Argentina expected the region to be swept up in a US-led free-trade initiative.

The failure of the Clinton administration to gain 'fast track' authority from the US Congress led to a reassessment of Argentine foreign policy priorities. As in Chile, this failure to achieve the 'fast track' caused considerable disruption to policy. In the circumstances, Mercosur took on a greater importance. It was, in the short term at least, the only game in town. However, with time Argentina has become less reticent about Mercosur and once again it is a central plank of Argentine policy. From the presidency of Dulhalde onwards, we have seen the development of a strategic alliance between Argentina and Brazil. The basis of this is the desire to create a functioning regional bloc with common positions in world affairs.[38]

Despite the political commitment of Brasilia and Buenos Aires, Mercosur was under pressure throughout the 1990s and economic difficulties towards the end of the decade saw some ruptures in the agreement. In response to economic crises, both Argentina and Brazil resorted to unilateral actions that breached the agreement.

---

35 Roberto Bouzas (ed.), *Realidades Nacionales Comparadas* (Buenos Aires, 2002), p. 14.

36 Laura Gomez Mera, 'Explaining Mercosur's Survival: Strategic Sources of Argentine–Brazilian Cooperation', *Journal of Latin American Studies* 37:1 (2005): p. 132.

37 María Alejandra Saccone, 'Aspectos políticos-diplomáticos de una nueva prioridad de la política exterior argentina: el Mercosur' in CIRIR (eds), *La Política Exterior del Gobierno de Menem. Seguimiento y reflexiones al promediar su mandato* (Rosario, 1994), p. 114.

38 Lincoln Bizzozero, 'Los Cambios de Gobierno en Argentina y Brasil y la Conformación de una agenda del MERCOSUR', *Nueva Sociedad* 186 (2003), p. 134.

Indeed, such were the problems in Mercosur between 1999 and 2001 that many were predicting the group's demise. And yet despite this, the members of the pact have restated their commitment to the organization. This is all the more interesting given the fact that the economic rationale for the group has faded somewhat.[39] The strong growth in intra-regional trade was not sustained and there have been some serious setbacks since the late 1990s. Trade between members declined for a time, and the institutional integrity of the agreement was challenged.[40] The continued existence of the pact may be best explained by its defensive functions. In economic terms, it allows Brazil and Argentine to face together the challenges of changing international trade and investment patterns. However, the principal motivation may lie in the political sphere. The agreement lends both parties some weight in negotiations with the United States on its FTAA initiative. In any bilateral negotiations both parties are extremely vulnerable to US pressure. This is all the more pertinent since the 1999 WTO meeting in Seattle where it became clear to developing countries just how little was on the table from the United States. The failure of the Cancun talks has further galvanized the position of developing nations. In this environment it makes more sense for Brazil and Argentina to stick together. In the case of the former, it would represent a serious challenge for a position built up over many years if Mercosur was to come asunder. For Argentina, the merits of going it alone in trade talks look questionable. Furthermore, the uncertainty generated by the attacks of 2001 on the United States has increased the sense of vulnerability of both countries and has tended to further emphasize the costs of going it alone.

There is something of a paradox with regard to the series of crises that have afflicted the Mercosur pact. As Gomez (2005) points out, the overcoming of repeated crises has given rise to a growing sense of the irreversibility of the project.[41] Moreover, as the project endures we see the development of shared instincts in the area of international relations. The constant contact and the struggles to arrive at common positions may be leading to a convergence in terms of world views. The key element of any such world view has been and will continue to be the manner in which Brazil and Argentina view initiatives from Washington. Argentina faces a distinct set of options from those of Brazil. The relative decline of Argentine over the past half-century has meant that Argentina is not an equal partner to Brazil. This asymmetry remains one of the most serious challenges facing Mercosur. The decline in the relative power of Argentina also explains their motivation in that Mercosur does strengthen their foreign policy hand.[42] The dilemma for Argentina is whether or not it can adjust itself to Brazilian leadership. Despite the tradition of activism in Argentina and the occasional willingness of Brazil to follow an Argentine lead in

---

39 Laura Gomez Mera, 'Explaining Mercosur's Survival: Strategic Sources of Argentine–Brazilian Cooperation', *Journal of Latin American Studies* 37:1 (2005) p. 110.

40 In 2001 Argentina broke the agreement on Common External Tariff.

41 Laura Gomez Mera, 'Explaining Mercosur's Survival'.

42 Micheal Mecham, 'Mercosur: A Failing Development Project?', *International Affairs* 79:2 (2003): p. 385.

international affairs this remains a very real issue. The choice is not one of accepting Brazilian leadership or pursuing an autonomous foreign policy. The looming FTAA negotiations have thrown the country's options into sharp relief. The options are rowing in behind Brazil or accepting US hemispheric leadership.

Relations with Chile also improved with the return of civilian government. In 1984 the Tratado de Paz y Amistad was signed with Chile. Just a few years earlier, the two countries had been on the brink of war in a territorial dispute over border demarcations at Tierra del Fuego, in the far south. With the restoration of democracy in Chile in 1989, relations warmed considerably. A number of border disputes were resolved by the two governments and *la agenda clásica*, one dominated by territorial disputes and geopolitical rivalry disappeared to be replaced by talks over trade and infrastructure projects. Both civilian administrations had a common goal of protecting democracy and addressing issues around human rights. The nature of the transition in Chile was distinct from that of Argentina and this had an impact on relations between the two counties. Argentina represented the best example of the subordination of the military to civilian rule.[43] In Chile, the process of establishing civilian supremacy was much slower and the military continued to enjoy prestige and autonomy. This continued influence of the military in Chile has meant that even among the centre-left in Chile security related ideas are heavily militarized, as opposed to the more citizen-centric policies of Argentina.[44] During the 1990s there was a growing military imbalance in Chile's favour. In 1996, Chile had some 93,000 military personnel compared to 75,000 in Argentina. However, the government of Ricardo Lagos (2000–2006) has been more strident in attempting to restore the supremacy of the civilian administration and this has further improved relations. The overall picture is now one of warm relations. Trade and infrastructural links have grown and Argentina is now a key supplier of gas to Chile. Within Mercosur, Argentina was active in the process of Chile achieving associate membership. For Argentine policy planners, Chile is less important than Brazil in both economic terms and political terms and Chile's decision to negotiate a bilateral free-trade agreement with the United States sets the country apart from the two leading players in Mercosur.

Redefinition of Argentine Foreign Policy under Menem

For a time under Menem there was an explicit commitment to accepting US leadership. It is a fascinating time for analysts of Argentine foreign policy. The move was almost without precedent and was driven by a wholesale reappraisal of Argentina's position in the world. As Norden and Russell point out Argentina's 'transformation to the

---

43 Monica Hirst, 'Security Policies, Democratisation, and Regional Integration in the Southern Cone' in Jorge I. Domínguez, (ed.), *International Security and Democracy: Latin America and the Caribbean in the Post-Cold War Era* (Pittsburgh, 1998), p. 106.

44 Carlos Escudé & Andrés Fontana, 'Argentina's Security Policies. Their Rationale and Regional Context', pp. 66–67.

most devoted of US allies stands as a major break in the historical pattern of US-Argentine relations'.[45] It is perhaps no surprise that this process took place in the aftermath of one of the most difficult periods of Argentine history. With the nation's confidence sapped by shocking state violence, by hyperinflation and by defeat in the South Atlantic, *lo argentino* came to be less valued. This facilitated a challenge to Argentine traditions in foreign policy making. The narratives that sustained Argentine exceptionalism no longer had the same hold over the population. These narratives had for generations effectively precluded the country from falling into the orbit of the United States, but in the 1980s there was a questioning of these narratives and the identity they spawned. Menem's comments on Argentina's history are instructive: 'The past has nothing more to teach us ... we must look ahead, with our eyes fixed on the future. Unless we learn to forget we will be turned into pillars of salt.'[46] In Argentina as in Chile, the past and the future had become political positions and the outcome of the conflict between the two would have profound consequences for both domestic and foreign policy sets.

This criticism of Argentine foreign policy positions was aimed at the disjuncture between the reality of the Argentine position and its profile in world affairs. The argument posited was that a poor country like Argentina should not engage in foreign policies that carry a high cost. The priority of foreign policy should be the welfare of the citizenry and that welfare depended upon economic growth and not on posturing on the world stage. In particular, the 'Third Worldist' position adopted by Argentina over a number of decades was seen as offering few benefits to the country and of having a high potential cost in that it tended to irritate those countries that were at the centre of world finance. The alliance with the non-aligned and developing nations, it was argued, sent out the wrong messages to those who controlled international financial flows and if Argentina was serious in its desire to develop it would have to make itself more attractive. The debate was underwritten by the collapse of the import substitution model and a move towards economic liberalism. Trade and investment concerns, it was argued, would have to form the core of foreign policy.

The key theoretical concept in this debate was that of autonomy. Autonomy is never absolute in politics and is always relative, moreover, the amount of autonomy that can be enjoyed by poorer nations is limited. The richer, the more powerful, the more autonomy is possible. The question arises as to how much autonomy is worth and whether or not there is a willingness to trade it off for economic welfare. This may be something of a false dichotomy in that over the longer term economic growth will facilitate more freedom of action. In Latin America, autonomy has often been perceived as lacking and as a goal to be achieved. As a concept it has informed an important variant of International Relations theory, realism of the periphery.

---

45 Deborah L. Norden & Roberto Russell, *The United States and Argentina. Changing Relations in a Changing World*, p. 1.
46 Marguerite Feitlowitz, *A Lexicon of Terror. Argentina and the Legacies of Terror.*

Unlike the Anglo Saxon realist and neorealist schools, they paid special attention to the vertical dimension of power and, more particularly, to the phenomena of imperialism and the asymmetries of power between the United States and Latin America.[47]

This theoretical perspective, which informed the debate on Argentine foreign policy during the 1980s and 1990s, makes an important distinction between different forms of autonomous action; that which is destructive and that which benefits the country. Given the asymmetries that exist in the power relations of the Western Hemisphere it was questionable whether Argentina could derive any benefit from conflicts with the United States. Thus, it was recommended that Argentina should avoid such conflicts. In doing so, Argentina would accept its dependent position. Any recognition of dependency *could* result in solidarity with other developing nations. Instead, the option taken was to court the favour of the wealthy in order to escape this dependency. Autonomy of action had come to be seen as the ability to defy the United States, instead, it was argued, autonomy should be seen as the ability to serve the interests of the people, and their interests, it was argued, were best served by good relations with the US.[48]

Such views were reflected among Menem's ministers. Cavallo, the Economy Minister argued that temptation to *principismo* should be resisted.[49] He saw Argentine policy as laden with contradictions. Argentina was confronting a superpower whilst at the same time attempting to secure loans from it.[50] Di Tella another key figure in Menem's government stated:

> Algunos dicen que nuestra política es frívola. Bueno, en cierto sentido lo es. No hablamos de grandes glorias, sino de cosas prácticas: de cuanto nos prestan, que tasa de interés ...[51]

This focus on economics mirrored the Chilean experience. The old agenda disappeared to be replaced by a drive to succeed in the world economy. In many ways this move in Argentine foreign policy did not comply with classic realism in stressing the low politics of economic development and domestic priorities.[52]

---

47 Roberto Russell & Juan Gabriel Tokatlian, 'From Antagonistic Autonomy to Relational Autonomy: A Theoretical Reflection from the Southern Cone', *Latin American Politics and Society* 45:1 (2003), p. 6.

48 Ibid., p. 9.

49 Principismo means following ideas based on rhetoric and abstract principles.

50 Domingo Felipe Cavallo, 'La Inserción de la Argentina en la Primer Mundo 1989–1991' in *La Política Exterior Argentina y sus Protagonistas 1880–1995* (Buenos Aires: 1996). p. 36.

51 'Some say that our politics are frivolous. Well in a sense they are. We do not talk glory, but of practical things, how much we can borrow, at what interest rate....' Guido Di Tella, 'Política Exterior Argentina: Actualidad y Perspectivas 1991–1995' in La Política Exterior Argentina y sus Protagonistas 1880–1995 (Buenos Aires: 1996), p. 185.

52 Alfredo Bruno Bologna & Anabella Busso, 'La Política Exterior Argentina a Partir del Gobierno de Menem: Una Presentación' in CIRIR (eds), *La Política Exterior del Gobierno de Menem. Seguimiento y reflexiones al promediar su mandato* (Rosario, 1994), p. 23.

The United States and Argentina

The Menem government that took office in July 1989 afforded relations with the United States a privileged position in its foreign policy. This was a non-traditional position for a Peronist government and was brought about by a more explicit linkage between internal and external politics.[53] It was hoped that better relations with the US would facilitate the transformation of Argentine economy. This departure was prompted by the arguments inherent in *realismo periférico*, namely, that weak countries should eliminate confrontation with hegemons. Menem stressed that only economic growth and the well-being of the population gave a country presence in the world. Cisneros expresses the rationale behind the changing policy:

> For too long our government pursued foreign policies that neglected the economic and social well-being of our people. The aim was 'prestige' and the strategy frequently jingoistic, an attitude favoured by the ruling elite which inevitably led to confrontations (with the United States, with our neighbours, and in time with Great Britain).[54]

In practical terms, the new policy saw Argentina send warships to the Gulf during the first Gulf War and dismantle the condor missile project. Argentina abandoned the non-aligned movement, officially withdrawing in 1991. The official reason given was a dispute over a declaration on pluralism and freedom of expression, but the real motivation lay in its desire to improve relations with Washington.[55] At the United Nations where Argentina had voted against the United States on 87.5% of occasions, it adopted a considerably more benign attitude to the United States. The policy of automatic dis-alignment with the US was abandoned and Argentina's voting record came to resemble that of Spain or Italy. In hemispheric politics, the shift became apparent in March 1991 when Argentina voted for a US proposal before the Human Rights Commission to investigate human rights abuses in Cuba. Regionalism now fell down the list of priorities as relations with the US were deemed all important. In Brazil, there was little sympathy for the shift in Argentine policy.[56] The desertion of Argentina could effectively torpedo the regional project that lay at the heart of Brazilian foreign policy. Elsewhere in the region, Chile looked on in dismay as Argentina sought to become an associate member of NATO. The brazenness of Argentine attempts to court favour with the US was damaging its relations with its neighbours and undermining the long-term viability of the Mercosur project.

---

53 Ibid., p. 17.

54 Andrés Cisneros, 'Foreign Policy and Argentina's National Interests' in Lewis & Szusterman (eds), *Argentina Foreign Relations and the New Foreign Policy Agenda* (London, 1996), p. 16.

55 Bologna and Busson, 'La Política Exterior Argentina a Partir del Gobierno de Menem: Una Presentacion', p. 38.

56 Carlos Escudé & Andrés Fontana, 'Argentina's Security Policies. Their Rationale and Regional Context', p. 76.

The Argentine desire to negotiate a bilateral FTA, with the United States, if carried through, would lead to the effective dismantlement of Mercosur.

When in 1990 George Bush visited Buenos Aires, he was the first US president to do so since 1960. There is no doubt that Argentina was exceptionally keen to promote good relations with the US. Di Tella spoke of the need to maintain *relaciones carnales* with Washington.[57] Instead of leading the world against the United States, Argentina was leading the world in supporting the US. Such a policy was not without its critics. Political rivals within the country criticized the subservience of the Menem government. There was also the issue as to what were the tangible benefits accruing to Argentina from its uncritical support of the US.[58] A more nuanced critique pointed out that Argentine policy towards the US amounted to just the latest episode of Argentine exceptionalism. Tulchin makes this case:

> And yet there was evidence that the alliance with the United States had become but one more way to establish Argentine exceptionalism in the hemisphere and the historic drive to be in the lead remained powerful and in conflict with the new realism.[59]

Those who championed the new policy line argued that Argentina should leave behind is historic pretensions of greatness and leadership and yet it appears that these long-standing narratives found their way into this variant of realism.[60] The Argentine wooing of the US was exaggerated and overdone.[61]

In terms of its relations with the US over the longer term, the period after 1989 was the exception to the rule. Historically, Argentina has not had good relations with the United States. For the most of its history Argentina has defined its relationship with the United States in terms of autonomy.[62] Throughout the twentieth century relations have been distant. It is this key relationship that accounts for the many paradoxes in Argentine foreign policy. The anti-communist fervour co-existing with strong links to the Eastern Bloc, Argentine exceptionalism alongside solidarity with the Third World, wariness of Brazil and Mercosur alongside Latin-americanism. The contradictions in Argentine policy form part of a legacy of the century old tradition

---

57 Bologna and Busson, 'La Política Exterior Argentina a Partir del Gobierno de Menem: Una Presentacion', p. 31.

58 Figari, Pasado, Presente y Futuro de la Política Exterior Argentina. p. 226.

59 Tulchin, 'Continuity and Change in Argentine Foreign Policy', p. 167.

60 There is an interesting discussion to be had on the co-presence along with realism of other forms of political thinking. The existence and salience of the idea of 'manifest destiny' in the United States is a good example of this.

61 Tuchin argues that Argentina had swung from being the most vociferous opponent of the US to being its main supporter internationally. 'The problem with the exaggerated gestures is that they are consistent with a truly disturbing interpretation: that one of the most enduring myths of Argentine foreign policy lives on in a new form, the myth of Argentine world influence, of Argentine exceptionalism.' Tulchin, 'Continuity and Change in Argentine Foreign Policy', p. 190.

62 Norden and Russell, *The United States and Argentina. Changing Relations in a Changing World*, p. 190.

in Argentine foreign relations of confrontation with the United States. This is a country, which like the United States, sees itself as exceptional. This may be the heart of the matter.

The periods immediately preceding and following the Menem government were more in line with the longer trajectory of Argentine–US relations. Alfonsín chose to be more focused on regional politics and to retain close links with the non-aligned movement rather than develop closer relations with Washington.[63] Argentina became hostile to US policy in Nicaragua and finance minister Grinspun, an intimate friend of Alfonsín, pursued a strong anti-US line in his attempt to resolve the debt issue. Both men were aware that this anti-US line played well to large sections of the Argentine public.[64] It was this set of policies that generated criticism from realists who saw foreign policy as detached from the realities of international politics.

Since the mid-1990s, Argentine governments have, in general, committed themselves to the Mercosur project. As a project, Mercosur and economic integration with Brazil posed a challenge to the United States and other industrialised countries and this played well to the deep-seated urges of many Argentines.[65] Identity politics remains an important part of the picture. The default position of the Argentine public appears to be to set itself in opposition to the United States. The Mercosur project provides a vehicle for this desire to challenge the US, whilst the pact also offers the promise of development.

Recent Developments in Argentine Foreign Policy

Speaking on relations with the US, Argentina's cabinet chief said in January 2004: 'Carnal relations and automatic alignment (between the two countries) don't exist anymore.' His remarks refer back to Di Tella's call for closer relations with the US made more than a decade previously.[66] Though relations between Kirchner and Bush are said to be cordial, both a speech by the US State Department's assistant secretary of state for Western Hemisphere Affairs, Roger Noriega and the reaction in Argentina revealed the tension that exists between the two countries. Noriega spoke of a certain leftward drift in Argentine foreign policy and his disappointment at some of the positions adopted by Argentina. In response to Noriega's statements, Alberto Fernández, Kirchner's cabinet chief, observed that the US official's comments were 'impertinent' and Aníbal Fernández, Argentina's Interior Minister, found that Noriega's remarks were 'those of an insolent individual'.[67] The election of Kirchner

---

63 Eve Rimoldi de Ladman, 'Los Gobiernos Constitucionales de Argentina 1983–1998 Similudes y Diferencias de su Política Exterior' in Eve Rimoldi de Ladman (ed.), *Política Exterior y Tratados Argentina Chile Mercosur* (Buenos Aires: Ciudad Argentina, 1999), p. 111.
64 Tulchin, 'Continuity and Change in Argentine Foreign Policy', p. 175.
65 Ibid., p. 178.
66 http://www.americas.org/item_3.
67 http://www.americas.org/item_3.

in 2003 brought Argentina into line with Brazil in ideological terms. The centre-left politics of Lula and Kirchner make them less than comfortable in their dealings with the United States and has prompted both to develop strong alternatives to counter the bargaining power of the US. Their commitment to Mercosur is one such alternative and closer relations with the EU have been another. For Lapper (2003) closer relations with the EU is more in line with the centre-left politics of both leaders.[68,69] Even so, there are a number of difficult issues to overcome in Mercosur–EU talks, with the negotiations floundering on the issue of trade subsidies. However, the parties have agreed to extend the negotiating period into 2006.

The restoration of diplomatic relations with Cuba and the warm relations between Kirchner and President Chavez of Venezuela are examples of a shift leftward in the foreign policy of Argentina. In the case of Cuba, the failure of the Argentine foreign minister, Rafael Bielsa, to meet with dissident groups during a 2003 visit to Havana led to sharp disagreement between Buenos Aires and Washington. Similarly, closer ties with Chavez, seen within the US administration as a destabilizing force in South America, will further antagonize the US State Department. The granting to Venezuela of Associate Membership of Mercosur in July 2004 prompted Kirchner to state: *'for Argentina it is not only an honor, it is above all a necessity to have Venezuela with us, so as to deepen the changes that we want to bring about'*.[70] In early 2006, full membership for Venezuela looks to be within the grasp of Chavez. This can only add to the complexities of US–Argentine relations. The scenario is further complicated by Argentina following Brazil in developing closer ties with China. In part, these links are explained by strong trade flows between the two countries. China is now the fourth largest destination for Argentine products and exports for the first four months of 2004 amounted to US$807 million, this a 66% increase on the previous year. The desire to pursue an independent (from the United States) foreign policy is also an important part of the picture.

It is the outside environment, in particular the dynamic of inter-hemispheric relations that constitutes the main driver of the Mercosur project. In the case of Argentina, since the election of Kirchner there has been deterioration in relations with the United States and this makes Mercosur an even greater priority. In Argentina, as in Brazil, Mercosur is taking on a less economic and more political hue. This is an interesting departure. At the outset, the Mercosur project had a political component for Argentina, but it was also the case that this project was distinct from previous attempts at regional integration in that it *was* economically driven. During much of the 1990s, the steep rises in intra-regional trade and the positive effect Mercosur was having on inward investment maintained the economic rationale for the project. The economic case has since declined for Argentina, but the political case has strengthened. The reason behind this dichotomy is the increasing disjunction between the areas of

---

68 Richard Lapper, *Financial Times* 17/07/2003.

69 In May 2006 EU-Mercosur trade talks were on hold pending the conclusion of the Doha round of world trade negotiations.

70 http://www.venezuelanalysis.com/articles.php?artno=1214.

domestic and foreign policy. In the case of Argentina and Brazil, the Mercosur pact has had little enough impact on domestic policy. There is a lack of coordination at the level of domestic policy. This has led to a number of problems, as each country has tended to act in a unilateral fashion in the face of domestic economic difficulties. In Brazil, in particular, domestic pressure groups have been vocal in their opposition to Mercosur arrangements when they perceive them as contrary to their wider interests. The drive to deepen Mercosur in the area of the coordination domestic policy has come from Argentina who seek greater institutional arrangements to counter the Brazilian desire for autonomy of action. Such arrangements would act as a corrective to the power imbalance that exist between Argentina and Brazil. In the realm of foreign policy however, the cooperative instinct has been more highly developed. The imperative to develop common positions in wider international trade talks has fed the development of a common mindset among foreign policy elites.

In Brazil, the commitment to Mercosur has been strong and it constitutes a core element of Brazilian foreign policy. Historically, Argentina's allegiance to the project has been less forthright. However, since the attempt in the 1990s to court favour with the US, the nature of that engagement has strengthened. Kirchner's administration has given new impetus to the regionalist politics. In this context, the co-existence of disputes over domestic economic policy and cooperation in Argentina's and Brazil's dealings with the wider world are best seen as a testament to the durability of pact.

The changing priorities in Argentine foreign policy have been demonstrated by the tougher stance on the Falklands/Malvinas question pursued by the Kirchner government. Since his inauguration, relations between Britain and Argentina have come under strain as Kirchner has made a point of reasserting Argentina's claim to sovereignty over the islands. During Menem's government, the Falklands/Malvinas question was subordinated to the policy of re-establishing the pro-western credentials of Argentina. Such was the transformation in Argentine–British relations that during the Gulf War, Argentina was supplied with Rolls Royce parts for its Frigates in return for backing the US-led coalition in the Gulf. Kirchner has reactivated a dormant but, over the longer term, a central element in Argentine foreign policy.

In Kirchner's foreign policy we are seeing a reconnecting with key themes of Argentine foreign policy over the longer trajectory. Reticence about closer ties with Washington has been the default position of the Argentine foreign policy for over a century and the desire to foster close relations with Europe has also been an important part of Argentine political culture for generations. Argentine sovereignty over the Falklands/Malvinas has also been a long held position. There is also a strong precedent for engaging with emerging economic powers around the world as a way of resisting US attempts to isolate Argentina within the hemisphere. What is somewhat novel is the strong commitment to its neighbour Brazil. Particularly in the foreign policy arena, the Kirchner government has thrown its weight behind close relations with Brazil and the success of the Mercosur project.

Conclusions

The history of Argentine foreign policy since World War Two shows the country attempting to come to terms with its decline in the world. The period from 1880–1930 was a time of profound transformation in Argentine society as it changed from being a sparsely populated backwater to a country which had a standard of living comparable to many wealthy European countries with, seemingly, the potential to become a first rate power. Many of the patterns of thought relating to Argentine position in the world were laid down during these decades. Argentina adopted a relatively high profile on the international stage. As early as the Great War, Argentina attempted to set itself apart through the pursuit of an ethical foreign policy and it built upon the legalism of the Drago Doctrine. The basis of Argentine hostility to US hegemony in the Western Hemisphere has a number sources. The similarity in output terms in the late nineteenth and early twentieth centuries led to Argentine products being excluded from US markets and this caused resentment among the Argentine elite. Culturally, this same elite saw themselves as primarily European and this constituted another point of departure from the United States. Furthermore, the success of this period gave rise to feelings of self-confidence that did not sit easily with US notions of manifest destiny and its willingness to intervene in the internal affairs of countries south of the Rio Grande.

Argentina is an interesting example of the disjuncture of historical narratives with the reality of power relations. It is this disjuncture that gave rise to the *realismo periférico*, so prominent in the 1990s. Scholars within this variant of realism have pointed to the destructive nature of Argentine foreign policy in the period since World War Two. They have highlighted the continued hostility towards the US and the fact that the United States was now the sole superpower and its good offices were needed more than ever for Argentina to develop economically. There are fortuitous occasions where realism can co-exist with strong national narratives. Argentina, post-dictatorship, was not such a place. The narratives which drove Argentine exceptionalism and the strong desire for autonomy in international affairs were devalued by the experience of dictatorship, economic collapse and defeat in war. For a brief period, a stark version of realism triumphed. As in the Chile of the early days of the *concertación*, it focused on the mundane and had no place for the Argentine sense of self. Again echoing the Chilean experience, economics and trade came to dominate the discourse of foreign policy making.

The period from the mid-1990s onwards saw the country move in a new direction again. On this occasion, the move did manage to incorporate many of the longer held elements of the Argentine identity. Mercosur is indistinguishable from Argentine–Brazilian relations. The group signifies their alliance in world politics, it demonstrates their shared reluctance to afford the US the opportunity for hemispheric leadership. As a project, Mercosur is flawed and dogged by disputes, however, as a shared vehicle for Brazilian and Argentine foreign policy ambitions it does offer potential. In both cases, it offers at least an approximation between the perceived historical trajectory of the nation and the political realities of the age. It offers Argentina, through its cooperation with Brazil, the ability to be a protagonist in international politics. Its participation in the project is of profound importance in the development of hemispheric and wider relations. It is true that the asymmetrical nature of the relationship between Argentina and Brazil is potentially the undoing of the alliance. If this is not managed carefully and Brazil does not take seriously enough its responsibility to mitigate some the effects of this imbalance, the Argentine commitment may flag and it may opt for another course. But, as long as Mercosur remains integration with Brazil and not integration into Brazil, Argentina should remain on board.

Map of Brazil

Chapter 4

Brazilian Foreign Policy

Introduction

Brazil is a country of some 186 million people, and is slighty smaller than the United States. In 2005, it had the world's tenth biggest economy. The size, the population and the economic weight of Brazil afford the country a higher profile in world affairs than either Argentina or Chile. Brazil has some 14,691 kilometres of borders with its neighbour, most of which are in more remote areas of this vast country. During the twentieth century, the country has come to occupy a more prominent position in the world polity. This was due to both economic growth and its perceived leadership role in South America. More typically, Brazil's diplomats have felt somewhat marginalized in world affairs. The desire to be a global actor has been a constant theme in Brazilian foreign policy over many decades. In the first decade of the twenty-first century this theme is exemplified in the campaign to be part of the United Nations Security Council. For many in Brazil, this would signify that the country has finally taken its rightful position among the world's great powers.

In the past, this desire to gain recognition beyond Latin America has tended to distance Brazil from its near neighbours. The prioritizing of the relations with the great powers has a long history. In the nineteenth century, the diplomatic priorities lay with maintaining good relations with Great Britain. During the twentieth century priorities changed and Washington became the focus of Brazilian diplomacy. In both cases economics and the politics of development determined the country's foreign policy decisions. In the nineteenth and first part of the twentieth century Britain was Brazil's banker, and in the twentieth century, the United States became the dominant trade partner and source of foreign direct investment. The relationship with Washington has been the key component of Brazilian diplomacy over the past century and interfaces with virtually all other aspects of Brazilian foreign policy. There have been many ups and downs in Brazil–US relations, Brazil has not always shared the same set of priorities as the United States. Since the end of the Cold War these differences have been more apparent, but the desire to pursue a foreign policy line independent of Washington has a long history. The drivers behind this desire to distinguish themselves from Washington are varied and are not shared universally among the Brazilian elite. Here, as elsewhere in Latin American, there is a nascent anti-Americanism. It is a tendency that gains influence periodically.

There is also a Latin Americanist strand to Brazilian foreign policy. However, in this regard, the case of Brazil is somewhat different to that of its neighbours in the Southern Cone. Firstly, there is the legacy of the Brazilian colonial experience.

From the Treaty of Madrid in 1750, Brazil was a Portuguese colony and this placed the territory in a distinct set of geopolitical relations and, in particular, ensured a particularly close relationship to Great Britain. Secondly, Brazil remained a monarchy for much of the nineteenth century and thus was less inclined to support ideologies emanating from the republican regimes elsewhere on the continent. Over the decades, this history has fed those political tendencies that have sought to set Brazil apart from the rest of South America.

The size of Brazil also has a profound impact. This has created a very particular set of beliefs amongst Brazil's political elite. In the first instance it causes them to be inward looking in that expansion has taken place inside the country's borders. Brazil has had to wrestle with its own frontiers and break down internal boundaries. The size of the country has also presented problems, and good governance has been hard to achieve with local power bases being a consistent feature of Brazilian politics. During the twentieth century, the size and the economic potential of Brazil has supported ideas of international grandeur and of activism on the world stage. These desires have taken sustenance from the growing industrial base of the country. Regional leadership has been a goal of the Brazilian foreign policy establishment for many decades now and this has shaped both the nation's engagement with other Latin American countries and with the United States. In the case of the former, the desire to be seen as the region's lead nation has meant that care is taken to foster warm relations with its neighbours. The engagement with Argentina is seen as central in this regard. In the case of relations with the US, the desire for regional leadership has run counter to the preponderance of US power in the Western hemisphere. This conflict of interests comes into stark relief in the debates that surround the merits of Mercosur and those of a hemispheric free-trade area of the Americas. For Brazil the establishment of a FTAA would signal the end of any pretensions of regional leadership it may have had and firmly establish the United States as the hegemonic power in the Americas.

A further consideration in any analysis of Brazilian foreign policy is the role played by imperative economic development. This has been the centrepiece of state policy throughout much of the twentieth century. Foreign policy is, in large part, designed to facilitate Brazil's development and therefore any change in economic thinking feeds into the construction of foreign policy. The end of the import substitution model of economic development drove the changes towards free trade and export led growth. The imperative of economic growth in Brazil, as elsewhere in the continent, frames the nature of the country's engagement with the United States. The costs associated with poor relations with the US are potentially very high in terms of economic development. There is a premium price on maintaining cordial relations with Washington. In 2005, Lula's attempt to distance himself from some of the more radical positions adopted by Hugo Chavez of Venezuela illustrates this pragmatic approach to hemispheric relations. For Brazil, hemispheric relations are shaped by the imperative of economic growth *and* the desire for regional leadership.[1]

---

1 Peter H. Smith, *Democracy in Latin America* (Oxford, 2005), p. 126.

In the long term these two goals are eminently compatible, however in the short-term conflicts with the US are costly and so a balance needs to be struck between the two.

In one important sense, the international environment has been stable for some time, that is in the continued power of the United States. How to manage this relationship has been at the heart of Brazilian foreign policy. At various junctures the Brazilians have courted the United States in order for regional leadership to be bestowed upon the country and at other times Brazil has resisted US interference in the region in order to attain that same leadership status. Over recent decades, both politically and economically there have been profound changes in the international system. There have been periods when the international environment has not been conducive to maintaining an independent foreign policy. The 1980s was one such period, the combination of high debt levels and a spike in interest rates left Brazil with little room for manoeuvre and the cost of defying the hemispheric hegemon became very high.

The nature of Brazilian national identity also shapes the construction of foreign policy. The political culture and the nature of the identity are partly dependent on the nature of the political regime in place. In 1964, the Brazilian armed forces took control of the government. It would be 1985 before the country returned to civilian rule. During these two decades a particular notion of 'Brazilianess' was developed. One of the key determinants of state policies in the 1980s and 1990s, across the Southern Cone, was the manner in which civilian government dealt with the legacy of military. In Brazil the armed forces had almost 20 years to propagate their vision of the country and pursue their policy goals. The nature of the transition to civilian rule in Brazil was less traumatic than that in Argentina and in fact shared some of the characteristics of *transición pactada* in Chile. As a result, discontinuities in policy were less a feature of the Brazilian transition.[2]

Some degree of continuity was also maintained by the nature of the institutions charged with managing Brazil's external relations. The *Itamaraty* (the Foreign Ministry) has a long history of autonomy within the Brazilian political establishment and those occupying other parts of the political system rarely challenge its policies. As in the case of both Argentina and Chile, we have a configuration of influences on foreign policy formation in Brazil. The forces at work are similar in all three cases but their relative importance is different in each case. The size and the geopolitical ambition of Brazil tend to colour all parts of the system. Its potential leadership role in the continent shapes Brazil's relations in the region, with the United State and in the wider world.

---

2   Transición pactada means agreed transition.

Historical Antecedents

Brazilian history shares some features with its Latin American neighbours. The initial process of colonization was difficult with many of the settlers killed, though the type of sustained resistance to colonial rule witnessed in Chile was absent. The geography of Brazil has had an impact on the history and the mentality of the Brazilians. The awareness of the 'big country' gives Brazilians a confidence in their dealings with the outside world with this applying to both business people and the administrators.[3]

Other aspects of Brazil's history also mark it out from its neighbours. Brazil was a Portuguese colony and for much of the nineteenth century was presided over by a royal family with their roots in Portugal. Portuguese political, cultural and economic values would have a profound effect upon the country.[4] From the latter half of the seventeenth century until independence in 1822, Portugal was the dominant power in Brazil. The Dutch invasion in the first half of the seventeenth century was the last attempt by a foreign power to invade the country. Brazil became increasingly important to the Portuguese and the colony became a Principality and the title of "the Prince of Brazil" was afforded to the heir to the Portuguese throne. Though it was never to be invaded again by foreign armies, Brazil was not immune from the fallout from European geopolitics. The Portuguese allied with Britain in the War of Spanish Succession and Brazil paid the price with punitive French raids on Rio de Janeiro in 1710 and 1711. The alliance between Portugal and Britain led to the growth of British economic power and political influence in the Principality. A key date for Brazil's distinct historical trajectory was the Treaty of Madrid signed in 1750. Known as the 'Boundaries Treaty' it allowed Portugal to keep Rio Grande del Sol together with the Amazon and the Spanish to secure the River Plate area and the Philippines. Thus, the division between Spanish America and Portuguese Brazil became formalized. A separate political culture emerged with one of the key differences being the more benign relations that existed between the locals and the Portuguese. Elsewhere in Latin America considerable tension arose between the creoles and the *peninsulares*. Another set of repercussions resulted from the fact that Brazil alone was Portuguese speaking in a predominantly Spanish America. This, together with Brazil retaining a monarchical regime for the much of the nineteenth century, saw the country reaching out beyond the continent, first to Britain and later to the United States in order to avoid isolation among the Spanish speaking republics that came to dominate the continent of South America.[5]

The Napoleonic Wars had a profound affect across Latin America. In the case of Brazil it led to the amazing spectacle of a European court relocating across the

---

3   Andy Klom, 'Mercosur and Brazil: a European Perspective', *International Affairs* 79:2 (2003): p. 351.

4   Joseph Smith, *History of Brazil, 1500–2000* (London, 2002), p. 1.

5   Frank D. McCann, 'Brazilian Foreign Relations in the Twentieth Century' in Wayne A. Selcher (ed.), *Brazil in the International System: The Rise of a Middle Power* (Boulder, 1981), p. 2.

Atlantic Ocean. In 1807, rather than face capture by the advancing French armies the Prince Regent, Dom João, chose to flee to Brazil. Some 40 ships and 15,000 individuals left Lisbon for Rio de Janeiro. The implications of the move were profound. The British, who had encouraged the move, were the main beneficiaries and a new commercial treaty in 1810 afforded preferential treatment to British imports into Brazil. The power and influence of Britain was exemplified in the local expression; *para ingles ver* (for English eyes) expressing a desire to show the best aspects of Brazil to the English. For McCann (1981) the desire to show its best face to the outside world is tied up with unease about the racial mix of the country.[6] The eighteenth and nineteenth centuries saw a massive influx of slaves from Africa. In this context, diplomacy became an idealized environment where a false reality could be created and the racial mix of Brazil could be shut out.

The achievement of independence in 1822 was a less traumatic affair than elsewhere on the continent, with the King's son prompting the breakaway from Portugal and its increasingly vocal Cortes (parliament). The founding of an independent Brazil was not accompanied by the same levels of violence seen elsewhere on the continent when the Spanish colonies broke free of Madrid. A year after independence the Brazilian writer and political activist José Bonifácio wrote:

> What a picture unhappy [Spanish] America shows us! For fourteen years its peoples have torn themselves to pieces because, after having known a monarchical government, they aspire to a licentatious liberty. And having swum in blood, they are no more than victims of their own disorder.[7]

Brazil then has its equivalent of the Chilean refrain *no pasa nada en Chile*[8] and Brazilians were similarly convinced of their exceptional status in Latin America.

The founding myths of the country are less connected to military success than is the case in either Argentina or Chile. There was no military tradition to speak of right through until the mid-nineteenth century. The radical ideas, which fed the republican movement elsewhere on the continent, were contained in Brazil and the monarchy remained in control. There were some revolts in the 1830s, but these were put down and the period of the Second Empire, from 1841–1889, was relatively calm.

> Despite the frequent changes of government, Brazilian politics during the Second Empire was more stable and peaceful than in the rest of Latin America.[9]

Brazil faced similar problems to its neighbouring republics in achieving recognition. Although opposed to the idea of monarchy, the United States, under Monroe, was the first country to grant recognition to Brazil. Interestingly, the

---

6 Ibid., p. 3.
7 Smith, *History of Brazil*, p. 83.
8 No Pas Nada en Chile mean Nothing happens in Chile. This was seen as a positive characteristic whereby Chile was portrayed as an oasis of calm.
9 Ibid., p. 54.

position of Brazil on the Monroe Doctrine evolved in a different fashion from its neighbours in that Brazil was much more positive on the desire of the US to prevent European interference in the Americas.[10] This response to the Monroe Doctrine was no indication that national sovereignty was any less important to the Brazilians and during the nineteenth century the country became increasingly assertive in its dealings with the great powers of the day. During the 1860s, Brazil, during separate incidents, was able to withstand diplomatic pressure from both Britain and the United States. In the case of the dispute with Britain, the Brazilians responded to a blockade of Rio de Janeiro by demanding compensation and when this was not forthcoming they broke off diplomatic relations and were ultimately successful in resolving the matter.

In the main, Brazil's frontiers with its neighbours are located in remote and sparsely populated areas. This and the absence of valuable natural resources in these zones have tended to militate against inter-state violence involving Brazil. However, in response to a strident Paraguayan dictator, Francisco Solano López and his interference in Uruguay and an incursion into Brazilian territory, Brazil joined with Argentina and Uruguay and fought the War of the Triple Alliance (1864–1870). Brazil contributed most to the victory of the allies. In the aftermath there was an increased rivalry with Argentina as its neighbour sought to rectify a perceived military imbalance. This rivalry between the two countries, which predated the war as Brazil had sought to limit the influence of the Rosas, became a central element of Brazilian diplomacy for many decades to come.

As foreign minister between 1902 and 1912, Rio Branco constructed the institutional basis of the *Itamaraty*, or the Brazilian Foreign Ministry. Throughout the twentieth century this institution enjoyed a good deal of power and prestige in Brazil. In part its autonomy is explained by non-partisanship in the area of external relations. Rarely did foreign policy become a political matter in Brazil.[11] Historically, this is also explained by the absence of a strong and vibrant democratic political culture in Brazil.[12] The early part of the twentieth century also saw a change in the focus of Brazilian foreign policy reflecting the changes in global geopolitics. From the second half of the nineteenth century the United States became an increasingly important export market and source of capital. This process accelerated in the first decades of the twentieth century and the US displaced Britain as the primary focus of Brazilian diplomatic activity. Brazil had sought to gain leverage locally through what is perceived as its special relationship with Britain.[13] Throughout much of the

---

10 Ibid., p. 129. Rio Branco, for many the architect of twentieth-century Brazilian diplomacy, was not hostile to the US Monroe Doctrine and indeed argued that Latin America should look to the US for protection from European aggression.

11 McCann, 'Brazilian Foreign Relations in the Twentieth Century', p. 3.

12 Leslie Bethell, 'Politics in Brazil: From Elections without Democracy to Democracy without Citizenship' in Maria D'Alva Kinzo & James Dunkerley (eds), *Brazil Since 1985. Economy, Politics and Society* (London, 2003).

13 'With England's friendship we can snap our fingers at the rest of the world.' Smith, 'History of Brazil', p. 80.

twentieth century Brazil would pursue the same strategy with the United States. The US came to be considered a tacit ally capable of enhancing Brazil's power in its dealings with its neighbours.[14] At the turn of the century, Brazil believed it had constructed a special relationship with Washington, and had hoped to be the 'first among equals'. It was not, however, afforded that status.[15] Relations with the United States will be examined in more detail below.

Brazil's engagement in world affairs during the twentieth century is best characterized as a series of false dawns and disappointments. The policy of 'approximation' (*aproximação*) or close relations with Washington yielded mixed results. Given the risk of alienating the rest of Latin America, the United States has been reluctant to side with one particular country against another, at least on a consistent basis. Brazil's pursuit of an elevated status with the US tended to alienate its neighbours. They became less likely to support any scheme that implied Brazilian leadership. This is particularly true in the case of Argentina, and the dilemma as to how to pursue good relations with both the US and Argentina has been a consistent problem for foreign policy planners in Brazil. This has been all the more difficult to resolve because of long periods of strong anti-Americanism amongst the Argentine political elite.

Brazil entered both World Wars on the same side as the United States. In the aftermath of World War One Brazil was humiliated by its marginalization at the Versailles Conference. The Brazilians felt they had recovered some of their status in the League of Nations where the country was recognized as one of the founding members and afforded one of the non-permanent seats on the Security Council. In a policy that mirrors current Brazilian policy in relation to the United Nations, the *Itamaraty* fought for a permanent seat. It is worth noting that resistance to such a development was not confined to the Great Powers. The granting of a special status to Brazil had never been acceptable to other Latin American powers.[16] This remains the case. In the inter-war years Brazil was unable to gain a permanent Security Council seat and by putting herself on a par with Germany in its campaign to get onto the Security Council only succeeded in generating ridicule in Europe. The active role played by Brazilian combat forces in World War Two again raised hopes that the country would be granted a permanent Security Council seat at, on this occasion, the United Nations. Again such ambitions were to be thwarted.

In the period following the war the goal of *grandeza nacional* was still a long way off. The ambition for a leadership role in South America had not been fulfilled. Brazil remained a country marked by terrible poverty, stark inequalities and occupied a position at the margins of world polity. For generations, the particularist tendencies

---

14 Maria Regina Soares de Lima, 'Brazil's Response to the "New Regionalism"' in Gordon Mace & Jean Philippe Therien (eds), *Foreign Policy and Regionalism in the Americas* (Boulder, 1996), p. 139.

15 David R. Mares, 'Violent Peace, Militarised Interstate Bargaining in Latin America', p. 66.

16 Peter H. Smith, *Democracy in Latin America*, p. 136.

in the country, that is those that saw Brazil on the cusp of greatness, had been denied any real sustenance from global politics. Post-war an alternative narrative began to gather strength, namely, that Brazil like other third world countries was the victim of an unfair system of international trade.[17]

In 1964, the Brazilian military overthrew the government of Goulart. The Brazilian military had long played an active role in politics and there had been previous coups, however the military coup of 1964 was different in that it was not a brief corrective action.[18] The military were to remain in power for 21 years. The idea that the military had the function of defining permanent national objectives emanated from the influential *Escola Superior de Guerra*. In 1968, the National Security Council was created and the constitutional reform of 1969 charged this body with the task of 'fixing the permanent objective and basis of national policy'. The Medici regime, which in 1969 succeeded that of Castelo Branco, adopted a 'non-political stance' in that it sought to rise above society and its competing pressure groups.[19] The military also placed great emphasis on cultivating Brazilian nationalism and linking Brazilian national life to the armed forces.[20] The armed forces, whilst sharing with the Chilean and the Argentine militaries the desire to use the ideology of nationalism, were less radical in the changes they sought to impose on the country. Rhetorically, though they were committed to liberal ideas, state involvement in the economy continued to grow. Of the hundred most powerful enterprises in Brazil, in 1970 40 were state controlled and by 1972 this had risen to 46.[21] Economic development and national security were linked. The major threat to national security was perceived to come from the nation's poor.[22] Thus, development was a security issue and was not left exclusively to the private sector. In comparison to its Southern Cone neighbours, during the 21 years of military rule the levels of

---

17 Ex-President of Brazil Fernando Henrique Cardosa was a prominent figure in the development of dependency theory. See Fernando Henrique Cardoso, *Dependency and Development* (Berkeley, 1979).

18 The military played an important role in Brazilian politics and without their consent, the so-called dipositivo militar, it was impossible to govern. The armed forces were disunited and that faction of the armed forces which opposed government policies needed to be neutralized. Alain Rouquie & Stephen Suffern, 'The Military in Latin American Politics Since 1930' in Leslie Bethell (ed.), *The Cambridge History of Latin America* Vol. 6, *Latin America since 1930* (Cambridge,1994): p. 252.

19 Thomas E. Skidmore, *The Politics of Military Rule* (Oxford, 1988), p. 106.

20 Levine and Crochihi cite passages from material circulated by the Grupo da Educacão Moral e Civica. 'Brazil, to us in 1973, in the tenth year of the revolution, is an enormous land distinguished by its greatness among nations of South America, it is a land of hope, destined for power and world leadership ... The security of every Brazilian and the safety of every Brazilian institution is guarded by the nation's armed forces.' Robert M. Levine and John J. Crocitti (eds), *The Brazil Reader: History, Culture, Politics* (Durham, 1999), pp. 258–259.

21 Rouquie & Suffern, 'The Military in Latin American Politics Since 1930', p. 255.

22 Martin T. Katzman, 'Translating Brazil's Economic Potential into International Influence' in Wayne A. Selcher, *Brazil in the International System: The Rise of a Middle Power* (Boulder: 1981), pp. 104–105.

repression were relatively low. In the 1970s, the security apparatus came to dwarf its supposed enemies. Here as elsewhere the military were associated with nationalism but the relatively conservative path adopted by the Brazilian military in the economic sphere and the somewhat less malign security apparatus meant there was less of a rupture in the patterns of governance. The Argentine and the Chilean people both emerged from the period of military rule traumatized, but this was less the case in Brazil. As a consequence there was less soul-searching and re-examination of what it meant to be Brazilian. Under the Sarney government the military remained strong and retained a good deal of influence. The first Sarney cabinet included six general officers on active duty. Only from 1990s onwards did civilians begin to take power back from the military.[23]

Relations with the United States

Given its aspirations for regional leadership, Brazil's relations with the US are crucially important. Whilst this aspiration has long been an element of Brazil's foreign policy, there has been less consistency in its relations with the United States. The distinction between strategic goals and tactical considerations is useful in this context. Good relations with Washington is not a strategic goal. Instead positive relations with Washington are seen as a means to achieving economic growth and ultimately development, this in order to cement its position of regional leadership. Following the World War Two, US policy began to run counter to what the Brazilian political establishment perceived to be in their interests. The stress Washington placed on the role of the private sector challenged the economic nationalism and statism prevalent in Brazil.

By the late 1950s, the policy of courting favour in Washington was yielding less and less. In terms of aid, assistance from Washington represented an ever-smaller amount compared to Brazilian state spending. Under the leadership of Quadros and later Goulart, Brazil began to pursue a much more independent line in foreign policy. The military government headed by Branco which came to power in 1964 quickly repudiated the radical nationalism that had preceded it and re-established close relations with Washington. The United States were pleased with the outcome of the coup and relations during much of the 1960s were warm with Brazil in receipt of both US aid and Washington's support in attracting finance capital into the country. However, this renewal of the tactic of 'approximation' under Castelo Branco was relatively short lived and with the arrival of Costa e Silva foreign policy again became more independent. Rhetorically at least, the policy was portrayed as nationalist, this to avoid any leftist connotations, but the regime's analysis of power relations in the world placed less emphasis on East–West relations and more on North–South divisions. This new 'Third Worldist' perspective was in evidence when

---

23 Rouquie & Suffern, 'The Military in Latin American Politics Since 1930', p. 292.

Brazil took a leading role in establishing the Group of 77 in the UNCTAD forum in 1968.[24]

The oscillation between cordiality and tension continued in the late 1960s and well into the 1970s. The role of the US in facilitating loans was appreciated and on Washington's side the shift towards a more favourable investment climate was well received. However, tensions were never far from the surface. Widespread human rights abuses caused concern in the United States and resulted in a freezing of aid for a time in 1968. By mid-1969 realist tendencies in Washington had once again come to the fore and the aid was reinstated. Despite expressions of concern, the human rights record deteriorated further in 1969 and 1970. Notwithstanding the human rights rhetoric emanating from the United States, the Nixon administration was a staunch ally of the Medici regime and strongly appreciated their anti-communist credentials.

Both Brazil and the United States were committed to fighting international communism and suppressing left-wing insurgencies in Latin America. However, on other matters there were sharp differences between the two countries. One case in point was the issue of nuclear proliferation. This controversy clearly showed the limits of US influence in Brasilia. In 1974, the US company Westinghouse lost a valuable contract to build nuclear power stations in Brazil. The contract was awarded to a supplier from the Federal Republic of Germany. The failure of the US Atomic Energy Commission to guarantee supplies of uranium is said to have predicated the change.[25] As part of the new arrangement the Brazilians gained control over the complete fuel cycle. The key point here is that such control afforded the Brazilians the opportunity to develop a nuclear weapons programme. The nuclear detonations by India had stimulated interest in both Brazil and Argentina. Despite intense pressure from the US on the issue of control of the fuel cycle, the Brazilians refused to back down. In part this can be explained by a change in policy towards the US adopted by the Geisel government. The United States was no longer to be seen as an indispensable ally and Brazil would afford itself more room for manoeuvre on a variety of issues.[26] Under Geisel (1974–1979) there were parallels with US foreign policy in that ideological frontiers and security were priorities. However, Brazilian nationalism was an important element of the policy mix and led to a more strident and at times defiant line in its dealings with the United States. From the mid-1970s having certain policy goals in common with Washington would not be sufficient to ensure warm relations.

Predictably relations worsened with the arrival of Carter into the White House. The issues of nuclear proliferation and human rights were a priority for the new administration. The incoming Secretary of State, Christopher Warren appealed to Brazil to come into line on the nuclear issue and once again the appeals were rejected. The Harking Bill of 1976 linked aid to human rights records and the first

---

24 Smith, 'History of Brazil', p. 235.
25 Thomas E. Skidmore, *The Politics of Military Rule*, p. 194.
26 Ibid., p. 194.

report produced on Brazil in 1977 was highly critical. The reaction in Brazil to this criticism from the United States was extremely negative and Foreign Minister Silveira denounced what he defined as interference in Brazil's internal affairs. In response, a number of agreements in the area of military cooperation were cancelled. Despite it indisputable anti-communist credentials, Brazil under the Geisel regime could no longer be seen as simply being in the orbit of the United States. Between 1974 and 1980 Brazil exchanged ambassadors with China, concluded the nuclear alliance with Germany, supported the Arab position in the Middle East conflict, recognized the MPLA in Angola and weakened its military alliance with the United States.

The issue of autonomy is a long-standing concern in Brazil and across the Americas. It relates to the asymmetrical power relations on the hemisphere with a huge preponderance of military and economic power lying with the United States. The issue that arises for actors in such a system is that autonomy can have a price. If a country in such an environment chooses to follow an independent line they risk antagonizing the United States and this can have far-reaching consequences. For a nation state like Brazil, with pretensions of regional leadership, such issues are all the more pertinent. Similar and perhaps more explicit debates on this subject have taken place in Argentina.[27]

The issue of autonomy is closely tied to the reputation in the international system and this is turn brings us to long-standing concerns in Brazil and elsewhere on the issue of parity and fairness in the international system. The long-term goals of Brazil have been national greatness and economic development. There have been occasions on which the former has had to be sacrificed for the latter. The key relationship here is that of Brazil and the United States. If the United States comes to dominate the hemisphere Brazil cannot achieve her goal of regional leadership. Soares de Lima identifies three influential intellectual forces in Brazil.

1. Nationalism
2. The notion of Centre-Periphery (as put forwards by CEPAL)[28]
3. Realist thinking in the area of international relations[29]

All three conspire to make Brazil resist US domination in South America. However, unlike elsewhere on the continent, such ideas are unwritten by the notion of Brazil as a 'big country' with a corresponding national destiny.[30] Brazil's ambitions to counter US hegemony also finds expression in its insistence not to see Latin America as one

---

27 During the 1990s the position of peripheral realism became an important strand of opinion in debates on the future direction of Argentine foreign policy.

28 La Comisión Económica para América Latina.

29 Cited in Pedro Da Motta Veiga, 'Brasil a inicios del nuevo milenio: Herencias y Desafíos de la Transición' in Roberto Bouzas (ed.), *Realidades Nacionales Comparadas* (Buenos Aires, 2002), p. 72.

30 Andy Klom, 'Mercosur and Brazil: a European Perspective', p. 354.

security system but instead to stress the existence of South America as a separate security entity.

The nature of the environment in which the nation state finds itself in is also important. In the case of the Brazilian desire to pursue a more independent foreign policy and to be less beholden to the United States, the political and economic environment was critical. Over the past number of decades the environment has been unstable, some times being more favourable to Brazil and other times less so. The 1970s were a propitious time for Brazil to distance itself from the United States in that in economic terms Brazil was less dependent on the United States. The rise of Japan and Europe as world trading powers ensured that Brazil had alternative destinations for its products and other sources of investment capital. In security terms also, the advent of détente has lessened the tension between East and West and so the logic of the Cold War was less pressing in Brazil's dealings with third parties. Thus, Brazil felt able to resist United States' calls for a boycott of the Moscow Olympics and a grain embargo on the Soviet Union.

The 1980s saw the international environment for Brazil become much harsher and this in turn tended to restrict the nature of Brazil's autonomy. Around Latin America the 1980s became known as the 'lost decade'. The new circumstances afforded the United States the ability to exert more control within the Western Hemisphere. The imperative of economic growth continued, driven at least in part by the severity of the country's social problems, but the country was in severe debt. In 1980, the country was ill prepared by the sudden tightening of monetary policy in the US and Europe and a sharp rise in interest rates left Brazil floundering. Brazil became, 'just another supplicant at the IMF', hardly befitting a nation that aspired to great power status. The advantage of independent decision making in the economic field, which the military had enjoyed since 1967, disappeared.[31] Its dependence on international financial institutions exposed the country to outside pressure, particularly from the United States.

For decades Brazil had based its development on the idea of import substitution industrialization (ISI). The logic behind this policy was that the Brazilian state would create an environment favourable to domestic industry, irrespective of foreign interests. The whole rationale of the foreign ministry, the *Itamaraty*, was based upon the politics of ISI and decisions on overseas trade were traditionally taken not by the Trade Ministry or the Finance Ministry but by the *Itamaraty*, an institution deeply committed to the idea of import substitution.[32] The debt crisis of the 1980s undermined this policy set. The experience of Brazil in the Uruguay GATT round is instructive. Initially Brazil adopted a policy that resisted the inclusion of services in the GATT negotiations. There was also resistance to the creation of a new regime in the area of intellectual property rights. The driving force behind these initiatives was the United States. On this occasion Brazil was unable to resist US pressure. The leverage the United States could exert on the debt issue made Brazil very vulnerable.

---

31 Thomas E. Skidmore, *The Politics of Military Rule*, p. 233.
32 Ricardo Wahrendorff Caldas, *Brazil in the Uruguay Round* (Aldershot, 1998).

Furthermore, with the economy already in trouble, the threat of trade sanctions carried more weight and Brazil was forced to climb down on both the services issue and that of intellectual property rights.

The 1980s also saw a more strident attitude on world affairs taken by Washington. Carter was gone and Ronald Reagan was in the White House and this signalled a major shift in foreign policy that was keenly felt across Latin America. Congress began to pursue a more activist line in world affairs in identifying those countries that attempted to resist US policy. The United States Special Trade Representative was encouraged to take action against such states. The so-called 'special 301', a trade sanction instrument, was put into affect against Brazil. According to Correa (2000), Brazil was further singled out because of her leadership status in Latin America and amongst the G77, and the so-called Gang of Five.[33] The *Itamaraty* believed it spoke for Latin America as a whole. This conceit proved costly with the United States determined to isolate Brazil and India, the two countries it perceived as at the head of the resistance to its policy goals.

Brazil's experience in the 1980s left a lasting legacy. There was a widespread realization that ISI and pro LDC policies were not yielding the desired results. Even within the *Itamaraty* there was a move towards a more pragmatic policy and an acceptance of the need to move towards a more market orientated philosophy. This did not mean that Brazil would return to a policy of 'approximation' with the United States. There was a brief period during which Collor sought to move the country in that direction. Warm relations also existed between Cardoso and Clinton.[34] However, the *Itamaraty* strongly resisted any moves that would bring Brazil into the political orbit of the United States. There was a belief that development would be more achievable if the country focused on export markets. The strategic goals of regional leadership and economic growth remained. In order to achieve these Brazil would turn her attention towards her neighbours.

Brazil in the Southern Cone

The key relationship for Brazil in the region is that with Argentina. Historically, the rivalry between the two countries has conditioned relations with the United States. Both Buenos Aires and Brasilia have sought to gain the upper hand over its neighbour by courting favour with the United States. In each case, the benefits accruing from such a policy were limited. Within the context of regional politics, Brazil has sought, traditionally, to limit Argentine influence and ally itself with Chile. However, the rapprochement between Brazil and Argentina that began in the 1980s has the potential to reshape international relations in the Southern Cone. For Hurrel,

---

33 C. Correa, *Intellectual Property Rights, the WTO and Developing Countries: The TRIPS Agreement and Policy Options* (London, 2000), pp. 170–171. The Gang of Five consisted of Brazil, Argentina, India, Egypt and Yugoslavia.

34 Susan Kaufman Purcell, 'The New US–Brazil Relationship' in Susan Kaufman Purcell & Riordan Roett (eds), *Brazil Under Cardoso* (Boulder, 1997), p. 89.

there has been a tremendously significant shift in the historic pattern of rivalry and geopolitical competition between Brazil and Argentina.[35] The attempt to foster improved relations with its neighbours began under the tenure of Figueiredo. His visit to Buenos Aires in 1980 was the first visit by a Brazilian president to Buenos Aires since Vargas in 1935. Figueiredo was also to visit Venezuela, Paraguay and Chile. Both the collective weakness of the Latin American nations and the poor relations between Brasilia and Washington helped generate a more appreciative atmosphere. Brazil was neither seen as pursuing an expansionist agenda nor as acting as a surrogate of the United States.[36]

The improvement in relations gathered pace after the military in Brazil handed back power to a civilian president. Both Argentina and Brazil now had civilian governments. The signing of the Iguaçu Declaration in 1985 by Raul Alfonsín and José Sarney created a commission to study the issue of regional economic integration thus signalling the desire for closer contacts. Three years later, the two governments signed the treaty of Integration, Cooperation and Development. In 1991 Brazil and Argentina, together with Uruguay and Paraguay, signed a customs union which became known as Mercosur.

During the early 1990s, the good relations with Argentina were consolidated. This change in regional dynamics marked a sea change in the pattern of inter-state relations in the Southern Cone. A new type of relationship with Argentina was established, one anchored in a new Brazilian approach in international relations.[37] It also reflected a realization in Brazil that its relations with Argentina were potentially of a similar magnitude, in respect of its ability to project itself internationally, as those with the United States. The same is true at a regional level, where Brazil's influence depends to a large extent on relations with Buenos Aires.[38] Two options exist in order to achieve regional leadership and global projection. The traditional route pursued by Brazil had been to align itself closely to the United States and be afforded the position of regional leadership by Washington. This has not proved a fruitful strategy. The second option has been the improvement of relations with its neighbours and the convergence of their interests with those of Brazil. Since the mid-1980s this has been the dominant line of thinking. Good relations with Argentina are the linchpin of such a strategy. There are advantages and disadvantages to such a position, on the one hand Brazil escapes the shadow of the United States and is able to pursue a more autonomous line in its dealings with the rest of the world. On the negative side in attempting to create this regional bloc Brazil risks antagonizing Washington.

---

35 Andrew Hurrel, 'Security in Latin America', *International Affairs* 74:3 (1998): p. 534.

36 Smith, 'History of Brazil', p. 239.

37 Bouzas (ed.), *Realidades Nacionales Comparadas*, p. 73.

38 Maria Regina Soares de Lima, 'Brazil's Response to the "New Regionalism"', p. 157.

Long-standing geopolitical rivalries with Argentina had to be put aside before such an approach became possible and a degree of trust could be built-up. The mid-1980s was a propitious time in this respect for both countries had civilian presidents and it was a time of transition during which a cooperative approach to regional relations underwrote the process of democratization. The importance of this transition will be examined below.

Brazil has invested considerable political capital in the project of regional integration and the nightmare scenario is that Washington would succeed in luring Argentina away from the Mercosur project through offering a bilateral trade agreement.[39] Whilst this is a new phase of Brazil-Argentine relations, problems have arisen between the two. Initially relations between Kirchner and Da Silva were exceptionally good. The two newly elected presidents shared a leftist perspective and the warmth of the relationship led them to being dubbed Latin America's 'Romeo and Juliet'. However a series of trade disputes have soured the relationship somewhat.

Hemispheric free trade is another possible scenario and is a rival to Mercosur as an agreement. This idea has been posited over a number of years and has received a good deal of support from the administration of George W. Bush. Such a treaty would challenge the logic of smaller regional treaties. However, the idea has less support in Brazil. Even amongst the business elite, the Mercosur project has enjoyed more support than signing up for a hemispheric free-trade agreement under the leadership of the United States.[40] It is this issue of US leadership that deters Brazil from entering such an arrangement. Campaigning during the presidential election in 2002 Da Silva argued:

> under present conditions, the FTAA will not be a free-trade agreement but a process of the economic annexation of the continent by the United States, with extremely serious consequences for the productive structures of our countries.[41]

The concern in Brazil over FTAA is still rooted to some extent in the centre-periphery analysis and the belief that the import substitution model has yet to be completed.[42] Clearly economic thinking in Brazil has moved on since the 1970s, but the idea of Brazil having to fulfil an industrial destiny remains. One can also detect elements of realist thinking. The *Itamaraty* continues to view the world through a realist prism and so all initiatives such as the FTAA have their roots in the power relations of the day.

---

39 Amaury de Souza, 'The European Union, Mercosur and New World Order' in Álvaro De Vasconcelos & Helio Jaguaribe (eds), *The European Union, Mercosul and the New World Order* (London, 2003), p. 181.

40 Maria Regina Soares de Lima, 'Brazil's Response to the "New Regionalism"', pp. 154–155

41 Nicola Philips, 'Integration and Subregionalism in the Americas', p. 340.

42 Ibid., p. 341.

Brazilian reluctance to join the FTAA is based on a well-founded estimate that particularly with American non-tariff barriers, a regime of free trade will systematically favour the US.[43]

There is also the question of Brazilian leadership in the region and how this would be damaged by an arrangement that clearly is led by Washington. Hence, on the basis of the long-term strategic goals of Brazilian foreign policy planners, Brazil is bound to resist such an initiative. At stake is Brazilian political leadership in the Southern Cone, its economic development and its autonomy.

The other option that exists for Brazil, and similarly for Argentina, is to use Mercosur as a bargaining chip in the negotiation of any FTAA. The existence of such a pact does give the two principal protagonists some extra leverage. In such a scenario Mercosur would be a stepping-stone on the way to achieving a more equitable hemispheric free-trade area. There are a number of important variables in this situation. Firstly, there are the economic fortunes of Mercosur to be considered. If the enterprise is not seen to be successful it will neither offer a viable alternative to FTAA nor be a valuable bargaining position. Over the past decade or so Mercosur has had some mixed fortunes. During the first period of agreement, there was substantial growth in intra-regional trade, between 1991 and 1997 there was a fourfold increase in intra-regional trade. From 1991–1995, the share of intra-Mercosur trade as a proportion of the total trade of the four members doubled.[44] However, in the late 1990s the agreement ran into a series of crises and in 1999 Brazil unilaterally devalued its currency, this move having a substantial negative impact on the Argentine economy.[45] In terms of intra-regional trade flows, the initial momentum of Mercosur stalled somewhat in the late 1990s. Another concern for the agreement's supporters has been the components of that trade. Too little of the trade has been comprised of goods with a high value-added content and has its origins in less dynamic areas of the economy. The picture is mixed and since 2002 there has been some more positive economic data emerging from the Southern Cone suggesting that Mercosur is getting back on track.[46]

Given the urgency attached to economic development it is difficult to make too strong a distinction between the economic and the political aspects of the agreement. However, there are increasingly some more explicitly political aspects to the

---

43 Álvaro De Vasconcelos & Helio Jaguaribe (eds), *The European Union, Mercosul and the New World Order* (London, 2003), p. 238.

44 Mario E. Carranza, 'Can Mercosur Survive? Domestic and International Constraints on Mercosur'.

45 The fall-out from this episode was considerable and trust between the two countries was badly damaged. The implication of Brazil's actions for its neighbour Argentina was that in difficult times Brazilia would sacrifice the interest of the collective (Mercosur) in favour of those of the nation state. Argentina responded by placing restrictions on Brazilian imports. Only negotiations at the highest level were able to diffuse the situation. Indeed for Carranza (2003), the agreement itself has only survived due to presidential diplomacy.

46 http://www.wto.org/english/news_e/pres04_e/pr373_e.htm.

agreement. Hence, it is not only the economic situation which will determine its success but also the political dynamics at play. Mercosur is more than simply a trading arrangement, that is to say, it is informed by more than simply a desire to increase trade flows. This political element of the agreement has tended to be ignored with analysts concentrating on the economic aspects of the bloc.[47] The political aspect of the agreement lies in two interconnected areas, the desire to promote regional solidarity and the wish to dilute US power in the region. It will not be economics on its own that will determine the fate of Mercosur, the dynamics that underpin the political rationale behind the project will also play a part. The politicization of the agreement damages prospects of any FTAA. Now the agreement is more than an economic one, it becomes less easy to bargain for inclusion in a wider trade agreement and makes negotiations with the US more complicated.

For Parish, there was a determination during the Cardoso presidency to build Mercosur as an autonomous bloc without North American involvement. Speaking in Quebec in 2001, the then President Cardoso made an interesting distinction: 'The FTAA is a choice, but Mercosur is destiny.'[48] It is a hybrid of pragmatism and grander notions of national destiny that inform Brazil's commitment to Mercosur. The commitment may also reside in the fact that in Mercosur, Brazil has been able to pursue its two great strategic goals simultaneously, economic development and the political grandeur of Brazil. Since the early 1990s, the international projection of Brazil has been intimately related to the success of this regional initiative. In speaking with and for South America, Brazil can realize her longer-term strategic ambitions.

For Hugueney regionalism has become a key element of Brazilian foreign policy:

> The building of a politically, economically and culturally integrated area in South America, with projections in Latin America, the Caribbean and Africa, is certainly a top priority for Brazilian diplomacy in coming decades.[49]

In Latin America there has been a long and unhappy tradition of regionalism. The example of Mercosur is different in many respects. The ideological drivers of the project are different today then they were in the past. There is much more pragmatism as to how to achieve development. Although the centre-periphery analysis has not disappeared, liberal economic values have been embraced as a mechanism to achieving economic growth. This has been true of both Brazil and Argentina.

With both Da Silva and Kirchner in office in Brazil and Argentina respectively, we have two leaders who are committed to Mercosur and anxious to resist US

---

47 Mario E. Carranza, 'Can Mercosur Survive? Domestic and International Constraints on Mercosur', p. 71.

48 Amaury de Souza, *The European Union, Mercosur and New World Order*, p. 201.

49 Clodoaldo Hugueney, 'Brazilian Foreign Policy at the Beginning of the Twenty-First Century' in Álvaro De Vasconcelos & Helio Jaguaribe (eds), *The European Union, Mercosul and the New World Order*, p. 216.

projection in the Southern Cone region. The shift to the left in Latin America from the end of the 1990s, of which Lula da Silva and Kirchner are part, has created a more positive environment for Latin Americanist initiatives. Traditionally the Right in Latin America (in an echo of the European experience) have been more sceptical of regional initiatives and more pro-Washington.

Outside the Americas, the European Union has been supportive of the Mercosur project. Again, relations with the United States form an important part of the picture. Relations with the US have traditionally been the dominant aspect of Brazilian foreign policy, certainly since the decline of Great Britain in the early twentieth century. But:

> the Mercosur project has in effect pushed Brazil in the opposite direction; US difficulties with Mercosur and Mercosur's strong relations with the EU have been crucial factors in inclining Brazil's foreign policy towards the EU.[50]

The presence of the EU in world polity, allow the Brazilians to play the 'European card' in its dealings with the US, a tactic that some European states are happy to encourage.[51] The EU–Mercosur relationship is in line with the long-standing preference with the EU of dealing with other regional blocs and encouraging the establishment of South–South political entities. The Essen European Council of December 1994 approved negotiations with Mercosur and a first agreement was formalized in 1995. Latin America was already considered a key component to the EU's global political strategy.[52] Since the mid-1990s, the relationship between Europe and Mercosur has been further strengthened by strong flows of investment into the continent from Europe. Trade and investment grew enormously through the 1990s. EU exports to Mercosur rose from €6 billion in 1990 to €24 billion by the end of the decade. Investment from Europe demonstrates a similar pattern. In the mid 1990s EU investment in the region amounted to around €1.6 billion which by the end of the 1990s had risen to some €26 billion in a single year. Spanish companies have been particularly active in the region investing heavily in both financial services and the utilities sector. In 1997 the EU overtook the United States as the principle investor in Latin America.[53] In the first decade of the twenty-first century Brazil (and so Mercosur)[54] is a global trader and the EU has become a significantly more important market than the US.[55]

Asia is also a growing market for Brazil and Mercosur generally. Both Japan and increasingly China are important trading partners. The Mercosur's internal market is also substantial and constitutes an important destination for the products of all the

---

50 Klom, 'Mercosur and Brazil: a European Perspective', p. 356.
51 Ibid., pp. 356–357.
52 Hazel Smith, *European Union Foreign Policy and Central America* (New York, 1995), p. 166.
53 Klom, 'Mercosur and Brazil: a European Perspective', p. 355.
54 Brazil accounts for some 2/3 of Mercosur GDP.
55 Nicola Philips, 'Integration and Subregionalism in the Americas', p. 336.

participants. The countries of Mercosur have diversified in terms of the destinations for their products. Trade relations with North America remain important but they are no longer dominant and this fact has afforded Brazil more flexibility in its dealings with Washington. For Brazil, FTAA is a choice but not a necessity.

This declining reliance on the United States in trading terms affects any assessment of Mercosur's prospects. Carranza (2003) suggests that the real question is whether or not the Mercosur agreement will be superseded by a wider hemispheric arrangement.[56] Given the diversification of trade flows from the Southern Cone, Mercosur may be a durable arrangement. As global traders, the countries of the region may benefit from a more autonomous status. For the dominant player in the group, Brazil, the political price of accepting US leadership may be too high given the other trading options available.

The important question is related to the durability of the arrangement. Paul Cammack argues:

> The Mercosur is an ineffectual regional association with little remaining capacity to contribute to regional or global integration, and little capacity to promote other goals ... It is likely to be marginalised by profound differences of perspective between its major partners, and overtaken by broader processes such as the move towards a Free-trade Area of the Americas.[57]

The preference for the United States is that the sub-regional bloc will be erased by hemispheric arrangements; 'subregional blocs, especially in the view of US business and members of congress have little political relevance'.[58]

The costs of failure are high for both Buenos Aires and Brasilia. Both gain considerable international projection from the existence of Mercosur. Brazil, on occasions, is happy to follow the Argentine lead on many international issues and at the same time Argentines are content to punch beyond their weight. Philips (2003) argues that external negotiations are constituting the 'glue' of Mercosur and progress is being made in terms of the construction of common positions, for example in the opening offers in the FTAA negotiations.[59] The alternative to Mercosur also holds the bloc together. In both countries, there are strong ideological and historical reasons to resist falling into a US-led hemispheric pact. Mercosur holds out the hope of resisting the satellization of South America.[60] It is also the case that no dispute is worth a return to the past. The unwillingness to go backwards may be amongst the more potent ideas sustaining the Mercosur project. In Brazil, Argentina and Chile nationalist narratives have all been tarnished by the experience of military rule. In

---

56 Carranza, 'Can Mercosur Survive? Domestic and International Constraints on Mercosur' (2003).
57 Philips, 'Integration and Subregionalism in the Americas', p. 339.
58 Ibid., p. 338.
59 Ibid., p. 341.
60 Vasconcelos & Jaguaribe, *The European Union, Mercosul and the New World Order*, p. 236.

each case, exceptionalist ideologies are less acceptable. For much of the twentieth century intra-regional relations were marked by rivalry and at times hostility. Wider global relations were dominated by strong links with the United States. Much of the second half of the century saw the region dominated by violent military dictatorships and then there was the complete debacle of the 'lost decade' of the 1980s. 'Mercosur was built upon decades of dictatorship.'[61] The agreement offers its members a distinct future and herein lies its power.

Transition and Continuity

The transition from military rule to civilian rule in Brazil was less abrupt than the case of Argentina. The transition process was agreed and the military were close to their immediate successor, José Sarney, who took office in 1985. Furthermore, the military had not left office completely discredited as they had in Argentina. The Brazilian military were a more successful agent of modernizing and so retained a degree of prestige and political leverage as a consequence.[62] This meant that the military continued to exert some control over policy making long after their departure from office. Smith (2005) outlines four stages in the democratization process in Latin America: military control, military tutelage, conditional military subordination and civilian control. Brazil and Chile, in the initial period of the transition to democracy, are both categorized under military tutelage.[63] Such close involvement of the military tended to militate against rupture in policy sets and this included, to some extent, the area of foreign policy.

The existence of the powerful and autonomous Foreign Affairs Ministry, the *Itamaraty*, lent further continuity to the area of foreign relations. The *Itamaraty* had over the years secured a high degree of control over policy making and their influence extended into other parts of the government.

> Decisions in Brazil regarding international trade are not taken by the trade minister or by the finance minister, as might be expected, but by the Ministry of Foreign Affairs (*Itamaraty*).[64]

During the 1980s the *Itamaraty* continued to be influenced by the centre-periphery critique developed by CEPAL and into the 1980s there was a strong belief that international trade was zero sum game. As an institution, it was convinced that it spoke for Latin America as a whole. Caldas (1998) goes so far as to further suggest that the *Itamaraty* had a hidden agenda to exercise hegemony over third world

---

61 Klom, 'Mercosur and Brazil: a European Perspective', p. 355.
62 Arturo C. Sotomayor Valazquez, 'Civil-Military Affairs and Security Institutions in the Southern Cone: The Sources of Argentine–Brazilian Nuclear Cooperation', *Latin American Politics and Society*, 46:4 (2004), p. 43.
63 Peter H. Smith, *Democracy in Latin America* (Oxford, 2005).
64 Caldas Wahrendorff, *Brazil in the Uruguay Round*, p. xxi.

countries. The economic shock of the 1980s brought more pragmatism to the foreign ministry and over the next decade there was an acceptance of the role of the free market. However, this was a tactical switch with the centrepiece of policy remaining regional leadership and economic development.

To some extent, the foreign policy-making establishment was insulated from outside forces. The fragmentation of the political parties in Brazil tended to militate against a firm policy line on foreign policy emanating from the Congress. In comparison with Argentina, the Brazilian elite governed a less democratic country and so was insulated, to some extent, against popular opinion.[65] In a sense then foreign policy formation has been protected from developments in the wider domestic political arena. However, the return of civilian government in 1985 did result in change in that the presence of civilian presidents in both Argentina and Brazil facilitated closer relations between the countries. The Brazilian armed forces still had a powerful role in government.[66] But, the handover to civilian rule in the two countries did foster a more open and trusting environment in bi-lateral relations. Though the new dispensation facilitated a change in intra-regional politics, it did not lead to much questioning of the wider strategic goals of Brazil.

Elsewhere in the Southern Cone, post-dictatorship, there were many more doubts expressed on the very nature of the *national* project. In the years following the handover to civilian rule in Chile, the country fell into a certain listlessness in foreign policy terms.[67] In Argentina there was a period of profound reflection after the departure of the military from power. In both cases the historical role of the nation had come into question. This was less the case in Brazil. The historical goal of the nation remained regional leadership and development. Many of the patterns of diplomacy, which took hold in the 1990s and the early twenty-first century had precedents during the military regime. The rapprochement with Argentina had begun before the military's departure from power and hostility to US involvement in South American affairs was well established by the mid-1970s. Links with Third World countries were both stridently pursued by the military regime of Geisel and by the left-wing government of Lula. The major changes in policy terms were the destruction of the Vargas legacy. The state was no longer to be the engine of economic growth and policy import-substitution was substituted for one of market led growth. These, though substantial, were tactical changes in direction and new positions were adopted in international trade negotiations but it did not mean that the Brazilians fell in behind the United States as an advocate of free trade. Brazil developed her own perspective on free trade and this for the most part was sharply at odds with the position of the United States.

---

65 Carlos Escudé & Andrés Fontana, 'Argentina's Security Policies. Their Rationale and Regional Context', p. 76.

66 Rur Diamint, 'Security Challenges in Latin America', *Bulletin of Latin American Research* 23:1 (2004): p. 51.

67 Jorge Heine, *Timidez o pragmatismo? La política exterior de Chile en 1990*.

The Lula Effect

Lula da Silva was elected president of Brazil in 2002. It marked an important event in Brazilian history in that it is the first left-wing presidency elected by the mass of the Brazilian people.[68] Klom (2003) argues that his election is unlikely to cause profound changes in the country's foreign policy. He writes:

> Under a Lula government a shift in foreign policy emphasis could occur; however, the broad tradition of Brazilian foreign policy and the stabilizing 'Itamaraty factor' will ensure that Brazil does not stray far from its established path.[69]

Similarly, Costa Vez argues that under Lula there was no deviation from the central foreign policy themes of previous government, but nor, he argues, were Lula's policies a mere continuation. Lula affected a change of emphasis, stressing his willingness to take a leadership role in South America, and Mercosur is a test case in this regard.[70]

During the second term of the Cardoso administration, Brazilian diplomacy was defined by three major policy lines. Firstly, the definition of a regional project for the country. Secondly, achieving better market access and opening new export markets. Thirdly, the construction of new international alliances. In many respects this agenda was overtaken by the events of September 11, 2001 with the attacks on the US by Islamic militants. This checked developments in the above areas as security issues came to dominate international relations for a time. The international environment that greeted the Lula government remained uncertain, even so the government did adopt some underlying principles in the conduct of foreign policy.

1. The subordination of foreign policy to the development goals
2. The reaffirmation of national sovereignty
3. The use of external trade as a mechanism for growth
4. The construction of alliances, global and regional, in favour of development.[71]

The themes expressed above are familiar and they all have precedent in previous administrations. Continuity remains important, as does the continued input of the *Itamaraty*. The continued power of this institution has been cited as a source of

---

68 Note that in the previous elections in the 1950s and 1960s the electorate constituted a small percentage of the general population. The first election with a franchise that extended to the mass of Brazilians was in 1989.

69 Klom, 'Mercosur and Brazil: a European Perspective', p. 366.

70 Alcides Costa Vaz, 'El Gobierno de Lula Una Nueva Política Exterior', *Nueva Sociedad 187* (2003): pp. 146–147.

71 Ibid.

conflict in dealings between the Brazil and the United States.[72] The desire to ensure policy stability, and in particular to protect the longer term goals of Brazilian foreign policy still informs the Brazilian foreign ministry. That said, internal interest groups do have a strong interest in the outcome of trade talks with some favouring a more positive line on the FTAA initiative. However, the fact that business groups are split on this issue lessens their impact and adds to the influence of the foreign ministry.

In its dealings on trade matters with the US, Brazil has taken a strident position since the election of Lula da Silva. However, again in examining these positions we find parallels with the past. In the run up to the GATT round in 1984 the military regime under João Baptista de Oliveira Figueiredo resisted the inclusion of services and intellectual property rights in the negotiations. In 2003 Lula's government adopted a similar position during negotiations on the proposed FTAA. The military regime failed to maintain its position, in many respects it was untenable because of leverage the US could exert on the debt issue. The balance of power has shifted somewhat (though this may be a temporary phenomena) and Brazil has recently maintained its strong line in trade talks. In the mid-1980s the United States sought to isolate Brazil from other developing countries and in 2003 Washington has adopted a similar strategy. Peru, Costa Rica and Colombia have all been warned that joining Brazil in attending G22 meetings will mean that they are ineligible for membership of any FTAA deal.[73] Once again Brazil is perceived as a leader of those developing countries that would defy the United States in trade talks.

> But the FTAA has been afflicted instead by international politics. Brazil evidently sees it as an extension of Nafta, with the US playing the hegemon. Brazil favours instead an expansion of Mercosur which it dominates.[74]

The goal of regional leadership remains a high priority for Brazil. For well over a decade this has constituted the core of the country's foreign policy. The region encompasses more that the countries of Mercosur and includes Latin America and South America in particular. Brazil has sought to extend its influence more widely across the continent, whilst at the same time seeking to preserve the coherence of the Mercosur group.

In any analysis of the international relations of Latin America, and of Brazilian foreign policy in particular, the relatively benign nature of the environment in security terms forms an important part of the picture. Compared with South Asia and the history of Europe over the past century, Latin America has experienced less inter-state violence. In the Southern Cone, Brazil had been used as a counter-weight in struggles between countries that often have their roots in the nineteenth century. Historically, Chile has sought close relations with Brazil based upon their mutual distrust of Argentine intentions. In the past Brazil reciprocated to some extent based

---

72 Peter Hakim, president of the Inter-American Dialogue raises this issue of the role of the Brazilian foreign ministry in talks on the FTAA, *Financial Times* 27/11/03.
73 Peru became an associate member of Mercosur in August 2004.
74 Baldwin & Bhagwati, *Financial Times* 18/12/2003.

primarily on rivalry in the River Plate region. Bolivia, for its part, has sought Brazil's 'good offices' in attempting to gain the upper hand in its battle over access to the Pacific through what is now Chilean territory. In recent decades rapprochement with Argentina has meant the traditional dynamic of relations in the Southern Cone has broken down. Relations are now less about the strategic balance of power and more about increasing Brazilian influence in the continent. In this regard one of the primary tasks of Brazilian diplomacy has been to avoid antagonizing one side or another in their particular disputes and so Brazil has shown a marked reluctance to be drawn into local conflicts. Brazil has also sought to reassure its neighbours on their fears over Brazilian leadership. This has become a key task in Brazilian diplomacy. In seeking to improve its contacts with other nations on the continent, Brazil has to compete head on with the United States who during the administration of George W. Bush has sought to undermine Brazil's influence in the region. This rivalry is at its starkest in the case of Colombia, where the increasing role of the US military in aiding the forces of the State against left-wing guerrillas has caused concern in Brazil. Relations with allies of the US creates problems, close links with enemies of the US also cause difficulties in Brazil-US relations. The United States has sought to isolate Cuba for half a century now. Over the decades, Brazilian governments have adopted various policies on Cuba. One of the first acts of the military regime in 1964 was to sever links with Cuba. However, in common with all other Latin American states Brazil now has diplomatic relations with the Castro government. Since the inauguration of Lula de Silva, relations with Cuba have become warmer. This may be explained by some ideological common ground with Havana, but there is also a desire to more clearly delineate Brazilian foreign policy from that of the United States.

Similar issues arise in Brazil's relations with Venezuela. The coming to office of Hugo Chavez has caused a good deal of concern in Washington. Relations between the Chavez government worsened still further when a coup attempt in 2002 failed. The apparent support the coup leaders had garnered in Washington caused much ill feeling when Chavez returned to office. This pattern of tense relations and rhetorical exchanges became established over the next few years. Under Lula, Brazil's relations with Chavez have been cordial and this is another source of irritation in Washington. Brazil has though at times become uneasy about the extent of Chavez's anti-US rhetoric and sought to distance itself from some of the more stridently anti-US positions adopted by Chavez. Foreign policy since Lula's election may have seen some changes of emphasis, but it remains essentially pragmatic and focused on Brazil's long-term goals. In 2005, Chavez stepped up efforts to gain full membership of Mercosur for Venezuela. To lend some weight to Venezuela's attempts to integrate with its neighbours, Chavez has invested heavily around the Mercosur area. Eventual Venezuelan entry could drive a further wedge between the Mercosur countries and Washington.

Since Lula da Silva's election, there has been greater emphasis on relations with other developing countries. This policy is not without precedent and under the military in the 1970s and early 1980s Brazil developed extensive ties with the developing world. The desire on the part of the *Itamaraty* to seek a leading role among developing countries has been present for some time.[75] In recent years Brazil has developed close links with China, India and South Africa. On this occasion this drive is not informed so much by ideological concerns on the nature of the global economy, but by more practical considerations. The goals of the policy have been twofold, firstly to open markets for Brazilian good and services. The Lula government see great potential in such trade arrangements between developing nations. Secondly, Brazil sees such linkages as offering potential leverage in wider negotiations on trade. Such countries are less vulnerable to intense pressure from the United States. Such tactics are not without risk, Brazil's mobilization of the group of 21 developing countries at the failed WTO talks in Cancun enraged Washington.[76] Lula has extended his diplomatic/trade offensive to North Africa and the Arab world in general. By generating such a dense set of relationships, Brazil feels more able to withstand US pressure on the FTAA issue. In wider global trade talks Brazil is seeking to generate alliances within and outside Latin America to wring concessions out of the United States and other rich nations.

The Future Outlook/Conclusions

Lula during his election campaign compared FTAA to annexation. He has since lowered the rhetorical temperature but many of his advisors remain deeply unenthusiastic about the project.[77] These reservations are shared within the Ministry of Foreign Affairs who see the FTAA as being at odds with their longer term ambitions for the country. Since 2003, Brazil has adopted a trenchant position in FTAA talks. It suits policy planners in Brazil to drag out negotiations as long as possible. Brazil would not wish to be excluded from such an arrangement but has its own set of preferences. The delay in achieving the FTAA will allow Brazil to pursue other options.

Among the questions that arise are how long can Brazil keep up its resistance to an hemispheric trade pact and what would determine its any change in its position? The key here is Brazil's relationship with its main Mercosur partner, Argentina. If this relationship remains strong, then politically at least, Mercosur continues to have a future. There is also the state of Brazil's wider relations in the continent and beyond. If these remain vibrant and strong Brazil will feel that it can exercise some influence in global trade diplomacy. Brazil's position depends upon the progress of Brazil's economic development. If this continues, inward investment flow will remain relatively strong and if the country's exporters can still find buyers, then Brazil's foreign ministry can enjoy some autonomy of action. If however, we see another severe setback in economic terms then priorities may change.

---

75 Caldas Wahrendorff, *Brazil in the Uruguay Round*.
76 De Jonquieres and Lapper 2003, *Financial Times* 17/11/2003.
77 Ibid.

In Brazil over the course of the twentieth century, the relationship between the goal of *grandeza nacional* and the achievement of economic growth has been a complex one. Good relations with the United States were for a time seen as a guarantee of both. Close relations with the US afforded the nation prestige, in effect bestowing regional leadership upon Brazil, and at the same time US approval was seen as an essential element of any development strategy. That sacrifices have been made in terms of autonomy in the pursuit of economic growth is understandable. The imperative to develop is urgent in Brazil where social problems associated with poverty are extremely acute. There is a useful distinction to be made between long and short-term objectives. Economic development serves the goal of autonomy and influence. Therefore it may be worth making some sacrifices in the short term to secure long-term strategic goals. By the 1970s, there was a certain disillusionment in that close relations with the US did not appear to be delivering. Politically, Brazil began to move out of the orbit of the United States. This trend has continued ever since. In the 1980s, circumstances dictated that Brazil comply with certain US policy goals, but this was a very grudging compliance.[78] In the 1990s Brazil resumed its trajectory that had its roots in the independent line pursued by the Goulart administration in the 1960s. During the terms of Cardoso and Lula da Silva, the relationship between growth and autonomy has been less problematic. The diversification of Brazil's export markets and sources of investment are an important part of the picture. Asia and Europe both represent important centres of trade for Brazil. The Mercosur project, born in the shadow of the generals, represents the ideal type for Brazilian foreign policy planners. It generates economic linkages and encourages inward investment.[79] Thus, using the developmental criterion, it has a positive role. At the same time, Mercosur lends much more credibility to Brazil's pretensions to be a global player and increases its power in its ongoing dealings with the United States.

In many respects it is this relationship with the US that remains the key in any assessment of likely outcomes. Taken over a longer trajectory Brazil appears to be distancing itself from the United States. This has been a long-term goal of the Foreign Ministry. Though we live in a world where in terms of hard power the United States dominates, its influence in terms of soft power is on the wane. In particular trading patterns in South America are such that Washington cannot exert the influence it enjoyed in previous decades. Ironically perhaps, the collapse of the ISI model and its embracing of export led growth has seen Brazil become less dependent on, and more strident in its dealings with the United States. All this should inform any prognosis on the future of the Mercosur project and whether it will be subsumed by a hemispheric free-trade project. There are a number of reasons for suggesting that Brazil will attempt to stay with and even strengthen Mercosur. Firstly, trade and investment no longer flow along longitudinal lines in and out of Brazil. This affords Brazil greater

---

78 'There is no doubt that Brazil's position on IPRs in the Uruguay Round changed because of the use of sanctions', Caldas Wahrendorff, *Brazil in the Uruguay Round*, p. 219.

79 Klom, 'Mercosur and Brazil: a European Perspective'.

freedom of action. Brazil's diplomatic efforts have been designed to enhance this process of reduced dependence on North America. Certainly, the profile of Brazil in global trade talks is growing. This happened in the 1970s and 1980s, however, on this occasion Brazil's strength derives in large part from its success in world trade markets and this adds durability to the position it has adopted.

The principal risk lies with the willingness of its allies to pursue the same course of action as Brazil. If Brazil can retain close relations with its principal partner, Argentina, maintain close relations with the EU, and develop its links with other developing countries then its current strategies will endure. The state of relations with Argentina is central. In 2005, Rafael Bielsa, the Argentine Foreign Minister spoke of a 'regression' in relations with Brazil. The main difficulty arises from the asymmetrical power relations between the two countries. Unless this is addressed, Argentine opinion could become alienated from the Mercosur project. Tokatlian sums up the situation thus: 'After more than 100 years, we have overcome a relationship based on rivalries but we have still not managed to create one based on friendship.'[80] This key relationship will have to be managed more effectively if Brazil hopes to sustain the Mercosur project.

Brazil's strategy also depends to a large part on the nature of the international environment. As a middle ranking power, Brazil's options in terms of shaping this environment are limited. A number of other major players welcome the presence of Mercosur in trade talks. Brazil uses Mercosur as leverage and other powers use its existence to maximize their negotiating positions. The gambit by the EU in April 2004 to offer Mercosur some attractive trade concessions in order to split the opposition to the Common Agricultural Policy is a case in point. India, during 2004, has been extremely receptive to overtures made by Brazil on bilateral trading links. In a globalized world where soft power is so effective, Brazil, the global trader, is thriving.

---

80 Cited in Raymond Colitt & Alan Thomsom, *Financial Times* 7/05/05.

Map of Chile

Chapter 5

Chilean Foreign Policy

Introduction

Chile is a long country, it is more than 4000 km from Arica in the North to the southernmost tip of the country. It is narrow land with an average width of just 180km. Excluding claims to a portion of Antarctica, the land area of the country is 756,252 square km. The shape and topography of the country gives rise to a complex security situation. Long borders and a history of tensions with its neighbours have given rise to a tradition of strategic thinking in Chile.[1] This said, the country has had no international wars for more than a century. In 1881 the frontiers with Argentina were drawn and in 1883, in the aftermath of the War of the Pacific, the Treaty of Ancon settled the frontier with Peru. However, in both cases a number of border issues remained unresolved. Two decades later, the 1904 Treaty of Peace and Friendship was signed with Bolivia, the other protagonist in that war, but the agreement failed to bring closure to the various issues at stake. Border disputes and tensions continued to shape Chilean relations with its neighbours throughout much of the twentieth century and the issue of Bolivian access to the Pacific remains an obstacle to the normalization of relations between the two countries. The War of the Pacific has cast a long shadow over Chilean diplomacy.

Chile, not unlike its Southern Cone neighbours, has endured a traumatic recent past. Any explanation of Chilean foreign policy over the past 30 years is not complete without reference to these events. A military coup took place on September 11, 1973. It was the culmination of a period of intense political instability.[2] During

---

1 Francisco Rojas Aravena, *Chile–Peru: revisando las agendas con una mirada de futuro in Chile: entre la II cumbre y la detención de Pinochet* (Santiago, 1998), p. 88.

2 The election of the Popular Unity government in 1970 with just over one third of the popular vote released strong desires for reform from both within the political caste and outside. The UP (Unidad Popular) government was a broad left-wing coalition that included some radical tendencies, indeed within the coalition it was the Chilean Communist Party which frequently found itself urging caution. Allende's government combined a strong respect for the institutions of the Chilean state with a messianic desire to better the position of the working classes. There were elements though whose aspirations went further and included a dismantling of the state. Carlos Altamirano, a prominent member of the Socialist party summed up the approach: 'The bourgeois state in Chile will not serve as the basis for socialism and it is necessary to destroy it.' The UP's analysis of the social order was strongly Marxist, and for them it was the capitalist mode of production that was to blame for the predicament of the country's poor. The government moved quickly to nationalize large sectors of the economy.

its 16-year tenure the military undertook a policy of removing the state from the economic activity of the country. During the 1970s the state's holdings in the economy were systematically sold off at what many believe to have been a knock down price.³ Much of the thinking behind the neo-liberal policies adopted by the military came from the so-called 'Chicago Boys', a group of young Chilean economists who studied in the University of Chicago in a department headed up by Milton Friedman. Their free market perspective sat well with the declared intention of the military to bring an end to the 'clientelistic' relationship between the state and the people. In Chile, this policy represented a dramatic break with the past. The state had long involved itself in the economic and social life of the country, even before Allende came to power in 1970 the state was an 'awesome set of structures and institutions'.⁴ No less than 40% of the economy was already state-owned with another 30% dependent on state funding.⁵ From the 1950s onwards, governments across the continent had, under the influence of Raul Prebisch, the head of ECLAC (Economic Commission for Latin American Co-operation), adopted interventionist policies. Tariff barriers were raised and a policy of import substitution was pursued. The military immediately abandoned this approach; tariff barriers were lowered, subsidies were withdrawn and large parts of industry went into decline. The result was massive de-industrialization and huge unemployment. The military did enjoy some conventional macro-economic successes. Inflation was reduced and the state budget was brought back under control.⁶ Foreign investment returned to the country, and during a brief period in the 1980s, the economy enjoyed strong growth, with exports performing particularly well. The impressive growth experienced by the country during the 1990's has for some been proof that the policies of the military government sowed the seeds of future success. Such a view informed much of the political discourse in Chile in the early years of the transition to democracy.

Within a year the UP had nationalized the banks and mining sectors. For some though, events were not moving fast enough. Some farm labourers and factory workers, often under the leadership of MIR (Moviemento Izquierda Revolucionario) activists, began to take over their places of employment. These so-called tomas proceeded apace around the country with calls for restraint being ignored. With the forces of law and order effectively held in check by the government, there seemed to be, for many people, nothing in the way of revolution or anarchy, which one depending on your standpoint. The reaction of the more conservative elements in Chilean society was one of alarm and they quickly set about defending their interests. Militias were established, middle class women were mobilized and a policy of economic non-co-operation was initiated. Employers formed associations to protect their interests. This atmosphere of crisis persisted throughout the Allende administration and formed the backdrop to the coup of 1973.

   3   Eduardo Silva, *The State and Capital in Chile. Business Elites, Technocrats and Market Economics* (Boulder, 1996), p. 122.

   4   Arturo Valenzuela, *The Breakdown of Democratic Regimes in Chile* (London, 1978), p. 13.

   5   Hickman, *News from End of the Earth. A portrait of Chile* (London, 1998), p. 95.

   6   Brian Loveman, *The Legacy of Hispanic Capitalism* (New York, 1988), p. 328.

It is however, in the area of human rights that the most important legacy of the military dictatorship may lie. This remains a highly contested area and there are those who have sought a *punta final* or full stop to the debate and legal processes surrounding state violence between 1973 and 1990. The abuses have been comprehensively documented.[7] The arrest of Pinochet in London in 1998 and the many ongoing legal processes have raised the profile of the human rights abuses of the past. The fact that the Lagos government has been less reticent in discussing past abuses has also contributed to a renewed debate on the nature of military rule. For many, it was a dark period in Chilean history with thousands killed and tens of thousands tortured. The legacy of these human rights abuses has touched the very collective identity of Chilean society.[8]

For the Chilean political class after the departure of Pinochet, rational political action offered a way of changing the political climate in the country. The language of the *Concertación* was designed to limit occasions of conflict in a deeply divided society.[9] This was true of both domestic and foreign policy. Such was the focus of the new regime on economic utility in its dealing with the international community that the authorities were accused of running a vacuous and meaningless foreign policy.[10] Chile's diplomatic activity throughout the transition had, as its overriding aim, the re-insertion of the country into the international community. In other words, it sought the normalization of relations with the outside world, this after the isolation experienced during the Pinochet years. The re-establishment of ties with its neighbours and trading partners would serve to facilitate the penetration of overseas export markets and to attract much needed foreign investment. The drive for acceptance around the world was fuelled in part by the desire to prevent a return to autocratic rule at home through institutionalizing democratic linkages with other states.

In terms of the discipline of International Relations, there is an important difference between realist thought and the type of debate that has occurred in Chile over the last decade or so. The Chilean political class has sought to protect itself from what they perceive as dangerous forces in society and have deliberately sought to insulate themselves from these forces through focusing on the rational, scientific and technocratic elements of governance. Realist thinkers on the other hand have tended to ontologize the disengaged perspective. In other words, whereas the Chilean elite, post-Pinochet, sought redemption with instrumental reason and social responsibility, realist thinking has attempted to naturalize this position.

The political elite's commitment to social responsibility explains the focus on economic development. Throughout the 1990s, it constituted a key driver of

---

7 Ascanio Cavallo, Manuel Salazar & Oscar Sepúlveda, *La Historia Oculta del Régimen Militar* (Santiago, 1997).

8 Roniger & Sznajder, *The Legacy of Human Right Violations in Latin America* (Oxford, 1999).

9 Jeffrey Puryear, *Thinking Politics: Intellectuals in Democracy in Chile* (Baltimore, Maryland; London, 1994).

10 Jorge Heine, *Timidez o pragmatismo? La política exterior de Chile en 1990* (Santiago, 1990), p. 1.

foreign policy in Chile. This is reflected in the infrastructure afforded to economic foreign policy with *La Dirección General de Asuntos Económicos Internacionales* and PROCHILE both having a prominent role. During the 16 years of military rule (1973–1990), great emphasis was placed on this element of foreign policy and, to some extent, this emphasis on trade matters has been inherited from the Pinochet regime. In the early days of civilian rule this prompted Heine (1990) to criticize the foreign policy of the coalition on the grounds that it was overly focused on trade.[11] Whilst there is a degree of continuity between this economically focused foreign policy of both the military and civilian governments, there are some differences, albeit subtle. In many respects, the concentration on economic foreign policy by the Pinochet regime was enforced. Its political isolation was such that its energies were displaced into the economic sphere. In the case of the coalition government, the policy of encouraging trade co-existed with a policy designed to promote democracy and human rights. Indeed, these three strands formed the basis of Chilean foreign policy throughout the period of transition. This said, the government of Aylwin did pursue a low profile on the international stage. The reasons behind this policy are complex and relate in part to the domestic political scene and the continuing influence of the military and the political dislocation caused by years of authoritarian rule. The domestic political situation cannot be ignored in any analysis of the Chilean foreign policy. Another of the internal drivers of policy was the nature of the debate around Chilean identity and the country's place in the world. In many respects, the trauma of the dictatorship had put much of this debate on hold. Today, the debate on Chile's role in the Mercosur project has brought these issues to the fore again.

The fact that domestic politics have a strong impact on foreign policy even at periphery, where constraints of power are at their most severe, is evidence of the saliency of such domestic factors in the field of International Relations. Not only is regime change important, the nature of any transition to democracy is also critical. In terms of foreign policy making among the principal countries of the Southern Cone, the nature of the transition to democracy is seen as a crucial determinant of foreign policy in the 1990s.[12] In the case of Chile, the military retained a degree of political influence in the system of governance after their formal departure from government. This influence was exercised through political allies in the Chilean Congress and through the formal mechanisms enshrined in the Constitution. These provisions were only reformed in 2004.

A number of exogenous factors are also prominent in shaping Chilean foreign policy. With civilians back in power in 1990, governments around the world were more favourably disposed towards Chile. That said, the world had changed considerably in the intervening 16 years. In terms of global politics, the Cold War had run its course. Much of the activity of the Pinochet government had been framed in the logic of the Cold War. After 1990, any imperative that had existed to defend the country from Marxist interference disappeared. Chile had to face a situation

---

11 Ibid.
12 Mónica Hirst, 'Los claroscuros de la seguridad regional en las Américas',

whereby the United States was important to Chile but the region was less strategically important to the United States. This lack of attention towards South America was mirrored to some extent in Europe where the collapse of the Eastern bloc caused diplomatic energy to focus on Eastern Europe, the reunification of Germany and the eventual expansion of the European Union. The war in ex-Yugoslavia also served to divert attention from the continent. Furthermore, for both United States and Europe the 1990s was a decade in which the Gulf and the Middle East were to retain a high profile. All these political factors conspired to lower the profile of South America in the wider world.

Given this environment, it is perhaps not surprising that the countries of the region began to look to one another as both diplomatic and trading partners. This process of regional integration was more intense on the eastern side of the Andes with Argentina and Brazil making great strides in their bilateral relations. The Chileans were somewhat more reticent in this regard. Chile's relations with the Mercosur nations did though improve with time. Insulsa Foreign Minister in the mid 1990's wrote:

> We think that Chile has to define herself as a Latin American country, not just for historical reasons or due to values, but also for national interest in this period of globalisation. Chile, due to her size, economic capacity, and geographical location cannot function isolated in the world.[13]

In order to pursue her rightful position in the continent, Insulsa recognized that the Chilean people had to challenge some of their historical attitudes towards their fellow South Americans.[14] Such attitudes have their roots in certain interpretations of nineteenth-century history. These have impacted upon Chilean identity and in turn on the country's international relations. The public, up and down the continent have for generations been inculcated into their respective nationalist traditions and Chile is no different in this regard. The effects of such narratives on policy are hard to gauge but large nationalist constituencies have been produced and thus need to be addressed.

Historical Antecedents

The early history of Chile's relations with its neighbours represents a valuable line of enquiry in the task to understanding the contemporary environment within which foreign policy is formed. The nineteenth century was the formative period of the Chilean nation state and it was during this century that the foundations of Chilean nationalism were laid down. Post-Pinochet, policy planners sought to form their relations with the outside world on a rational basis but nationalist sentiment remains

---

13 José Miguel Insulsa, *Ensayos Sobre Política Exterior de Chile* (Santiago, 1998), p. 64.
14 Ibid., pp. 82–83.

an important constraint upon policy making.¹⁵ Any innovations in this area of foreign relations, particularly with regard to its neighbours, are liable to run the gauntlet of nationalist sentiment.

The acceptance of the Republic of Chile as part of the family of nations was long and drawn out. Their fellow Latin American republics were quick to recognize the country. The United States did not delay long after the defeat of the Royalist forces and in 1823 it began formal dealings with Santiago. However, European states were much slower to respond. The fact that Latin America had been under the jurisdiction of the Spanish monarchy meant that there was a certain reluctance in the major European capitals to grant recognition. The influence of powerful monarchical states goes some way in explaining the delay but the power politics of the time also played an important role. Chile came to feel sacrificed on the altar of European power politics, and after the initial cordial relations O'Higgins, the founding father of the Chilean nation, was to feel cheated by Britain.¹⁶ London's need to maintain close relations with other European colonial powers and an anxiousness to avoid a damaging precedent being set for other colonial subjects made London cautious in its dealings with Santiago.

It was for Chile not just a matter of simple recognition. Chilean political leaders wanted to be accepted as equals. In the first decades of the nineteenth century Chilean foreign policy was less about marking out an identity of its own and more about simply gaining *an* identity.

> It was necessary to demonstrate to the world that which we really were. To demonstrate that we were an orderly country and respectful of judicial norms; that we had culture and we were worthy to form part of the international community on equal terms. This would be the task of early diplomacy.¹⁷

Chilean diplomacy was marked by a desire for acceptance and equal treatment. This concern over equality of treatment was to be a constant theme over the next two centuries, with Chile remaining insistent that it be afforded the same rights as other nation-states. The emphasis placed on formal legal structures by the Chilean jurist, Andres Bello, was in part an expression of this desire. The existing system of international relations was seen as insufficient to guarantee Chilean equality of

---

15 Van Klaveren, 2000. In 1996, Alberto van Klaveren was appointed Director for Policy Planning at the Foreign Ministry, a position which he left in May 2001 to become Chilean Ambassador to the European Union. As Director for Policy Planning, Mr van Klaveren gave advice on foreign policy issues to the Minister of Foreign Affairs. He also supervised speech writing on international issues for the President of the Republic and the Minister of Foreign Affairs. In November 2000 he granted the author an interview during which he expressed these beliefs.

16 Luis Melo Lecaros, 'Trayectoria del Ministro de Relaciones Exteriores y las Problemas en la conducion de la diplomacia Chilena' in G. Walter Sanchez & L. Pereira (eds), *150 Anos de Política Exterior* Chilena (Santiago, 1977), 108.

17 Ibid., p. 119.

esteem. Bello wanted to see the introduction of a new system governed by legal structures. This *activismo*, as it has been termed by Chilean commentators, has been an important strand of thought throughout the country's history.[18]

The dominant historical discourse in Chile has been based on the claim that the country's internal stability formed the basis for its successes during the nineteenth century. Relative to its neighbours the Chilean authorities were successful in the rapid establishment of a strong state structure. By the mid-nineteenth century, Chile was stable and had avoided some of the difficulties that had beset other countries in the region. The contrasting fortunes of other Latin American states led to a strong tendency in Chile to ascribe their good fortune to a set of characteristics that were said to be particular to Chile. It was argued that the racial mix of the country had afforded it a predisposition towards hard work and the long Araucanian war had instilled a sense of discipline in the nation. The qualities of the Chilean people were elevated to great heights and they continued to support chauvinistic tendencies, particularly towards their northern neighbours.

Conversely, we also see an acceptance that Chile shares many characteristics with its neighbours. It is too simplistic to see these ideological processes as occurring on a single temporal plane. Rather it is that diverse elements of the historical consciousness of the Chilean people exist contemporaneously. What we have is the co-presence of seemingly paradoxical beliefs. There is both a strong belief in the exceptionalist position that sharply differentiates Chile from its neighbours *and* a tendency to identify with their fellow Latin Americans. Whilst it is the case that the strong nationalist position tends to be common among the rightist parties, to ascribe such belief system to one element in Chilean society or another is again to oversimplify. They can co-exist in one segment of the population or another. They can even co-exist within individuals.[19]

The arrest of, the then, Senator Pinochet in Spain is instructive in this regard. One of the positions adopted by those attempting to repatriate Pinochet was that by attempting to put him on trial the Spanish were behaving like a colonial power. Such a critique of colonialism is rarely made in such rightist circles but it is available in that it constitutes part of Chilean national identity. In this case it was conscripted into the cause of securing Pinochet's return to Chile.

The debate as to the future direction of Chilean foreign policy is in part played out in the national consciousness of the country. Various positions within the debate are underwritten by historical episodes that support their position. Long-term institutional stability, the military triumphs of the late nineteenth century and recent

---

18 Manfred Wilhelmy, 'Hacia un Análisis de la Política Exterior Chilena Contemporáneo' in *Estudios Internacionales*, 48 (1979): p. 447.

19 The arrest of the then Senator Pinochet in Spain is instructive in this regard. One of the positions adopted by those attempting to repatriate Pinochet was that by attempting to put him on trial the Spanish were behaving like a colonial power. Such a critique of colonialism is rarely made in such rightist circles but it is available in that in constitutes part of Chilean national identity. In this case it was conscripted into the cause of securing Pinochet's return to Chile.

economic success support the exceptionalist thesis. On the other hand, the shared legacy of an imperial past, the political philosophy of Bolivar, the heroism of San Martin, and the resistance to US interventionism all highlight a shared past and, to some extent, a shared Latin American identity. The recent struggles for democracy across the continent serve to underwrite this identity.

The War of the Pacific was a key moment in Chilean history. The conflict was fought between Chile on one side and Peru and Bolivia on the other. It had its origins in a dispute over the mineral rich northern desert and was sparked off by a change in Bolivian fiscal practices in regard to Chile firms. Many though saw this war as an example of Chilean expansionism. In diplomatic terms the war was a disaster. Chile's insistence on keeping the territorial gains generated hostility across Latin America and beyond. The consequences were long lived, and over the next three decades Chile found herself isolated in the region. Disputes related to the War of the Pacific continue and to this day they impact upon Chile's relations with Peru and Bolivia.

The war also caused a marked shift away from a legalist and activist tendency in the country's foreign relations. Anxious to hold on to her spoils, Chile was increasingly reluctant to involve herself in any hemispheric initiatives that could have exposed her to compulsory arbitration with Peru over the disputed cities of Tacna and Arica. In such a self-confident mood Chile had little need for such legal instruments, and, along with the United States, she resisted any attempts to restrict her freedom of action. Indeed Chile, with the United States, rejected the Calvo Clause, an Argentine initiative designed to prevent the intervention of outside powers on behalf of the private interest of their citizens. The reasoning in Santiago was that some of the countries in the region were too underdeveloped to afford them such complete sovereignty.[20]

After the War of the Pacific Chile had reached a stage in her journey where she could now focus on other goals. Newspapers predicted a great future for the country. El Mercurio of January 22, 1881 editorialized:

> Chile's greatness was now immense and all other nations acknowledge it ... How could its glory be greater? Is there any other Latin American nation that has accomplished so much?[21]

However, the War of the Pacific and its aftermath was the high point of Chilean power. After 1891 Chile as a regional power was on the decline. This was the year of the Chilean civil war. For those convinced of the need to preserve internal discipline in order to succeed internationally, the evidence is clear, as are the lessons that can be drawn; the country never fulfilled its national destiny due to internal dissent. This belief in the need for internal discipline also has its roots in the centuries-long Araucanian Wars and forms part of the ideology of those that overthrew Allende's government in 1973. Many working in Chilean foreign relations stress the importance

---

20 Frederick B. Pike, *Chile and the United States* (New York, 1983), p. 126.
21 Ibid., p. 35.

of internal politics. According to Orrego Vicuna, 'Internal politics are absolutely inseparable from international politics: a country that fails internally is condemned to fail externally.'[22]

Accordingly, in a competitive environment it is crucial to maintain order. This has been the argument pursued by influential groups within Chile. In the recent decades it has found its expression in the views of General Leigh, one of the architects of the 1973 *coup d'etat*, on the need to cut out the 'cancer' of Marxism from Chilean society.[23] In this instance, the imperative for action internally has its source partly in the external environment. The struggle against Marxism/left-wing politics was seen as transcending national borders with the threat seen as coming from both within and outside the country's borders.

Throughout the nineteenth century, the United States was seen as a rival to Chile in its quest for Pacific hegemony. Chileans saw themselves as competing with the United States in the region. Already fraught relations were damaged further during the War of the Pacific and its aftermath. North American interventions in the conflict were seen as favouring Peru. The result was, according to Varas that, 'this behaviour influenced the negative image of the United States held by Chile and increases the distrust that already existed'.[24] For Pike (1983) and Guerro Yoacham (1977) the War of the Pacific generated an enduring distrust of the United States.[25] The US role in the Patagonian dispute also caused rancour in Chile. The United States this time was seen to be favouring Argentina. The situation was to deteriorate still further in 1891 when the United States effectively backed the losing side in the Chilean civil war. The sentiment of anti-Americanism has deep roots in Chilean politics, fed in large part by the events described above. It has been identified as a salient theme in Chilean foreign relations dating back to Francisco Bilboa in the nineteenth century. It has been bolstered by a continent-wide *hispanismo*, one component of which is the identification of the 'Anglo-Saxon' north of the continent as being materialistic and lacking the depth of the Hispanic culture south of the Rio Grande.

Chilean Excepionalism

It might be going too far to suggest that identity politics dominate foreign policy making. However, such belief systems do at times constitute important barriers to policy initiatives. Public opinion across the continent remains extremely sensitive

---

22 Francisco Orrego Vicuna, *La Participación de Chile en el Sistema Internacional* (Santiago, 1974), p. 16. See also, *Insulsa, Ensayos Sobre Política Exterior de Chile*.

23 Cited in Lois Hecht Oppenheim, *Politics in Chile. Democracy, Authoritarianism, and the Search for Development* (Boulder, 1999), p. 3.

24 Pilar Alamos Varas, 'Algunas Fuentes Históricas de la Política Exterior de Chile', *Estudios Internacionales*, 126 (1999): p. 29.

25 Frederick B. Pike, Chile and the United States & Christián Guerro Yoacham, 'Chile y Estados Unidos Relaciones y Problemas 1812–1916' in Walter G. Sanchez. & L. Pereira, (eds), *150 Anos de Política Exterior Chilena* (Santiago, 1977).

to historical issues or *la agenda clásica* and Chile is no different in this regard. Importantly, there resides in the historical narratives of Chile the basis of a scepticism towards Latin American solidarity, a strong basis for isolationism and a suspicion of the United States and Europe. Insulsa sees a struggle taking place between the self-interest of integration and a traditional reluctance to establish closer linkages with Chile's neighbours and this is in large part driven by identity politics.

> The process of the economic, physical and political interaction of Chile with the countries of Latin America, in the framework of the strategic option of Mercosur, is under way, though we still have to overcome many obstacles, the major part of which usually lie in our own idiosyncrasies and mentality.[26]

Historical narratives in Chile tended to support the belief held by a section of the political elite that notions of Latin American solidarity were purely rhetorical. In part, such thinking was fuelled by geopolitical ideas. These ideas were imported into the country at the end of the nineteenth century from Europe and have had a particularly strong influence within the country's military schools. In a scenario of eternal competition between nation states there was little room for regional solidarity. Scepticism vis-à-vis Latin American solidarity has a long history and dates back to the aftermath of the War of the Pacific in the nineteenth century. In the late nineteenth century such a position was already well established and many already doubted the merits of close relations with Chile's Latin neighbours who were seen as untrustworthy.[27]

On the political level, one strand of thought in Chile has argued consistently that the country is best served by distancing itself from its neighbours. Alamos Varas (1999) and Sanchez (1977) identify this isolationist perspective as a persistent position in Chilean politics.[28] It is a strand of thinking that very much depends on a particularistic view of the country, on the belief that Chile has itself a unique mission to carry out. During the military government this vision gained much ground. This type of foreign policy position sees entry into regional accords as a sign of weakness as such agreements undermine Chile's claim to be a particular case, for why, after all, would a country with such a glorious past as Chile throw in her lot with the likes of Peru and Bolivia? A disinclination to form links with other Latin American countries is often accompanied by a dismissive attitude toward pan-Latinamercanism. Orrego Vicuna writes:

---

26 Insulsa, *Ensayos Sobre Política Exterior de Chile*, pp. 82–83.
27 Robert Burr, *By Reason or Force* (Berkeley, 1965), p. 65.
28 Alamos Varas, 'Algunas Fuentes Históricas de la Política Exterior de Chile' & Walter G. Sánchez, 'Las Tendencias Sobresalientes de la Política Exterior Chilena' in Sánchez & Periera (eds), *150 Anos de Política Exterior Chilena*.

If there is one institution in Latin America that is characterised by verbalism and fragility, that institution is Latin American solidarity, it has never manifested itself in concrete terms in those circumstances when it was needed.[29]

Whilst continental solidarity was largely idle talk, the Pacific, for Orrego Vicuna, constituted an important symbol of expansion. Essentially, we see one goal or desire preferred over another, only the latter project is a uniquely Chilean project. The idea of a Pacific destiny for the country sits well with this type of thinking, conjuring up an image of a nation looking proudly out to sea turning its back on its less illustrious neighbours. Gustavo Lagos who in 1972 maintained that by joining the Andean Pact Chile had gone from being a leading country to a marginal one typifies such attitudes.[30] The military government was quick to withdraw from the pact.

For generations the country had prided itself on its relative institutional stability. Whilst the overt involvement of the military in politics was common in neighbouring countries, this was less the case in Chile. This vision of history fed into local sayings such as *no pasa nada en Chile* (nothing happens in Chile) and the notion that the Chileans were the 'English' of Latin America. The coup of 1973 put an end to this aspect of national self-identity. The sheer brutality of the coup and its aftermath meant that Chileans were suddenly held to be more like their neighbours. The paradox is that the great proponents of Chilean exceptionalism, through their actions in September 1973, did considerable damage to those same ideas. This view is reflected by Wilhelmy and Fuentes (1997), who maintain that the dictatorship put an end to exceptionalism in Chile's foreign policy.[31] Chile was no longer the democratic star in the region.

The Nature of the Chilean Transition

The process of democratization in Chile under Aylwin was one of the least successful in the region in terms of subordinating the armed forces to the civilian authorities. In Chile, the military retained a broad degree of prerogatives and economic advantages, which included a substantial involvement in a successful weapons industry.[32] The process of transition is referred to as *pactado* or agreed. In contrast with the Argentine transition, the Chilean military and their allies retained a degree of authority and the Constitution guaranteed that both the military and their supporters had an institutional role in the new administration. In such circumstances a sharp

---

29 Orrego Vicuña, *La Participación de Chile en el Sistema Internacional*, p. 155.

30 Manfred Wilhelmy, 'Hacia un Análisis de la Política Exterior Chilena Contemperaría' in *Estudios Internacionales*, 48 (1979): p. 465.

31 Manfred Wilhelmy & Cristian Fuentes, 'De la reinserción a la diplomacia para el desarrollo: política exterior de Chile 1992–1994' in Alberto Van Klaveren (ed.), *América Latina en el mundo* (Santiago, 1997), p. 233.

32 Monica Hirst, 'Security Policies, Democratisation, and Regional Integration in the Southern Cone' in Jorge Domínguez (ed.), *International Security and Democracy: Latin America and the Caribbean in the Post-Cold War Era* (Pittsburgh, 1998), p. 105.

break in policy was never likely and this cohabitation also, in part, explains the lack of policy direction and the low profile adopted by the new government. The fact the armed forces retained a high degree of autonomy served to limit the foreign policy options available to the civilian authorities. Internationalist in outlook, the civilian authorities were anxious to build relations with Chile's neighbours and beyond. However, the country's military were reluctant to enter into arrangements that would threaten their autonomy. In the 1990s Chile did not participate in UN peacekeeping missions and the military resisted arms control initiatives.[33] Chile has reduced her military expenditure in terms of a percentage of the national budget but it remains one of the highest in the region.[34]

The years between 1973 and 1990 was a time of relative isolation from the international community. The re-entry of Chile into the world community in 1990, which came about with Aylwin's assumption of the presidency, was marked by a certain reticence on the part of the new administration. In June of that year Enrique Correa, the Secretary General of the Government, spoke of his vision of the future:

> We are not looking for a boastful, nor forced return, nor do we want world, continental or regional leadership; we simply want to be a normal country and to be respected in the international community; to be visited by the presidents of the world and to be welcomed wherever we go.[35]

Correa's words highlight the low-key approach adopted by the new administration. Instead, Correa identifies the need for acceptance of Chile on the part of others. This policy of *inserción* has drawn criticism from some quarters in Chile for a lack of substance. Fermandios also accepts that in adopting a low profile the government of Aylwin did run the risk of creating a vacuum in policy terms: 'Its [Chile's] correct decision not to look for nor to feign the search for leadership does however run the risk of resulting in a lack of a foreign policy.'[36] The explanation for this low profile lies in a number of areas. Firstly, the developmental priorities of the first administration explain their cautious approach. The focus on trade led to a conservative attitude on the international stage. Secondly, as Silva (2003) has identified, post-Pinochet Chile was a much less politicized society and this also fed into the 'steady as she goes' attitudes prevailing at the centre of government.[37] Thirdly, there was the issue

---

33 Hirst, 'Security Policies, Democratisation, and Regional Integration in the Southern Cone', p. 110.

34 Hirst, 'Los claroscuros de la seguridad regional en las Américas', p. 90.

35 Quoted in Heine, 'Timidez o pragmatismo? La política exterior de Chile en 1990', p. 2. 'No Pretendemos un reingreso grandilocuente ni impulso, ni queremos liderados mundiales, continentales ni regionales; simplemente queremos volver a ser un país normal y respetado en la comunidad internacional; que seamos visitados por presidentes de todo el mundo y el nuestro sea bienvenido dónde quiera que vaya.'

36 Joaquín Fermandios, 'De una Inserción a Otra: Política Exterior de Chile, 1966–1990', *Estudios Internacionales*, 24:96 (1991): p. 454.

37 Patricio Silva, 'Doing Politics in a Depoliticised Society: Social Change and Political Deactivation in Chile', *Bulletin of Latin American Studies*, 23:1 (2004): pp. 30–42.

of civilian-military relations. In Latin American there is a tradition of using external relations to regulate the balance between the civilian and military power.[38] In Chile this balance was so fragile as to generate a degree of inertia in this and other policy areas. Fourthly, there is the issue of the damage done to Chilean political identity by 16 years of dictatorship.[39] It would take time for the civilian authorities in Chile to examine the questions pertaining to Chile's place in the region and in the wider world.

This low profile on the international stage was in contrast to both Allende's government and Pinochet's administration. Each, for very different reasons, had achieved a degree of notoriety in the world. During the Popular Unity administration, Chile was at the forefront of the campaign for new terms of trade between the rich North and the poorer South. For many, the election of a radical socialist government was a blueprint for the future. For those interested in radical change without a bloody struggle, Allende's Chile was, for a brief period, a beacon of light. Socialists in Europe followed the developments in Santiago with particular fascination. During the Pinochet years the country retained its high profile, it became the subject of much polemic around the world and the military authorities were infamous for human rights abuses. The experiment with neo-liberal economic formulas also attracted a good deal of attention. In the space of a generation the Chilean *polis* had played out two very different roles in front of the rest of the world. In a sense, this fitted in well with notions of Chile as an exceptional country; they would be the first to experience a genuinely democratic socialist revolution and then later they would be the pioneers of neo-liberal free market economics. Here, as elsewhere, it is often not a particular attribute that stabilizes the matrix of identity but rather the possession of 'particularness'. On the site of this 'particularness' attributes are placed, and then may be superseded later by others. In the case of Chile, for generations the country had a democratic tradition and it could, within the international community, play upon this social capital. With the coming to power of Pinochet, economic success became the country's attribute. Chile was the star player again.

In his paper on foreign policy during *la transcion*, Alberto van Klaveren identifies the three factors he sees as policy determinants; they are the impact of the Pinochet years, economics and history.[40] Of Van Klaveren's triad of determinants it is precisely the first two, Pinochet and economics that have tended to eclipse history. This is not a stable relationship and increasingly economics is becoming the predominant factor, while its prominence and the imperative of economic development has meant that history has been posited as a problem for more than a decade now. When we come to look at the period after the military regime, we are examining the effect of

---

38 Rur Diamint, 'Security Challenges in Latin America', *Bulletin of Latin American Research* 23:1 (2004), p. 44.

39 Tomas Moulian, *Chile Actual* (Santiago, 1997); Jocelyn-Holt Letelier, *El Chile perplejo. Del Avanzar sin Transar Al Transar sin Parar* (Santiago, 1999).

40 Alberto Van Klaveren, 'Inserción internacional de Chile' in Cristián Toloza & Eugenio Lahera (eds), *Chile en los noventa* (Santiago, 1998), p. 115.

the destruction of historical narratives on policy making. The state violence of the Pinochet administration rendered previously powerful national narratives inoperable. For a nation supposedly forged on the battlefield and famed for its institutional stability, the actions of the armed forces from 1973–1989 proved very damaging. The focus during these years was *la reinserción*, or the return to the fold. As with most 'returns', from the prodigal son onwards, there is a need for compliance and no real room for notions of leadership.

Internationally, Chile was fêted for its achievements both in the economic and political spheres. However, there were a number of countries whose citizens had faced human rights abuses, or that had been the location of criminal acts carried out by the Chilean secret service (DINA). This amounted to an unwelcome legacy for the civilian authorities anxiously trying to manage the transition to democracy. The most notable case was that of the assassination of Orlando Letelier. Letelier, a prominent member of the Allende government, was killed by a car bomb, in broad daylight, in the centre of Washington in 1976. Evidence of the involvement of Chilean military intelligence had come to light through the testimony of an ex-CIA operative who claimed to have worked with them on the attack. The United States demanded action, and two ex-DINA (later the CNI) were imprisoned. In 1998, Augusto Pinochet was arrested in London on an extradition warrant from a Spanish judge. The human rights abuses of the past again dominated Chile's engagement with the wider world and generated political tensions at home.

Development and Trade

In terms of Chile's policy towards the international community, Wilhelmy and Infante (1993) argue that the country, in the 1990s, was dealing with tangible economic themes.[41] Furthermore, there was an acceptance that Chile now had to operate in a harsh, highly competitive international climate. In such an environment high politics came to be seen as an indulgence. The political leadership recognized the dangers of adopting high profile positions internationally. Given the fragility of the internal political scene, the new government was unlikely to go out on a limb in terms of its foreign policy. It was a policy of 'steady as she goes' and the energies of the state were directed towards the economic area. Chile was going to play to her strengths.

Development was the key point of reference for foreign policy makers. Diverse policies were associated with the idea of development, and so were strengthened. Import substitution was once the basis of development, later it became radical neo-liberal economics, and finally the slightly toned down version of neo-liberalism adopted by the centre-left coalitions that followed authoritarian rule. The policy of insertion into the international economy was now the pathway to economic development. Development was the primary duty of coalition diplomacy, only this

---

41 Manfred Wilhelmy and Maria Teresa Infante, 'La Política Exterior Chilena en los Anos 90: El Gobierno del Presidente Aylwin y Algunas Proyecciones' in *Estudios Sociales*, 75:1 (1993), p. 101.

time ideological content was not going to inhibit progress. The stress on economics is partly explained by the urgency to address the problem of social debt. This phenomenon of the *deuda social* has been identified as a legacy of the Pinochet regime.[42] This debt also obliged the government to prioritize external cooperation in housing, health and education and poverty reduction programmes.

The country was thirsty for foreign investment and this became a basic objective of the *Concertación* governments.[43] Furthermore, a primary objective of *la inserción* was to consolidate and expand export markets. Copper remained an important source of export earnings throughout this period, though its relative importance did decline somewhat as other sectors of the economy broke into world markets. However, the industrial content of Chilean exports remained low. In terms of both the internal market and the industrial base, the Chilean authorities put less emphasis on these areas than either Argentina or Brazil. This in part explains the different priorities in terms of trade negotiations in Santiago. Access for Chilean exports has long had priority over attempts to protect aspects of the local economy.[44] This difference in emphasis is driven not by ideology but by distinct relations of production and these will not change in the short term. Chile will continue to base its growth on export growth whereas Argentina and Brazil look more to their internal markets to generate growth. The scenario is, though, a complex one. Garreton argues that it is just this predominance of primary exports which makes markets of the Southern Cone all the more important for it is in the Southern Cone that Chilean exports of goods with a high industrial content are concentrated.[45] In general terms, during the latter part of the twentieth century the patterns of trade altered. Proportionately, the US declined in importance as a market to the point where foreign trade is now divided in four practically equal parts; Europe, North America, Latin America and Asia.

Foreign policy during the first years of the *Concertación* amounted to the self-conscious privileging of economics and trade over other considerations. The motivation, as we have said, was development and there was a desire to take advantage of what was perceived to be a great opportunity. For domestic policy, this meant taking the heat and the history out of political practice. There was a great deal of fear of an 'irruption' from the past, that the passions generated by the Pinochet regime would destabilize the transition.[46] Production, consumption, trade flows and investment occupied prime positions. Notions of efficiency and competitiveness, particularly striking during the presidency of Frei, dominated the political discourse.

---

42 B. Bosworth, R. Dornbusch & R. Laban, *The Chilean Economy, Policy Lesson and Challenges*.

43 Van Klaveren, 'Inserción internacional de Chile', p. 127.

44 Roberto Bouzas (ed.), *Realidades Nacionales Comparadas* (Buenos Aires, 2002), p. 224.

45 M.A. Garreton, 'El Difícil Reintento de un Proyecto de País. La Sociedad Chilena a Comienzos de Siglo' in Roberto Bouzas (ed.), *Realidades Nacionales Comparadas*, p. 278.

46 Alexander Wilde, 'Irruptions of Memory: Expressive Politics in Chile's Transition to Democracy' in *Journal of Latin American Studies* 31:2 (1999).

Changing Global Environment

Changes in Chile at the close of the 1980s mirrored changes in the wider world. As civilians returned to office after 16 years of military rule, we were witnessing the fall of communism in Europe and the privileging of democratic principles across the world. In regional terms, Chile was the last of the three major powers in the Southern Cone to return to civilian rule. The end of the Cold War signalled an important change in the patterns of world politics. This change also had implications for Chilean internal politics as the rhetoric of military authorities emphasized their role in the battle to defeat communism. With the collapse of the Eastern Bloc this rationale for their actions disappeared. For hemispheric relations, there was a change in the dynamics of the relationship between the United States and Latin America. Hirst (1998) argues that the Southern Cone came to occupy a marginal spot in the wider world's strategic agenda.[47]

The new environment was unipolar. The United States emerged as the dominant world power. Chile's reaction to this new state of affairs was more circumspect than that of Menem's Argentina. This said, good relations with the United States were a high priority during the 1990s. This was in part driven by a desire to gain access for Chile to the North American Free-trade Area. With the US Congress's refusal to grant the Clinton administration the right to pursue a 'fast track' negotiation with Chile, this initiative initially floundered.

Whilst good relations with Washington are a central plank of Chilean foreign policy, the position adopted by Chile during the United Nations debate on the second Gulf War is instructive. At the time, in 2003, Chile was one of the non-permanent members of the UN Security Council. Despite being under enormous pressure from the United States and enduring some criticism from within Chile, the government of Ricardo Lagos refused to endorse the position of the United States on the Security Council. In terms of the priorities of Chilean foreign policy there were important issues at stake. The wish to restrain US interventionism and maintain a strong legal framework for the conduct of international relations informed the Chilean position. This episode is also interesting in that it serves to illustrate the limits of US hegemony in Latin America.

The principle goal of Aylwin's government was to achieve reinsertion in the diplomatic system. With the departure of Pinochet, insertion in the political system became possible. So complete was the isolation of the military that this element of government practically disappeared between 1973 and 1989.[48] The foreign relations of the military regime reach its nadir in 1980 when Pinochet was forced, in mid-air, to turn back and abandon a trip to the Philippines. In stark contrast, Aylwin's first

---

47 Hirst, 'Security Policies, Democratisation, and Regional Integration in the Southern Cone'.

48 Rodrigo Egana, 'Balance y Perspectivas de la cooperación internacional' in Marcelo Garcia, *Mas Allá de las Fronteras* (Santiago, 1994), p. 427.

foreign visit to Europe was notable for the warmth of the reception that greeted him.

Bolivia and Peru

Historically, Chile's relations with its northern neighbours, Peru and Bolivia have been difficult. This is particularly true in the case of the latter whose relationship with Chile has been poisoned by the legacy of a nineteenth-century war. During the War of the Pacific Chile fought and defeated both Bolivia and Peru and gained a valuable desert zone which now lies in the north of the country. The loss of this territory has been all the more bitter an experience for Chile's northern neighbours as the resources of the area, first nitrates, then copper, have proved to be enormously beneficial to the Chilean economy. It is the issue of Bolivian access to the Pacific that has been the most intractable problem. The failure to resolve this issue has seen bilateral relations frozen in a nineteenth-century mode, that is to say, dominated by the historical agenda. The historical agenda in the case of Chile's relations with its neighbours means border disputes born out of conflicts that date back over a century. Insulsa sees the historical agenda as still dominating the relationship with Bolivia and here we see the consequences of being unable to lay such considerations to one side.[49] Chilean–Bolivian relations have scarcely moved forward over the past 10 years. It is an interesting commentary that the improvement in relations with Peru which took place during Fujimori's tenure in office has been ascribed to the fact that his Japanese background meant he did not have the same historical sensibilities as most other Peruvians with regard to the War of the Pacific.[50]

As was the case with relations with Argentina, there was an attempt in the early 1990s to resolve all border issues with Peru. This initiative resulted in the Negotiating Commission whose purpose would be to resolve the issues pending from the Treaty of 1929. An agreement was reached in Lima in 1993, known as the Lima Convention, however this had not brought closure to those issues relating to Tacna and Arica and problems over the interpretation of the Convention remain. Relations with Peru have been improving slowly. An initiative by Chile in early 2005 to launch free-trade negotiations with Peru and Ecuador will build on a 1998 trade agreement with Peru. The desire to improve relations with Peru is in part driven by economic considerations. Peru is the third most important regional trading partner for Chile. Commercial relations between the two countries demonstrate good potential for growth, as in 2004 Chilean exports into Peru rose by over a quarter. Furthermore, Peru is the second largest recipient of Chilean investment with inflows of US$4 billion over the past decade.

---

49 Insulsa, *Ensayos Sobre Política Exterior de Chile*, p. 93.

50 Eve Rimoldi de Ladman, 'Los Gobiernos Constitucionales de Argentina 1983–1998 Similudes y Diferencias de su Politica Exterior' in Eve Rimoldi de Ladman (ed.), *Política Exterior y Tratados Argentina Chile Mercosur* (Buenos Aires: Ciudad Argentina, 1999), p. 63.

Relations with Bolivia remain dominated by the past. Access to the sea, or *mediterraneidad* continues to be a live issue into the twenty-first century. However, from 1978 the possibility of a 'corridor' to the Pacific was no longer open with the Peruvian rejection of a corridor along its border.[51] This problem of access to the ocean has poisoned relations between the two countries for generations and remains the central issue. In 1978 Bolivia cut diplomatic relations with Chile and they have yet to be re-established. Bolivia has repeatedly raised this issue at international arenas, both at the regional and global levels. At various points in history the Bolivian government has sought to garner support for its position within the Americas. From a Chilean perspective, this is a bilateral issue and Santiago has been reluctant to involve other parties in this dispute. It is interesting that the two countries have been unable to overcome the historical agenda. The price for a settlement may be too high in that after the Peruvian refusal to countenance a corridor along its border the other option to divide Chilean territory is seen as out of the question. Despite the absence of formal diplomatic channels, contact has continued and a number of agreements have been signed in the commercial area. However, trade levels between the two countries remain unimpressive with exports to Bolivia in 2004 accounting for 1.3% of the total, while imports of Bolivian products make up a mere 0.1% of the total. The explosion of anti-Chilean sentiment in Bolivia in 2003 over a proposal to export gas through Chile demonstrates the overlap between the areas of trade and foreign policy. The granting of associate status to both Chile and Bolivia by the Mercosur trading bloc in 1996 has not improved matters. In political terms the Mercosur members have designated Mercosur, Bolivia and Chile a 'zone of peace', even so, the relationship remains frosty. In early 2006, the election of Evo Morales marks a shift to the left in Bolivia. It remains to be seen whether this represents an opportunity to improve relations between the two countries.

Argentina

Chilean-Argentine relations have historically been difficult. Changes in the relative power of the two countries over the last century have been largely responsible. In the period when the basis for Chilean national identity was being laid, Chile was a recognized regional power. The fortunes of the country have since declined precipitously and nowhere has this decline been more evident than in its relations with Argentina. As Chile came to terms with the end of any aspirations of regional hegemony, she saw her neighbour's population grow, her economy expand and her military increase its capability. Although there were no wars during the twentieth century, tensions remained high on Chile's borders. This was particularly the case during the years of military government. Disputes surrounding the Beagle channel brought the two countries to the point of war in 1979. The intervention of the Vatican averted open conflict. The Papal Treaties of 1984 opened up various possibilities for

---

51 Rojas Aravena, *Chile–Peru: revisando las agendas con una mirada de futuro in Chile: entre la II cumbre y la detención de Pinochet*, p. 90.

settling outstanding border disputes. It was though regime change in both countries that allowed a final settlement of these disputes. The departure of Pinochet from government in Chile in 1990 meant there were democracies in operation on both sides of the Andes, albeit a somewhat limited democracy on the Chilean side. This changed the atmosphere between the two countries and introduced a degree of trust between the two governments. Santiago and Buenos Aires no longer see themselves as engaged in a 'zero sum game'. In part, these changes can be explained by the formation of horizontal linkages between different national elites who share a common interest in preserving democratic rule in the region as a whole.

It is the relationship with Argentina that has shown the most radical alteration over time. After an initial period of some distrust, relations have become cordial. The civilian governments on both sides of the Andes have been determined to settle outstanding issues, and willing to make the necessary sacrifices to resolve their differences. The fact the two nations are now seen as more similar than they had been in the past has also facilitated better relations. The Argentine economy has been in decline whilst that of Chile has been in the ascendant. Whereas 30 years ago the two countries had little in common, this is no longer the case. This narrowing of the gap between the two countries has tended to smooth out some of the rougher cultural edges. Taking a long-term view, van Klaveren (2000) identifies a change in emphasis in Chilean foreign policy, which, he claims, is mirrored in the cultural sphere. Some 30 years ago Chile was seen and to some extent saw itself as an Andean country. However, over time, in political and cultural terms, the focus has shifted towards the Southern Cone of the continent.[52]

Good personal relations between Presidents Aylvin and Alfonsín aided the process of reconciliation. In August 1991, the two countries approved an historic agreement on the demarcation of the border between Argentina and Chile. Two areas of contention remained; the Laguna del Desierto and Campos del Hielos. The former was finally settled in 1995 and the latter soon after. This process was not without controversy with elements in Chile accusing their government of weakness. Despite such complaints, Chilean–Argentine relations did manage to move beyond the historical agenda. The explanation for this change is worthy of consideration, especially in view of the continued problems with Chile's northern neighbours. The first point to highlight is that of democratization, and with the advent of democracy in Santiago and Buenos Aires politics became more transparent and trust was more easily achieved. In the case of Chile, there was an anxiety to improve its relations with the outside world after the isolation of the Pinochet years and the settlement of outstanding issues with Argentina was part of this process. Throughout the 1990s, the economies of the countries became increasingly interconnected and this further cemented relations. Strategic issues began to drop off the agenda and trade issues became more important. Chile's association with Mercosur has further strengthened relations. The decision for Chile as to whether or not to pursue closer links with Mercosur, is more than simply an economic decision it is also political and relates

---

52 Van Klaveren interview (2000).

to profound questions as to Chile's future role in the region and in the wider world. These debates are intimately related to the country's relationship with Argentina. The profundity of changes in relations with Argentina opens the door to the Mercosur project.

The United States

Whilst it was true that the United States had been relatively swift in recognizing the country, it did in the same year proclaim the Monroe Doctrine. Although the declaration was well received by some in Latin America, in that it outlined US hostility to any future European intervention in the hemisphere, it was also seen as evidence of the hegemonic intentions of the United States' government.

It is the concern over unilateral US intervention that informed the Chilean position on Iraq in 2003. There were concerns expressed at home on the damage done to bilateral relations with the United States due to the position adopted within the Security Council. Indeed Errázuriz Correa argues that, Frei Montalva, Allende and Pinochet had all avoided positions that ran risks with the United States and so the stance adopted by the Lagos administration was stridently anti-interventionist.[53] Many in Washington working in the area of foreign policy, now stress the desirability of a more assertive US in the world. This has brought the issue of US intervention and extra-territoriality into sharp relief around the world, but such concerns have a long history in Chile and Latin America as a whole. In contemporary Chile, the issue of US interventionism has particular resonance. This is a time when the country is attempting, albeit slowly, to come to terms with a difficult and painful past. The role played by the United States in the *coup d'etat* of 1973 continued to be debated and makes up part of the backdrop to US–Chilean relations. The release of State Department papers by the Clinton administration stirred up the debate as to the role of the United States in the events of 1973. The sentiment of anti-Americanism has deep roots in Chilean politics, fed in large part by events described above. Suspicion of the United States is common across the continent and centres not only on cultural questions but also on the very practical question of US intervention outside its borders.

Whilst there is suspicion of the United States, there is also respect for that country's achievements. For many, the United States represents a paradigm of modernity, the lifestyle and economic success offering a way forward for the rest of the continent. There are deep divisions in Chilean society as to how to view the United States. The events of 1973 tended to confirm and exacerbate the existing left-right divisions on this issue. In general attitudes towards the United States remain ambiguous. It is true to say that much of what divides the Chileans from the North Americans are those same issues that unite the Chileans with the rest of Latin America. Joaquin Fernández argues that:

---

53 Hernán Felipe, Errázuriz Correa, *La diplomacia Chilena en la Segunda guerra de Irak Estudios Internationales*, 36 (2003).

Although this anti-Americanism is evident in the Chilean left and also present in different degrees across the whole political spectrum, in having a strong rhetorical bond it may be misleading. For the masses, the United States represents the paradigm of modernity, and in general is admired as a social and political model.[54]

The issue of membership of the North American Free-trade Association (NAFTA) was central to Chilean foreign policy in the 1990s. The Frei government invested a good deal of political capital in this project. The question of the time was whether or not Chile would be granted 'fast track' status in the negotiations by the US Congress. Failure in this area would see the process drag out over very many years. Fast track was the issue that exercised the Chilean editorial writers of the early 1990s, and scarcely a day went by without the issue generating headline news. The strong interest in NAFTA is explained by the perceived economic and political benefits of any agreement. Entry would ensure access of Chilean goods to what was then the largest market in the world. It would also be an important signal to the financial markets that the country had teamed up with the most powerful economy in the world. In political terms, the impact of NAFTA would have been two-fold; firstly, it would dispel any illusions on the part of the leftists that there was any alternative to pursing the free market model, and secondly, it would protect democratic structures from rightist elements.[55] The negotiations were to fail; internal political dynamics impeded the White House from initiating any 'fast track' process with the Chilean government. Relations with Washington did influence other aspects of Chilean foreign policy. Van Klaveren identifies a link between the NAFTA negotiations and Chile's policy towards her Southern Cone neighbours:

> as we know nothing happened, there was no fast track on the part of the United States, but we did not approach more Latin American countries at the time precisely because there was an expectation of a special relationship with the United States.[56]

The negotiation on the 'fast track' did hold up Chile's move towards closer relations with its neighbours and with disappointment in this area came a renewed impetus to improve relations with Mercosur. According to Feinburg the Chileans experienced something more than disappointment:

> The Chilean government was furious with the Clinton administration when it abandoned efforts to secure fast track authority, President Eduardo Frei complained bitterly to visiting Americans, making it clear that having been jilted first by Bush and then by Clinton, the Chileans considered the United States an unreliable ally.[57]

---

54 Joaquin Fermandois, 'Chile and the Great Powers' in Michael Morris, Great Power Relations in *Argentina, Chile and Antarctica* (Basingstoke, 1990), p. 79.
55 Van Klaveren, 'Inserción internacional de Chile', p. 124.
56 Van Klaveren interview, Santiago 2000.
57 Feinberg quoted in Riordan Roett, 'U.S. Policy Towards Mercosur' in Riordan Roett (ed.), *Mercosur Regional Integration, World Markets* (Boulder, 1999), p. 118.

The story of Chile's attempt to gain a free-trade agreement does not end here. The option continued to be pursued, although with less vigour than in the first half of the 1990s. Eventually an agreement was signed in 2003 and came into force on January 1, 2004. It was the culmination of 13 years of negotiations. Chile became one of the few countries in the hemisphere to be granted such an agreement. However, during this extended period of on-off talks Chile had become closer to her neighbours in the Southern Cone and Mercosur had become an increasingly important option for the Chilean government. Agreement with the United States now has fewer of the exceptionalist overtones that shaped the NAFTA debate in the previous decade.

Regionalism

During the early 1990's the watchword for Chilean diplomacy was 'open regionalism'.[58] It is possible to portray this as another example of the non-committal approach to the international community, but perhaps it should also be seen under the more positive banner of *reinserción*. The Chilean drive to re-establish contacts all over the world would not be hindered by an explicit commitment to one exclusive grouping or another. Thus, the one main objective of *la inserción* was the consolidation and extension of the country's export markets.[59] Today, those who wish to see Chile develop a closer relationship with its neighbours do not tend to employ the slogans of Bolivar. In their dealing with the United States they no longer oppose the virtues of Caliban to the materialist Prospero. Instead they stress the material benefits of integration. Again here we can see the dominance of the politics of development and its stress on tangible trade gains. Alongside Mexico, Chile has been the most active nation in the hemisphere in developing free-trade arrangements.

There are though some tensions in this area. On the one hand there is the treaty with the United States and APEC membership, on the other there is Chile's relationship with Mercosur. In trade terms, it is the issue of the external tariff that is the most difficult for Chile. In Mercosur the average tariffs are much higher than those of Chile. For the Chilean political class to throw its weight firmly behind the Mercosur project it would need to be convinced that no harm would be done to Chile's developmental prospects. From a political standpoint there are also elements of Chilean society that do not favour the Mercosur project. There are even elements within the coalition who would favour affording priority to relations with the United States.[60]

---

58 Alberto Van Klaveren, Hacia un regionalismo abierto in Estudio Internacionales (Santiago, 1997); Roberto Duran, 'Democracy and Regional Multilateralism in Chile' in Gordon Mace & Jean Philippe Therien (eds), *Foreign Policy and Regionalism in the Americas* (Boulder, 1996).

59 Van Klaveren, 'Inserción internacional de Chile', p. 122.

60 M.A. Garreton, 'El Difícil Reintento de un Proyecto de País. La Sociedad Chilena a Comienzos de Siglo', p. 284.

There are also integrationist elements within Chilean politics that seeks to establish closer links with her Latin American neighbours. This position has had some prominent advocates, Munoz (1989) argued that the first priority of Chilean foreign policy should be the achievement of autonomy for Latin America.[61] In Chile the renewal of 'Latin Americanism' can be dated from the settlement of the Tacna dispute in the 1920s and the realization on the part of the then President Alessandri that, given Chile's relative power position, it could no longer afford to be diplomatically isolated. Integrationists can be divided into various strands. The Frei Montalva presidency in the 1960s marked a return to some extent of the early activism of the Chilean State. He also showed a renewed 'Latin Americanism', and regional links were strengthened. The torch of integration was taken up with great enthusiasm by the Allende administration, but the ideological position was different. The line taken by this government has been labelled as revolutionary.[62] It was based on the ideology which saw the Latin American region as having been a victim of imperialism. From this perspective, notions about Chilean glory are both illusory and harmful in that they obscured the fact that Chile and all her neighbours have, over the years, shared the same fate. From this perspective Chile is a small power in an unjust world and there is nothing particularly special about that. However, this position did offer its adherents a basis for a much larger project, namely the emancipation of the poor of the Third World. It also allowed the representation of Chile as a particular case in that the country's respect for order and the country's constitution had presented her with the opportunity to be the first to achieve a democratic socialist revolution.

This position of the Lagos centre-left government, though somewhat more strident than its immediate predecessors on these matters, is still based on a pragmatic approach to international relations. There are those who are attracted to a regional project but the imperative of development and the domination of the soft politics of economic integration still hold sway. There will be many in Chile who are sympathetic to Lula's pronouncement on the need for South–South solidarity. But such ideas will also generate such unease with the Chilean body politic. The Mercosur project also causes some concerns in Chile in terms of the national autonomy. Mercosur is seen as being dominated by Brazil. To opt for the project is to accept Brazilian leadership. Given the different priorities of Brazilian foreign policy which aims for global projection and the distinct composition of the Brazilian economic base, the fear is that the pursuit of Brazilian foreign goals may be damaging to the Chilean national interest. The Chilean leadership have up until now jealously guarded their autonomy in the area of foreign relations. The fact that Chile depends upon foreign trade for some 70 per cent of its GDP explains the high priority attached to good international relations, the concentration upon fostering economic links and a reluctance to take risks internationally.

---

61 Heraldo Munoz, 'La agenda futura de la política exterior de Chile' in Heraldo Munoz (ed.), *Chile: política exterior para la democracia* (Santiago, 1989).

62 Wilhelmy, 'Hacia un Análisis de la Política Exterior Chilena Contemperaría', p. 445.

Regionalist projects also provoke of degree of scepticism in Chile. This sense of scepticism has a long history and represents an important strand of thought in terms of Chile's position in the continent. As we have seen, the reluctance to become involved in regional projects has a strong basis in elements of Chilean national identity. Unease on regional initiatives is not only based upon Chilean identity politics but also on doubts on the strength on Latin Americanism around the continent. Aravena (1998) argues that the very idea of Latin America, which conveys a sense of unity and common destiny, is in crisis.[63] The ups and downs of the Mercosur project have fuelled the doubts on the wisdom of integrating fully into the trade bloc. The economic difficulties experienced in Argentina have also raised concerns in Chile.

Conclusion

Since the return of civilian government to Chile in 1990 the authorities have rigorously pursued a policy of 'open regionalism'. Alongside Mexico they have been the most aggressive Latin American state in pursuing bilateral free-trade agreements. In 2003, Chile achieved a long-standing ambition of signing a free-trade agreement with the United States. Chile's dependence on export earnings and the centrality of development explain this focus on trade. During the same period, Chile's relations with Argentina improved dramatically and the Lagos government is sympathetic to the Mercosur project. There remains though some reticence on the issue of Mercosur, relating to the acute sensitivities in Santiago on trade issues and also fears on the wisdom of entering a trade bloc clearly led by Brazil. The nature of the Chilean economy is different to that of Brazil and the worry for policy planners is that Chile could pay a heavy price for the sake of Brazilian interests.

Chile's position in the hemispheric politics is complex. It has successfully negotiated a free-trade agreement with the United States. Like the US, it is broadly supportive of a free-trade environment across the hemisphere. However, Chile's centre-left government has an ideological affinity with Lula da Silva in Brazil and Kirchner in Argentina. The fact that Chile's Interior Minister, José Miguel Insulsa stood against the preferred candidate of the United States for the head of the Organization of American States in 2005 and that his victory was hailed by both Brazil and Venezuela is indicative the independence of Chilean foreign policy. The same can be said for Chile's dogged determination on the United Nations Security Council to resist US pressure over the war in Iraq. Chile's determination to build ties with Asia is another important part of the picture. Increasingly, China is becoming a major trading partner for Chile. The desire in Santiago to pursue an independent foreign policy has been underwritten by the country's economic success. The preference for an independent foreign policy has served Chile well in this regard and

---

63 Aravena, *Chile–Peru: revisando las agendas con una mirada de futuro in Chile: entre la II cumbre y la detención de Pinochet.*

there may be some resistance to fall in behind Brazil in its dealings with the wider world.

Identity politics also play a role in that there is a strong suspicion of Latin Americanism in Chile. In terms of its relations with its northern neighbours, identity and history figure large in relations with Peru and Bolivia. In both cases, and this is particularly true of Bolivia, so-called historical agenda of border disputes continues to dominate. Over the next decade the key question facing Chile is whether regional agreements with its southern Cone neighbours should be strengthened. With Brazil and Argentina being more strident in their resistance to US-led trade initiatives, Chile as an associate member of Mercosur, does face something of a dilemma. Both Argentina and Brazil derive a clear set of benefits from the existence of Mercosur. For Brazil it lends credibility to its ambition of regional leadership and for Argentina, the regional pact does give the country some leverage in that Brasília does at times follow Argentina's lead in world affairs. For Chile the benefits of closer association are less clear cut and the potential costs of closer association with the group are tangible in that it might adversely affect relations with Washington. The potential entry of Venezuela into Mercosur makes such a scenario all the more likely.

With the declining influence of the military and their allies in Congress the ruling centre-left coalition should have more room to manoeuvre.[64] The transition to democracy is now seen as largely complete, the management of civilian-military relations should decline in importance in terms of the setting of foreign policy priorities. This may have paradoxical effects, in that the need to use good relations with neighbours as a method of managing internal political dynamics may disappear. At the same time, with the subordination of the military to civilian rule, the impediments to a more cooperative attitude on matters of regional security may be overcome.

The choices available to Chile will in large part be determined by the political dynamics of the Western Hemisphere. George Bush's FTAA initiative looks, in the short term at least, to be running into serious problems. Over the next few years, Chile may simply choose to adopt a holding position and wait for what is a fluid political situation in South America to develop. There are elements, particularly on the left of Chilean politics whose instinct would be to pursue a more regionalist foreign policy, this tendency is held somewhat in check by the imperative to maintain good relations with the US and avoid any dislocations in trade flows. The politics of development remain paramount.

---

64 The election of Michelle Bachelet in January 2006 demonstrates the continued ascendancy of the Chilean centre-left.

Chapter 6

Conclusions

International relations in the Southern Cone are in a state of flux. During the 1990s, the countries of the region were struggling to overcome the legacy of many years of dictatorship. The process of transition impacted greatly on foreign policy formation in Argentina, Brazil and Chile. The Mercosur project was at least in part the product of the dictatorships. The determination on the part of civilian authorities to avoid a repeat of the human rights abuses of the 1970s and 1980s drove them to establish a more cooperative security regime in the Southern Cone. Their success in overcoming the historical agenda of border disputes and strategic competition bolstered the democratic process across the region. It allowed the newly elected authorities to wrestle control of foreign policy away from the military and to gain control of a key performative aspect of the state, the formation of foreign policy. The creation of a more benign environment in the Southern Cone meant that international affairs were less likely to intrude upon the process of democratization. Furthermore, the civilian authorities could find support from each other in their efforts to fully subordinate the armed forces in their respective countries.

Foreign policy came to be used as a method for managing the relationship between competing social forces, in this case, the armed forces of the region and civilian politicians. The nature of the transition to democracy was a central component of the formation of foreign policy since the departure of the armed forces from power. Whether or not there was continuity in foreign policy making was, to some extent, determined by the nature of those transitions. Sudden institutional rupture, as was experienced in Argentina, did lead to disruption in the area of foreign policy. This said, the legacy of dictatorship merits yet closer attention.

The abject failure of the military in Argentina impacted on Argentine society in general. It brought about a period of reflection as to what were the appropriate drivers of public policy. In the area of international relations during this period, there was a profound debate as to the purpose of foreign policy. Interestingly, this debate was accompanied by a reassessment of the basis of Argentine foreign policy during the twentieth century. Those around Menem and a number of discipline specialists identified what they regarded as a disturbing disjunction between the policy options pursued by successive Argentine governments and the realities of the distribution of power in the international system. This disjunction was attributed to the idiosyncrasies of the Argentine identity. The lack of correspondence between power politics and Argentine foreign policy affords us an opportunity to examine factors outside the normal parameters of international relations, namely the impact of internal political dynamics and national identity. Both in Argentina and in Chile, in the aftermath of the military dictatorship, there was a conscious decision on the part of the political elites to dispense with loftier notions of national destiny and introduce a politics based on rationality and responsibility towards the citizenry.

In Brazil, the situation was rather different in that there was greater continuity between the foreign policies pursued by the military and the civilian governments that followed. This continuity was facilitated to some extent by the fact that the political trauma caused by the years of military rule in Brazil was of a different order to that experienced in either Argentina or Chile. This is not to devalue the suffering caused by more than two decades of military rule, but the impact on the body politic was different. In both Chile and Argentina, in the aftermath of military rule, there was a period of reflection as to what were the appropriate values to be brought forward into the future. Part of this process involved a reassessment of the meaning and relevance of *lo nacional* in policy making. In Brazil, this process did not take hold in the same way. Another factor, which tended to militate against abrupt change in Brazil was the lack of a democratic tradition to match either that of Argentina or Chile. Moreover, professional diplomats who prided themselves on their relative autonomy from domestic Brazilian politics closely guarded the area of foreign policy formation. The *Itamaraty* valued their power in the setting of Brazilian foreign policy and to wrestle control away from them would have involved considerable political will and in recent times this has not been apparent.

Historically, the desire for autonomy has been an important ambition in international politics of the Southern Cone. The existence of a superpower in the Americas has had an important effect in shaping foreign policy formation in the region. From the first decades of the twentieth century, the United States displaced European powers as the dominant force in Latin America. This was particularly true of Central America and the Caribbean where the US has shown a strong propensity to intervene directly or indirectly in the politics of the region. South of the Isthmus of Panama, direct military intervention has been less common, nevertheless the United States has exerted a powerful role in South America. During the decades of the Cold War, the security interests of the United States were crucial in determining the political scene across the Americas. In the 1970s and 1980s, Washington shared an ideological commitment with a number of military dictatorships to eradicate leftist/communist opposition across the Americas. The military regimes in Argentina, Brazil and Chile had strong allies in Washington. Priorities changed during the presidency of Jimmy Carter during which human rights became an explicit priority for the government of the United States. With the inauguration of Reagan, normal service was resumed and the military regimes across the Southern Cone enjoyed reasonably good relations with the United States.

Given the power of the US, the temptation has always existed for the countries of the Southern Cone to try and attain a preferential relationship with the United States. For much the twentieth century, Brazil pursued just such a policy as it sought the status of regional leadership through its special relationship with Washington. Ultimately, Brazil did not derive sufficient benefits to sustain its pro-US diplomatic position over the longer term. By the 1970s, the perceived interests of Brazil and the United States began to diverge. This process of divergence has been accelerated by the formation of Mercosur. In effect, it has signalled that Brazil has chosen a different path in order to achieve its goal of regional leadership. Brazilian foreign policy in the 1990s and in the first years of the twenty-first century has been marked by a desire to create its own sphere of influence in South America and to resist the extension of US hegemony into what Brazil perceives as its natural sphere of influence. Central to this new approach has been good relations with Argentina, it is only with the cooperation of Buenos Aires that the Mercosur project, and Brazil's wider geopolitical strategy becomes viable.

The desire to pursue an independent foreign policy has been a key element of Argentine foreign policy for much of the last century. Independence from the United States was the main characteristic of this approach to international affairs. However, during the government of Carlos Menem, this policy was abandoned in order for Argentina to seek the kind of privileged relationship that previously Brazil had tried to achieve. Again, like Brazil before it, Argentina was ultimately unsuccessful in its quest and eventually came to commit itself firmly to the Mercosur project.

For Chile, the United States represents an extremely valuable trading partner. During the first half of the 1990s, Chile sought to gain access to NAFTA. This was the main element of Chilean foreign policy for a time and there was a good deal of frustration when the Clinton administration failed to persuade the US Congress to grant Chile 'fast track' status in negotiations. This setback caused Chile to reassess its foreign policy priorities and seek to improve its relations with Mercosur. Even so, in 2003, Chile became the first country in South America to sign a bi-lateral free-trade agreement with the United States. Chile remains an associate member of the Mercocur group. Chile has for a number of years pursued a balancing act; it has sought to maintain good relations with the United States whilst at the same time insisting on its right to pursue an independent foreign policy line. In terms of Chile's relationship with Argentina and Brazil, these are positive, but at the same time there is a desire in Chile not to damage its trading relationships elsewhere by committing itself to Mercosur. The external tariff regime of Mercosur is not seen as compatible with Chile's integration into the larger world economy.

All three countries share a common feature in that the hemispheric axis is no longer so dominant in terms of their international relations. In trading terms, the United States is no longer as important as it once was. Argentina, Brazil and Chile have valuable trading relationships with Europe (the EU is now Merocur's most important trading partner), and Asia. In terms of attracting international investment capital, Europe has overtaken the US as the principal source of funds for Mercosur countries. Brazil, in particular, has sought to intensify its diplomatic contacts with other medium-sized trading nations. During 2003, trade talks at Seattle and Cancun, Brazil has come to be perceived as a leading voice in the campaign on the part of the less developed nations for fairer access to markets in developed countries. Diplomatic and trading relationships are multi-dimensional and although relations with the United States are extremely important, they are just part of a larger picture. This drive to build a more diverse set of relationships is related to Brazil's more strident position in world and hemispheric trade talks. Historically, Brazil has been vulnerable to US pressure and has, in the past, had to pay a price for those foreign policy positions at odds with stated US policy preferences. In attempting to build a wider coalition of trading powers amongst developing countries, Brazil hopes to be able to resist such pressure in the future.

For Argentina, the risks of asserting an independent (from Washington) policy-line are outweighed by its desire to pursue an activist position in world affairs. Such positions also play well to a domestic audience who remain sceptical of US intentions in South America.

For Chile, tense relations between the US and Mercosur are unwelcome as Chile seeks to avoid alienating either its near neighbours or the United States. It may be that if the gulf widens between Brazil/Argentina and the United States, Chile may find itself in an increasingly uncomfortable position. Pragmatism is deep seated in the politics of the *Concertación* and the possibility of an increasingly anti-US line developing across South America will raise concerns in Santiago.

The growing profile of Venezuela in the regional politics of Latin America can only exacerbate this situation. Lula da Silva shares this concern, especially over the radical language adopted by Hugo Chavez in his speeches relating to the United States. Notwithstanding Brazilian reticence in this regard, Brazil has a much stronger rationale to dilute the power of the United States in the Southern Cone. Its ambitions of regional leadership would be severely curtailed if the US comes to dominate hemispheric politics. Hence, the construction of a regional grouping capable of resisting US diplomatic pressure and lending creditability to Brazil's goal of having a powerful voice globally.

The Americas are not a homogenous bloc in diplomatic terms. This fact has not been lost on EU trade negotiators who have sought to develop a close relationship with the Mercosur nations. Such a relationship offers benefits for both sides, as it tends to offset the powerful position occupied by the United States in world and regional trade talks. That the Americas is a diverse political system is clear from the political manoeuvrings of the European Commission which has sought to detach the Mercosur countries from the wider free-trade lobby. The ongoing contacts between the Mercosur and the EU send out a message to the wider world community that the nations of the Southern Cone have an independent voice and can pursue their own policy agenda. Mercosur offers the nations of the region something which they have sought over many generations; recognition and the affording of equal status by the wider world community. These have proved elusive in the past, the discourse on foreign policy in Argentina, Brazil and Chile has for generations focused on this issue of equity. In the case of the most powerful of the three, Brazil, its desire to be afforded equal status internationally has been a defining feature of Brazilian diplomacy during the twentieth century.

The study of foreign policy formation in the Southern Cone illuminates a number of issues that go to the heart of contemporary world polity. Firstly, the phenomenon of nation states making the transition from being lesser to more powerful entities merits attention. As the power of these nations increases so do their demands for autonomy and independence in the global political system. Currently, India is one such power and Brazil is another. The question that arises is that in a world where the US remains the dominant power, how will the configuration of power change in response to such emergent nation states? In the case of Brazil, its transformation takes place under the watchful gaze of the world's only superpower which, since the early nineteenth century, has jealously guarded the Western Hemisphere as its sphere of influence. Brazilian foreign policy represents a considerable challenge to policy planners in the US and this is reflected in the intense public debate as to the future trajectory of US–Latin American relations. Brazil's commitment to Mercosur reflects a realization that in order to pursue a genuinely autonomous foreign policy it requires an alliance with Argentina and the other member nations of Mercosur. In the short term, Brazil's priority is to resist the proposal from the United States for a hemispheric free-trade pact. Brazil's preference is to strengthen Mercosur.

A second related area, which is raised by the Mercosur project and the longer history of US-Latin America relations is that of the appropriate relationship between a global hegemon and the wider international community. The United States has been aggressive in pursuing its foreign policy interests in Latin America. Its power has prevented those outside the hemisphere from intervening in Latin American affairs, but the US has retained the right to intervene in the internal affairs of nations across the hemisphere. The nature of intervention has varied from the explicit support for one political grouping over another combined with accompanying warnings over future relations (Nicaragua 2004), to the funding of sympathetic political groups (Chile 1964–1973) and has included direct military intervention (Panama 2000). In Latin America, the problems associated with one dominant power in the world are brought into focus. The vibrant tradition in Latin America of legalism in international affairs is, in part, explained by the history of interventions on the part of the United States. This history also explains the dogged resistance on the United Nations Security Council on the part of both Chile and Mexico to US pressure over resolution 1441 on Iraq. The propensity of the United States to intervene across the hemisphere has also contributed to another persistent tendency in Latin American, that of anti-Americanism. This is not a universal phenomenon in Latin America but among the Left in particular there is a distrust of the United States. US interventionism in the 1970s and 1980s helped fuel this distrust. The unseating of the socialist Allende in Chile in 1973 with the complicity, if not the support, of the Nixon administration became a *cause célèbre* for socialists across the globe. At the time, there were voices in the US who cautioned their administration against becoming too associated with the repressive regimes of the Right which came to dominate the Southern Cone. For some in Latin America there is a strong resonance between the supportive attitude adopted by Washington towards the recent attempted coup in Venezuela and the hemispheric politics of previous decades. The continued US support for anti-Chavez factions and the fierce anti-Chavez rhetoric of the Bush White House is a source of worry on the continent and may be alienating even the more moderate countries like Chile. The history of the US intervention on the continent has meant that in Brazil for a number of decades, the United States has been seen as a security risk to that nation's sovereignty. At present there is a good deal of unease about the presence of US troops in Colombia and US military overtures directed at Paraguay.

Regionalism represents a third example of the salience of the politics of the Southern Cone. Mercosur is an interesting example of South–South regional cooperation. For those concerned over the power asymmetries between the wealthy North and the poorer South, Mercosur is a positive development in that such alliances potentially increase the bargaining power of developing countries. For the European Union too, regional arrangements like Mercosur are to be encouraged and this is reflected in the EU's positive attitude towards the pact. Initially, Mercosur was seen as, primarily, a trading bloc and was informed by a new economic pragmatism on the part of its members. The trade bloc was built upon liberal economic assumptions and was designed to encourage intra-regional trade. On both counts the bloc enjoyed considerable successes throughout much of the 1990s. However, toward the end of that decade there were a number of economic and institutional setbacks. The growth in internal trade stalled and indeed for a time went into reverse and for those favouring the strengthening of the pact, the reactions in Brasilia and Buenos Aires were far from encouraging. In the face of an economic downturn both Argentina and Brazil resorted to unilateral actions that challenged the institutional basis of the Mercosur agreement. It took intense presidential diplomacy to salvage the agreement. Interestingly, the agreement not only survived the unilateralist instincts of its members but in some ways Mercosur has grown in strength.

As the economic rationale has declined, it has been replaced by a more explicitly political rationale. Mercosur is still a trading bloc, but it is also the centrepiece of both Brazilian and Argentine diplomacy. The situation may be best described by reference to those forces that inhabit the Mercosur countries *and* those forces lying outside. In the main, the political elites in Argentina and Brazil have been unable to fully control those domestic forces who demand action if their economic interests are threatened. Hence, in the face of economic difficulties the state has tended to respond to the demands of these interest groups and this has generated a series of crisis within Mercosur. At the same time, there are those imperatives, which have their origin in the international political system, and these have tended to promote close cooperation between Argentina and Brazil. In particular, their shared goal to resist US hegemony in South America in the long term, and a US sponsored hemispheric free-trade agreement, in the short term, has given the two countries a sense of shared purpose. Thus, Mercosur has evolved into a more explicitly political arrangement with one of its primary functions being to increase the relative power of its members in any negotiations with the United States. In the first half of the first decade of the twentieth century a more strident attitude to trade talks and wider geopolitical issues was evident in both Brasilia and Buenos Aires. The Chilean foreign ministry views this politicization with a sense of unease. It has long pursued a policy of open regionalism and has sought to simultaneously build good relations with its neighbours in the Southern Cone and with Washington. On the horizon, we have full Mercosur membership for Venezuela and this is liable to further complicate hemispheric relations.

Conclusions

In discussions on hemispheric relations, divergent ideologies are now part of the debate. Within South America, there is a growing concentration of left and centre-left governments and this is seen as both promoting cooperation between the nations of South America and stiffening their resistance to the politics of Washington. The existence of an interventionist Republican administration in Washington exacerbates an already difficult situation. With Brazil focused on achieving regional leadership and greater global projection, with Argentina determined to reassert its traditional independent line in foreign affairs and with the naked hostility towards the Bush administration that exists in Venezuela, it is difficult to see hemispheric relations improving in the short term and certainly the prospects for Washington hemispheric free-trade initiatives do not seem good. Over the past decade Mercosur has been transformed. It began as a free-trade association that the Menem government were prepared to dispense with in order to achieve a wider trade agreement with the United States, now that same agreement is seen as representing a bulwark against the FTAA. Mercosur has changed from being a vehicle of soft power to being an entity sustained by the hard politics of geopolitical ambition.

The asymmetrical power relations in the pact do represent a threat to the agreement. Argentina seeks independence and autonomy through its engagement with Mercosur. But, Argentina is unlikely to simply trade one distant hegemon for another. Brazil needs Argentine cooperation, and to secure this it needs to be willing to trade some of its manoeuvrability in its international affairs for a greater commitment from Argentina. Brazil will also be obliged to face down internal sectoral lobbies in order to strengthen the institutional integrity of Mercosur. In essence, Brazil will be obliged to sacrifice some of its power within the Southern Cone in order to gain greater presence in the international political system.

Democratization brought the countries of the region together. The simple fact that the civilian administrations across the region were engaged in a similar struggle cemented relations between them. However, it was more than simply a common project that drove regional relations. The civilian administrations used their foreign policy as a means to strengthen the process of transition from dictatorship to democracy. By forming alliances, they undermined the geopolitical discourse of their respective armed forces, they wrestled control of regional relations from the military and transferred it to those ministries seeking to engage cooperatively with neighbouring countries. Through closer cooperation, the civilian politicians ensured that the international environment became more predictable.

In Chile, where authoritarian enclaves survived for much of the 1990s, the civilian authorities struggled to engage in the type of security cooperation that existed between Brazil and Argentina. During the transition to democracy, the countries of the region attempted to come to terms with the human rights abuses of the 1970s and 1980s. In committing these atrocities the military authorities destabilized the body politic in all three countries. Across the Southern Cone, the military sought to produce social and political change. This was particularly the case in Argentina and Chile where the military authorities had ambitious plans to create a new social order. In seeking to achieve this through such brutal means they severely disrupted the nation's sense of itself.

In the aftermath of the dictatorships the politics of memory become important, the past and the future became political positions. In the public discourse of both Chile and Argentina we find explicit attempts to move away from the past. This tendency was strongest in the government of Eduardo Frei in Chile and Carlos Menem in Argentina. History, in both cases, was identified as a source of conflict. This is important because national identities rely upon history for their sustenance. As historical narratives became disrupted so identities became more fragile. There are many theoretical visions on the nature of identity but most coalesce around the idea of continuity and narrative form. These qualities became harder to sustain in the aftermath of the military regimes. In Argentina, this period of crisis resulted in a re-evaluation of *lo argentinidad* and led to the wholesale abandonment of Argentina's traditional stances in world affairs. In Chile the situation was different, the trauma existed but the la *transicion pactada* ensured a low-key re-engagement with world polity.

All three countries have largely completed their transition to democracy. However, the shadows of the generals still remain. In Argentina and Chile in particular, the spectre of the past plays a important role in the present in that the visions of 'Chileaness' and 'Argentineaness' as posited by the their respective militaries are no longer available in the present. In the main these were exceptionalist visions and their decline has been an important factor in promoting regional cooperation.

In theoretical terms, foreign policy formation in the Southern Cone represents a particular set of challenges. Development has always been a key function of the state in this part of the world. Historically, this has led to compromises being made around more traditional notions of sovereignty and autonomy in order to achieve economic development. This goal of development has been an important driver of foreign policy. More recently, the achievement of democracy has taken on a similar function. In both cases, domestic politics are important in determining foreign policy. In a comprehensive analysis of foreign policy formation, history is phenomena worthy of attention, historical narratives constitute identities and they also form a context for the present generation's decision makers. The social phenomena referred to above constitute the world occupied by Argentineans, Brazilian and Chileans. Their world is the New World, Post-Colonial, *Latino*, historically marginalized from global polity, underdeveloped, subject to intervention by the US, and traumatized by political violence. In order to give a full account of foreign policy formation in the Southern Cone, International Relations' theory needs to be able to take account of these characteristics. To achieve this, it needs to use multiple perspectives and to compliment realist insights with more interpretive approaches to international politics.

Bibliography

Alamos Varas, Pilar, 'Algunas Fuentes Históricas de la Política Exterior de Chile', *Estudios Internacionales*. 126 (1999): pp. 3–39.
Alconada Sempé, Raúl, 'Democracia Y Política Exterior 1983–1989' in Jalabe, Silvia Ruth, *La Política Exterior Argentina y sus Protagonistas 1880–1995* (Buenos Aires: Grupo Editor Latinoamericano 1996).
Alusuutari, Pertti, *Researching Culture* (London: Sage Publications, 1995).
Alvear, Soledad, 'Tiene América Latina un Papel Propio en la Comunidad Internacional', *Estudios Internacionales* 141 (2003): pp. 69–89.
Anderson, Benedict, *Imagined Communities* (London: Verso, 1983).
Angell and Pollack (eds), *The Legacy of Dictatorship: Political, Economic and Social Change in Pinochet's Chile* (The Institute of Latin American Studies. Liverpool: University of Liverpool, 1993).
Appleby-Hunt, Jacob, *Telling the Truth about History* (New York: Norton, 1995).
Arciniegas, German, *Latin America. A Cultural History* (London: Alfred A. Knopf, 1973).
Arendt, Hannah, *On Violence* (New York: Penguin Books, 1969).
Arendt, Hannah (ed. Peter Baehr), *The Portable Arendt* (New York; London: Penguin Books, 2000).
Armstrong, D.M., *A Materialist Theory of the Mind* (London: Routledge, 1968).
Arquilla, John & Moyano Rasmussen, 'Origins of the South Atlantic War', *Journal of Latin American Studies* (2001): pp. 739–775.
Ashley, Richard K., *The Poverty of Neorealism* in Keohane, Robert (ed.), *Neorealism and its Critics* (New York: Columbia University Press, 1986).
Atkins, Pope G., *Latin America in the International Political System* (Boulder, Colo: Westview, 1995).
Atkins, Pope, G., *Handbook of Research on the International Relations of Latin America and the Caribbean* (Boulder, Colo: Westview 2001).
Augelli, Enrico and Murphy, Craig, *America's Quest for Supremacy and the Third World. An Essay in Gramscian Analysis* (London: Pinter Publishers, 1988).
Aylwin Azocar, Patricio, 'Chile en el Camino Hacia la Paz y el Desarrollo' in *Forum Duesto Desarrollo y Paz an América Latina* (University de Duesto Bilbao, 1995).
Aylwin Azocar, Patricio, *La Transición Chilena Discursos Escogidos Marzo 1990–1992* (Santiago: Andrés Bello, 2002).
Balmaceda, Maria de los Ángeles, 'La Doctrina de la Seguridad Nacional como Sustento de la Política Exterior Argentina Durante el Gobierno Militar (1976–1982)' in Rimoldi de Ladman, Eve (ed.). *Política Exterior y Tratados Argentina Chile Mercosur* (Buenos Aires: Ciudad Argentina, 1999).

Baltra Cortes, Alberto, 'La Economía y su Influencia Sobre las Relaciones Exteriores de las Estados' in Sánchez, Walter G. & Pereira, L., *150 Anos de Política Exterior Chilena* (Santiago: Editorial Universitiaria Santiago de Chile, 1977).
Barthes, R., 'Introduction to the Structural Analysis of Narratives' in Onega, Susana & Garcia Landa, Jose Angel (eds), *Narratology* (New York; London: Longman, 1996).
Barton, Jonathan R. & Murray, Warwick E., 'The End of Transition? Chile 1990–2000' in *Bulletin of Latin American Research* 21:3 (2002): pp. 329–338.
Barton, Jonathan R., 'State *Continuismo* and *Pinochetismo:* The Keys to the Chilean Transition' in *Bulletin of Latin American Research* 21:3 (2002): pp. 358–374.
Barzun, Jacques, 'Cultural History as a Synthesis' in Stern, Fritz (ed.), *Varieties of History From Voltaire to the Present* (New York: Vintage, 1972).
Baudrillard, Jean, *America* (London: New York: Verso, 1988).
Baudrillard, Jean, Fatal *Strategies* (New York: Pluto, 1990).
Baudrillard, Jean, *The Illusion of the End* (translated by Chris Turner) (Cambridge: Cambridge Polity Press, 1994).
Baudrillard, Jean, *Simulacra and Simulation* (Ann Arbor: University of Michigan, 1994).
Bauman, Zymunt, *Life in Fragments. Essays in Post Modern Morality* (Oxford: Blackwell, 1995).
Beck, Peter J., 'International Relations in the Antarctica, Argentina, Chile and the Great Powers', Morris, Michael (ed.), *Great Power Relation in Argentina, Chile and Antarctica* (Basingstoke: Macmillan, 1990).
Benjamin, Walter, *Illuminations, Essays and Reflections* (London: Jonathan Cape, 1970).
Benjamin, Walter, *Selected Writings*, Michael W. Jennings & Marcus Bullock (eds) (Cambridge, Mass: Harward University Press, 1996).
Benjamin, Walter, *Charles Baudelaire* (London; New York: Verso, 1997).
Bennington, Geoffrey, 'Postal Politics and the Institution of the Nation' in Bhabha, Homi K (ed.), *Nation and Narration* (London: Routledge, 1990).
Bernal-Meza, Rual, 'Evolución histórica de las relaciones políticas económicos de Chile con las potencias hegemónicas: Gran Bretana y Estados Unidos', *Estudios Internacionales*, 113 (1993).
Berstein, C. Enrique, 'Chile y la Política de Defensa Continental Desde la Segunda Guerra Mundial hasta el Presente', in Sánchez ,Walter G. & Pereira L. (eds), *150 Anos de Política Exterior Chilena* (Santiago: Editorial Universitaria Santiago de Chile, 1977).
Bethell, Leslie, 'Politics in Brazil: From Elections without Democracy to Democracy without Citizenship' in D'Alva Kinzo, Maria & Dunkerley, James (eds), *Brazil Since 1985. Economy, Politics and Society* (London: University of London, 2003).
Bethell, Leslie, *The Cambridge History of Latin America* Vol III (Cambridge: Cambridge University Press, 1985).

Bethell, Leslie, *The Cambridge History of Latin America* Vol IV (Cambridge: Cambridge University Press, 1986).
Bethell, Leslie, *The Cambridge History of Latin America* Vol V (Cambridge: Cambridge University Press, 1986).
Bhabha, Homi K, 'Dissemination: time, narrative, and the margins of the modern nation' in Bhabha, Homi K. (ed.), *Nation and Narration* (London: Routledge, 1990).
Biersteker, Thomas J., 'Critical Reflections on Post-Positivism', *International Relations. International Studies Quarterly* 33 (1989): pp. 263–267.
Biersteker, Thomas, 'The "Triumph" of Liberal Economic Ideas in the Developing World' in Stallings, Barbara (ed.), *Global Change, Regional Response. The New International Context of Development* (Cambridge: Cambridge University Press, 1995).
Billig, Michael, *Banal Nationalism* (London: Sage Publications, 1993).
Birchill, Scott & Linklater, Andrew, *Theories of International Relations* (London: Macmillan Press, 1996).
Bizzozero, Lincoln, 'Los Cambios de Gobierno en Argentina y Brasil y la Conformación de una agenda del Mercosur in *Nueva Sociedad* 186 (2003): pp. 36–45.
Blakemore, Harold, 'Chile from the War of the Pacific to the World Depression 1880–1930' in Bethell, Leslie, *The Cambridge History of Latin America* Vol. V (Cambridge: Cambridge University Press, 1986).
Blest Gana, Alberto, *Martin Rivas* (Santiago: Editorial Renacimiento, 1981).
Bloom, William, *Personal Identity, National Identity and International Relations* (Cambridge: Cambridge University Press, 1990).
Bologna, Alfredo Bruno, 'Malvinas: Fin de la Política de Seducción' in CERIR (ed.), *LA Política Exterior Argentina 1998/2000 El cambio de gobierno ¿Impacto o irrelevancia?* (Rosario: Ediciones CERIR, 2001).
Boothby, Richard, *Death and Desire, Psychoanalytic Theory in Lacan's Return to Freud* (New York: Routledge, 1991).
Bosworth, B., Dornbusch, R. and Laban, R., *The Chilean Economy, Policy Lesson and Challenges* (Washington, DC. The Brooking Institution, 1994).
Bourdieu, Pierre, *Language and Symbolic Power*. Edited and Introduction, John B. Thompson (Cambridge: Polity Press, 1992).
Bouzas, Roberto (ed.), *Realidades Nacionales Comparadas* (Buenos Aires: Altamira, 2002).
Bowie, Malcolm, *Lacan* (Cambridge Mass: Harvard University Press, 1991).
Braudel, Fernand, *On History*. (translated by Sarah Mathews) (Chicago: University of Chicago Press, 1980).
Brennan, Timothy, 'The National Longman for Form', Bhabha, Homi K. (ed.), *Nation and Narration* (London: Routledge, 1990).
Brinckerhoff, Jackson John, *A Sense of Place, A Sense of Time* (Albuquerque: New Mexico Press, 1994).

Brooks Peter, 'Reading for the Plot' in Onega, Susana & Garcia Landa, Jose Angel (eds.), *Narratology* (New York; London: Longman, 1996).
Buck, Morss. *The Origins of Negative Dialectics. Theodore W. Adorno, Walter Benjamin and the Frankfurt School* (Hassocks: Harvester Press, 1977).
Bull, Hedley, *The Anarchical Society. A Study of Order in World Politics* (London: Macmillan, 1977).
Burke, Peter, *Vico* (Oxford: Oxford University Press, 1985).
Burr, Robert, *By Reason or Force* (Berkeley: University of California, 1965).
Bushell, David, 'The Independence of Spanish South American' in Bethell, Leslie (ed.), *The Cambridge History of Latin America* Vol. III (Cambridge: Cambridge University Press, 1985).
Busso, Anabella, 'LAS Relaciones Argentino–Americanas a Finales del Gobierno de Menem y en los Inicios de la Gestions de la Rua. Entre la continuidad y los condicionantes domésticos' in CERIR (ed.), *LA Política Exterior Argentina 1998/2000 El cambio de gobierno ¿Impacto o irrelevancia?* (Rosario: Ediciones CERIR, 2001).
Busso, Anabella & Bologna, Alfredo Bruno, 'La Política Exterior Argentina a Partir del Gobierno de Menem: Una Presentación' in CERIR (ed.), *La Política Exterior Argentina a Partir del Gobierno de Menem* (Rosario: CERIR, 1994).
Caldas, Ricardo Wahrendorff, *Brazil in the Uruguay Round* (Aldershot: Ashgate, 1998).
Calderon, Beatriz & Martin Carlos, *Construyendo Confianza: las relaciones chilenos–argentinos durante 1997* in *La política exterior chilena en el 97: los desafíos en la reinserción in Chile 1997. Análisis y Opiniones* (Santiago: Flacso, 1998).
Calvert, Peter, *The International Politics of Latin America* (Manchester: Manchester University Press, 1994).
Campbell, David, *Writing Security* (Manchester; New York: Manchester University Press, 1996).
Campbell, David & Dillon, Michael, *The Political Subject of Violence* (Manchester; New York: Manchester University Press, 1993).
Cardosa, Henrique, *Dependency and Development* (Berkely: University of California, 1979).
Carranza, Mario E., 'Can Mercosur Survive? Domestic and International Constraints on Mercosur, *Latin American Politics & Society* 45:3 (2003): pp. 67–103.
Carr, E.H., *International Relations between the Two World Wars* (London: Macmillan Press, 1947).
Carr, E.H., *What is History* (London: Macmillan Press, 1961).
Carrard, Philippe, *Politics of the New History* (Baltimore; London: Johns Hopkins University Press, 1992).
Cassirer, Ernst, *Symbol, Myth and Culture. Essays and Lectures of Ernst Cassirer*, edited by Verene, Donald Phillip (New Haven: Yale University Press, 1979).
Castañeda, Jorge G., 'The Forgotten Relationship' in *Foreign Affairs* 83:3 (2003).

Cavallo, Ascanio, Salazar, Manuel & Sepúlveda, Oscar, *La Historia Oculta del Régimen Militar* (Santiago: Editorial Grijalbo, 1997).

Cavallo, Domingo Felipe, 'La Inserción de la Argentina en la Primer Mundo 1989–1991' in CARI, *La Política Exterior Argentina y sus Protagonistas 1880–1995* (Buenos Aires: Grupo Editor Latinoamericano, 1996).

Caygill, Howard., 'Violence, Civility and the Predicaments of Philosophy' in Campbell & Dillon (eds), *The Political Subject of Violence* (Manchester: Manchester University Press, 1993).

Caygill, Howard, *Walter Benjamin. The Colour of Experience* (London; New York: Routledge, 1998).

Chakrabarti Pasic, Sujata., 'Culturing International Relations Theory: A Call for an Extension' in Lapid, Yosef & Kratochwil, Fredrich (eds), *The Return of Culture and Identity in IR Theory* (Boulder, Colo: Lynne Rienner Publishers, 1996).

Challener, Richard D., 'The French Foreign Office: The Era of Philippe Berthelot' in Craig, Gordon A. & Gilbert, Felix (eds), *The Diplomats 1919–1939 Volume 1: The Twenties* (New York: Atheneum, 1972).

Chanady, Amaryll (ed.), *Latin America and the Construction of Difference* (Minneapolis: University of Minnesota Press, 1994).

Chaneton, Juan Carlos, Argentina: *La Ambigüedad como destino La Identidad del País Que no Fue* (Buenos Aires: Editorial Biblos, 1998).

Chomsky, Noam, *On Power and Ideology, The Managua Lectures* (Boston: South End Press, 1987).

Child, Jack, *Antarctica and South American Geopolitics* (New York: Praeger, 1988).

Cimadamore, Alberto D., 'Crisis e Instituciones Hacia el MERCOSUR del Siglo XXI' in De Sierra, Jerónimo (ed.), *Los Rostros del MERCOSUR* (Buenos Aires: CLACSO, 2001).

Cisneros, Andrés, 'Foreign Policy and Argentina's National Interests' in Lewis, Colin & Szusterman, Celia (eds). *Argentina, Foreign Relations and the New Foreign Policy Agenda* (London: University of London, Institute of Latin American Studies Occasional Papers No 14, 1996).

Cocks, Geoffrey and Travis Thomas (eds), *Readings in the Method of Psychology, Psychoanalysis and History* (New Haven; London: Yale University Press, 1987).

Cohen, Anthony P., *The Symbolic Construction of Community* (London: Routledge, 1995).

Collier, Simon, *Chile from Independence to the War of the Pacific* in Bethell, Leslie (ed.), *The Cambridge History of Latin America* Vol III (Cambridge: Cambridge University Press, 1985).

Collier, Simon and Sater, William F., *A History of Chile 1808–1994* (Cambridge: Cambridge University Press, 1996).

Connolly, William E., 'Identity and Difference in Global Politics' in Der Derian, James & Shapiro, Michael J. (eds), *International/Intertextual Relations. Post Modern Readings of World Politics* (Lexington, Mass: Lexington Books, 1989).

Constable and Valenzuela, *A Nation of Enemies* (New York: W.W. Norton, 1991).

Conway, Daniel W. *Nietzsche & the Political* (London: Routledge, 1997).
Correa, C., *Intellectual Property Rights, the WTO and Developing Countries: The TRIPS Agreement and Policy Options* (London: Zed Books, 2000).
Correa, Errázuriz and Hernán Felipe, *La diplomacia Chilena en la Segunda guerra de Irak Estudios Internationales*, 36 (2003).
Correa, Sofia, 'The Chilean Right after Pinochet' in Angell and Pollack (eds), *The Legacy of Dictatorship: Political, Economic and Social Change in Pinochet's Chile* (The Institute of Latin American Studies. Liverpool: University of Liverpool, 1993).
Costa Vaz, Alcides, 'El Gobierno de Lula Una Nueva Política Exterior', *Nueva Sociedad* 187 (2003)
Cousino, Jose Antonio, 'La Inserción de Chile en el Pacifico 20 Anos Después' in *Estudios Internacionales* 126 (1999): pp. 40–60.
Cox, Robert W., 'Social Forces, States and World Orders Beyond International Relations Theory' in Keohane, Robert (ed.), *Neorealism and its Critics* (New York: Columbia University Press, 1986).
Cox, Robert W., 'Gramsci, Hegemony and International Relations: An Essay in Method' in Gill, Stephen (ed.), *Gramsci Historical Materialism and International Relations* (Cambridge, New York: Cambridge University Press, 1993).
D'Alva Kinzo, Maria & Dunkerley, James (eds), *Brazil Since 1985. Economy, Politics and Society* (London: University of London, 2003).
Dammert, Lucia & Malone, Mary Fran T., 'Fear of Crime or Fear of Life? Public Insecurities in Chile', *Bulletin of Latin American Research* 22: 1 (2003): pp. 79–101.
Da Motta Veiga, Pedro, 'Brazil in Mercosur: Reciprocal Influence' in Roett, Riordan (ed.), 1999.
Da Motta Veiga, Pedro (2002), 'Brasil a inicios del nuevo milenio: Herencias y Desafíos de la Transición' in Bouzas, Roberto (ed.), *Realidades Nacionales Comparadas*, Buenos Aires: Altamira.
Davis, Eugene, Finan, John J. & Peck, Taylor, *Latin American Diplomatic History* (Baton Rouge Louisiana State University Press, 1977).
de Calliers, Francois, *The Art of Diplomacy* (edited by Keens-Saper, H.M.A & Schweizer, Karl W (Leicester: Leicester University Press, 1983).
De Ercilla, *La Araucana* (Santiago: Clásico Castalia, 1979).
De Toro, Alfonso, 'Post-Coloniality and Post Modernity: Jorge Luis Borges: The Periphery in the Centre, the Periphery as the Centre, the Centre of the Periphery' in De Toro, Fernando & De Toro, Alfonso (eds), *Borders and Margins. Post-Colonial and Post Modernism*. Frankfurt: Vervuert Verlag, 1995.
De Toro, Fernando, 'From Where to Speak? Post-Modern/Post Colonial Personalities' in De Toro, Fernando & De Toro, Alfonso (eds), *Borders and Margins. Post-Colonial and Post Modernism*. Frankfurt: Vervuert Verlag, 1995.
De Vasconcelos, Álvaro & Jaguaribe, Helio (2003), *The European Union, Mercosul and the New World Order*, London: Frank Cass.

Deigh, John, 'Freud's Later Theory of Civilisation: Changes and Implications' in Neu, Jerome (ed.), *The Cambridge Companion to Freud* (Cambridge: Cambridge University Press, 1991).

Delaney, Jean H, 'Imaging *El ser Argentino*: Cultural Nationalism and Romantic Concepts of Nationhood in Early Twentieth-Century Argentina', *Journal of Latin American Studies* 34 (2002): pp. 625–658.

Der Derian, James, *On Diplomacy* (Oxford: Blackwell, 1987).

Der Derian, James, 'The Boundaries of Knowledge and Power in International Relations' in Der Derian, James & Shapiro, Michael J. (eds), *International/ Intertextual Relations. Post Modern Readings of World Politics*, Lexington, Mass.: Lexington Books, 1989.

Der Derian, James, *Anti-Diplomacy* (Cambridge MA: Blackwell, 1992).

Derrida, Jacques, *Writing and Difference* (London: Routledge and Kegan Paul, 1978).

de Souza, Amaury, 'The European Union, Mercosur and New World Order' in De Vasconcelos, Álvaro & Jaguaribe, Helio (eds), *The European Union, Mercosul and the New World Order* (London: Frank Cass, 2003).

Devetak, Richard, 'Critical Theory' in Burchill, Linklater, Devetak, Paterson & True, *Theories of International Relations* (London: Macmillan, 1996).

Diamint, Rur, 'Security Challenges in Latin America', *Bulletin of Latin American Research* 23:1 (2004): pp. 43–62.

Di Tella, Guido, 'Política Exterior Argentina: Actualidad y Perspectivas 1991–1995 in CARI (ed.), *La Política Exterior Argentina y sus Protagonistas 1880–1995* (Buenos Aires: Grupo Editor Latinoamericano, 1996).

Domínguez, Jorge I., *International Security & Democracy. Latin America and the Caribbean in the Post-Cold War Era* (Pittsburg: University of Pittsburg 1998).

Dostal, Robert J., 'Time and Phenomenology in Husserl and Heidegger' in Guigman, Charles (ed.), *The Cambridge Companion to Heidegger* (Cambridge: Cambridge University Press, 1993).

Drennan, Mathew P., 'The Dominance of International Finance by London, New York and Tokyo' in Daniels and Lever (eds), *The Global Economy in Transition* (London, New York: Longman, 1996), p. 133.

Dugini de de Cándido, Maria, *Argentina Chile Mercosur Cambios y Continuidades* (Buenos Aires: Ediciones Cuidad Argentina, 1997).

Duncan, James S. & Duncan, Nancy G., 'Roland Barthes and the Secret History of Landscape' in Barnes, Trevor J. and Duncan James S. (eds), *Writing Worlds. Discourse, Text and Metaphor in the Representation of Landscape* (London: Routledge, 1992).

Duran, Roberto, 'Lo Constante y lo variable de la política exterior chilena durante los anos 1974–1984' in *Revista de Ciencia Política* Volume VII, No 2 (1985).

Duran, Roberto, 'Democracy and Regional Multilateralism in Chile' in Mace, Gordon & Therien Jean Philippe (eds), *Foreign Policy and Regionalism in the Americas* (Boulder, Colo: Lynne Rienner Publishers, 1996).

Duran, Roberto, Quezada, Gonzalo & Avetikian, Tamara, 'La política multilateral de Chile entre 1945–1970. Análisis de algunas variables significativa' in *Revista de Ciencias Políticas* Volume V, No 2 (1983).

Eagleton, Terry, Jameson, Fredric and Said, Edward W., *Nationalism, Colonialism and Literature* (Minneapolis: University of Minnesota, 1990).

Ebel, Richard H., Taras, Raymond and Cochrane, James D., *Political Culture and Foreign Policy in Latin America* (New York: State University of New York Press, 1991).

Echeverria D.C. Gloria, 'La Controversia entre Chile y Argentina Sobre la Región del Beagle: Origin Desarrollo y Desenlace' in Sánchez, Walter G. & Pereira L. (eds), *150 Anos de Política Exterior Chilena* (Santiago: Editorial Universitaria Santiago de Chile, 1977).

Egana, Rodrigo, Balance y Perspectivas de la cooperación internacional' in García, Marcelo, *Mas Allá de las Fronteras* (Santiago: Editores Asociados Ltda., 1994).

Eguigunin, Juan Eduardo, *Relaciones Internacionales una perspectiva antropológica* (Santiago: Andrés Bello, 1987).

Emin Salla, Michael, 'Integral Peace and Power. A Foucauldian Perspective' in *Peace and Change* 23: 3 July (1998): pp. 312–332.

Ensalaco, Mark, *Chile Under Pinochet. Recovering the Truth* (Philadelphia: University of Pennsylvania Press, 2000).

Erik H. Erikson, *Childhood and Society* (New York: W.W.Norton and Company, 1963).

Errazuriz, Hernán Felipe, 'Las constantes de Nuestra política exterior' in *Diplomacia* 46 (1988).

Escala Esbocar with Fortin Gajardo, Fuentealba Jiménez, *Historia Dictá tica de Chile* (Santiago: Ediciones Hernández Blanco, 1985).

Escolar, Marcelo, Quintero Palacios, Silvina and Rebcratti, Carlos, 'Geographical Identity and Patriotic Representation in Argentina' in Hoosan, David (ed.), *Geography and National Identity* (Oxford; Cambridge, Mass.: Blackwell, 1994).

Escudé, Carlos & Cisneros, Andrés, *Historia de las Relaciones Exteriores Argentinas* http://www.argentina-rree.com/historia.htm.

Escudé, Carlos & Fontana, Andrés, 'Argentina's Security Policies. Their Rationale and Regional Context' in Domínguez, Jorge I. (ed.), *International Security and Democracy: Latin America and the Caribbean in the Post-Cold War Era* (Pittsburgh: University of Pittsburgh Press, 1998).

Fairclough, Norman, *Critical Discourse Analysis, The Critical Study of Language*, (London: New York: Longman, 1995).

Fausto, Boris, 'Brazil: The Social and Political Structure of the First Republic 1889–1930' in Bethell, Leslie (ed.), *Cambridge History of Latin America* vol. 5 (Cambridge: Cambridge University Press 1986).

Febreve, Lucian (ed. Peter Burke), *A New Kind of History* (London: Routledge and Kegan Paul, 1973).

Feitlowitz, Marguerite, *A Lexicon of Terror. Argentina and the Legacies of Terror* (Oxford: Oxford University Press, 1998).

Femia, Joseph V., *The Machiavellian Legacy. Essays in Italian Political Thought* (London: Macmillan, 1998).
Fermandois, Joaquín, 'Ideología y pragmatismo en la política exterior chilena durante la crisis del sistema política 1970–1975', *Revista de Ciencia Política* VII: 2 (1985).
Fermandois, Joaquín, 'De una Inserción a Otra: Política Exterior de Chile', 1966–1991', *Estudios Internacionales*, 96 (1991): pp. 433–455.
Fermandois, Joaquin, 'Chile and the Great Powers' in Morris, Michael (ed.), *Great Power Relations in Argentina, Chile and Antarctica* (Basingstoke: Macmillan, 1990).
Fermandois, Joaquín, 'Interpretación histórica de las relaciones hispano–chilena: el sentido de una pregunta', *Estudios Internacionales* (1999): pp. 127–128.
Fermandois, Joaquín, 'Una Década de Transformaciones Relaciones Exteriores de Chile' in Rimoldi de Ladman, Eve (ed.), *Política Exterior y Tratados Argentina Chile Mercosur* (Buenos Aires: Ciudad Argentina, 1999).
Ferris, Elizabeth G., Lincoln, Jennie K., 'Introduction to Latin America Foreign Policy: Latin American Government as Actors in the International System' in Ferris and Lincoln (eds), *Latin American Foreign Policies. Global and Regional Dimensions* (Boulder Colo: Westview Press, 1981).
Figari, Guillermo Miguel, *Pasado, Presente y Futuro de la Política Exterior Argentina* (Buenos Aires: Editorial Biblos, 1993).
Finan, John J., 'Foreign Relations in the 1930's Effects of the Great Depression' in Davis, Finan, Peck, *Latin American Diplomatic History* (Baton Rouge: Louisiana State University Press, 1977).
Finan, John J., 'Latin America and World War II'. Davis, Finan, Peck, *Latin American Diplomatic History* (Baton Rouge: Louisiana State University Press, 1977).
Fisher, Glen, *Mindsets: The Role of Culture and Perception in International Relations* (Yarmouth Me.: Intercultural Press Inc, 1988).
Foucault, Michel, *The Archaeology of Knowledge* (London: Tavistock, 1972).
Foucault, Michel, *Language, counter-memory, practice: Selected essays and Practices* (Oxford: Blackwell, 1977).
Foucault, Michel, *Discipline and Punish: the Birth of the Prison* (Harmondsworth: Penguin, 1979).
Foucault, Michel, *Questions on Geography in Power/Knowledge. Selections, Interviews and Other Writings 1972–1977* (Hassocks: The Harvester Press, 1980).
Foucault, Michel, *Nietzsche, Genealogy, History*, in Paul Rabinow (ed.), *The Foucault Reader* (Harmondsworth: Penguin, 1984).
Ffrench Davis lecture on Mercosur, at the Institute of International Relations (Santiago, Chile. November 2000).
Freeden, Michael, *Ideologies and Political Theory. A Conceptual Approach* (Oxford: Clarendon, 1996).

Freeman Smith, Robert, 'Latin America, The United States and the European Powers, 1830–1930' in Bethell, Leslie (ed.), *The Cambridge History of Latin America* Volume 4 (Cambridge: Cambridge University Press, 1986).

Freud, Sigmund, *Beyond the Pleasure Principle* (translated and edited by James Strachey) (New York: W.W. Norton and Company, 1961).

Freud, Sigmund, *Civilisation and Its Discontents* (translated by Joan Riveiere) (New York: Dover Publications, 1963).

Frosh, Stephen, *The Politics of Psychoanalysis* (London: Macmillan, 1987).

Fuchs, Stephen and Ward, Steven, 'What is Deconstruction, and Where and When Does it Take Place? Making Facts in Science, Building Cases in Law', *American Sociological Review* 59:4 (1994): pp. 481–500.

Gadamer, Hans-George, *Truth and Method* (London: Steed and Ward, 1975).

Galeano, Eduardo, *Las Vienas Abiertas de América Latina* (Mexico D.F: Siglo XXI, 1992).

Gazmuri, Cristián, 'The Armed Forces in Democratic Chile' in Angell and Pollack (eds), *The Legacy of Dictatorship: Political, Economic and Social Change in Pinochet's Chile* (Liverpool, 1993).

Gallo, Ezequiel, 'Argentina: Society and Politics, 1880–1916' in Leslie Bethell, *The Cambridge History of Latin America* Vol. 5 (Cambridge: Cambridge University Press, 1986), p. 409.

Garreton, Manuel Antonio, 'Political Democratisation in Latin America and the Crisis of the Paradigm' in Manor, James (ed.), *Rethinking Third World Politics* (London; New York: Longman, 1991).

Geertz, Clifford, *Towards an Interpretative Theory of Culture* (New York: Basic Books, 1973).

Geertz, Clifford, *Local Knowledge, Further Essays in Interpretative Anthropology* (New York: Basic Books, 1983).

George, Jim, 'International Relations and the Search for Thinking Space: Another View of the Third Debate', *International Studies Quarterly* 33 (1989): pp. 269–279.

Giddens, Anthony, *Sociology* (Cambridge: Polity Press, 1993).

Gill, Stephen, 'Gramsci and Global Politics: Towards a Post-Hegemonic Research Agenda' in Gill, Stephen (ed.), *Gramsci, Historical Materialism and International Relations* (Cambridge; New York: Cambridge University, 1993).

Gill, Stephen, 'Epistemology, Ontology and the "Italian School"', in Gill, Stephen (ed.), *Gramsci, Historical Materialism and International Relations* (Cambridge; New York: Cambridge University Press, 1994).

Gill, Stephen (ed.), *Gramsci, Historical Materialism and International Relations* (Cambridge; New York: Cambridge University Press, 1994).

Gill, Stephen, 'Transformation and Innovation in the Study of World Order' in Gill and Mittelman (ed.), *Innovation and Transformation in International Studies* (Cambridge; New York: Cambridge University Press, 1997).

Gilloch, Graeme, *Myth and Metropolis. Walter Benjamin and the City* (Cambridge: Polity Press, 1996).

Gilpin, Robert, *War and Change in World Politics* (Cambridge: Cambridge University Press, 1981).
Gilpin, Robert G., 'The Richness of Political Realism' in Keohane, Robert (ed.), *Neorealism and its Critics* (New York: Columbia University Press, 1986).
Glade, William, 'Latin America and the International Economy' in Bethell, Leslie (ed.), *The Cambridge History of Latin America* Vol. 4 (Cambridge: Cambridge University Press, 1986).
Gomes Saraiva, Miriam, 'Brasil y Argentina nos Anos 90: Diez Años de Política Externa' in CERIR (ed.), *LA Política Exterior Argentina 1998/2000 El cambio de gobierno ¿Impacto o irrelevancia?* (Rosario: Ediciones CERIR, 2001).
Gomez Mera, Laura 'Explaining Mercosur's Survival: Strategic Sources of Argentine–Brazilian Cooperation', *Journal of Latin American Studies* 37:1 (2005): pp. 109–140.
González, E. Javier, 'El Aporte de Portales a la Formación del Estado Nacional como base de una Política Exterior' in Sánchez, Walter G. & Pereira L. (eds.), *150 Anos de Política Exterior Chilena* (Santiago: Editorial Universitaria Santiago de Chile, 1977).
Grabendorff, Wolf, 'Mercosur and the European Union: From Cooperation to Alliance?' in Roett, Riordan (ed.), *Mercosur Regional Integration, World Markets* (Boulder, Colo: Lynne Rienner Publishers, 1999).
Gramsci, Antonio, *Selection from Cultural Writings* (David Fergae ed.) (London: Lawrence and Wishort, 1985).
Grugel, Jean, 'Latin America and the Remaking of the Americas in Gamble, Andrew & Payne, Anthony, *Regionalism and the World Order* (Basingstoke: Macmillan, 1996).
Guedes da Costa, Thomaz, 'Strategies for Global Insertion: Brazil and Its Regional Partners' in Tulchin, Joseph S. and Ralph H. Espach (eds), *Latin America in the New International System* (Boulder: Lynne Rienner, 2001).
Guerro Yoacham, Cristian, 'Chile y Estados Unidos Relaciones y Problemas 1812–1916' in Sánchez, Walter G. & Pereira L. (eds), *150 Anos de Política Exterior Chilena* (Santiago: Editorial Universitaria Santiago de Chile, 1977).
Guetzkow, Harold & Valadez, Joseph J., 'Simulation and "Reality" Validity Research' in Vasquez, John A. (ed.), *Classics of International Relations* (London: Prentice Hall, 1990).
Guignon, Charles (ed.), *The Cambridge Companion to Heidegger* (Cambridge: Cambridge University Press, 1993).
Habermas, Jurgen, *The Philosophical Discourse of Modernity* (Cambridge: Polity Press, 1987).
Hale, Charles A., 'Political and Social Ideas in Latin America' in Bethell, Leslie (ed.), *The Cambridge History of Latin America* Vol. 4 (Cambridge: Cambridge University Press, 1986).
Hamilton, Paul, *Historicism* (New York: Routledge, 1996).
Hamilton, Ken & Longhorn, Richard, *The Practice of Diplomacy* (London; New York: Routledge, 1995).

Hansen, Lene, 'RBJ Walker and International Relations: Deconstructing a Discipline' in Neumann, Iver B. and Waever, Ole (eds), *The Future of International Relations, Masters in the Making* (London: Routledge, 1997).

Hartlyn, Jonathan, 'Democracies in Contemporary South America: Convergences and Diversities', in Joseph S. Tulchin with Allison M. Garland (eds), *Argentina: The Challenges of Modernization* (Wilmington: Scholarly Resources Inc., 1998).

Hawthorn, Jeremy, *Cunning Passages, New Historicism, Cultural Materialism and Marxism in the Contemporary Literary Debate* (London: Arnold, 1996).

Hayman, Ronald, *Nietzsche A Critical Life* (London: Weidenfeld & Nicolson, 1980).

Heidegger, Martin, *Being and Time* (Oxford: Basil Blackwell, 1962).

Heine, Jorge, *Timidez o pragmatismo? La política exterior de Chile en 1990* (Santiago: Prospel, 1990).

Heine, Jorge, 'Qué Pasó, Tío Sam? Los Estados Unidos y América Latina después del 11 de septiembre', *Estudio Internacionales* 138 (2002): pp. 89–106.

Hepple, Leslie W. 'Metaphor, Geopolitical Discourse and the Military in South America' in Barnes, Trevor J. and Duncan, James S. (eds), *Writing Worlds. Discourse, Text and Metaphor in the Representation of Landscape* (London: Routledge, 1992).

Hernández, José, *Martín Fierro* (Barcelona: Editorial Juventud, 1995).

Hickman, John, *News from End of the Earth. A portrait of Chile* (London: Hurst and Company, 1998).

Hirst, Monica, 'The Foreign Policy of Brazil: From the Democratic Transition to its Consolidation' in Munoz, Heraldo & Tulchin, Joseph (eds), *Latin America in World Politics* (Boulder, Westview, 1996).

Hirst, Monica, 'Security Policies, Democratisation, and Regional Integration in the Southern Cone' in Domínguez, Jorge I. (ed.), *International Security and Democracy: Latin America and the Caribbean in the Post-Cold War Era* (Pittsburgh: University of Pittsburgh Press, 1998).

Hirst, Monica, 'Mercosur's Complex Political Agenda' in Roett, Riordan (ed.), *Mercosur Regional Integration, World Markets* (Boulder, Colo: Lynne Rienner Publishers, 1999).

Hirst, Mónica (2003), 'Los claroscuros de la seguridad regional en las Américas', *Nuevo Sociedad*, 185, pp. 83–101.

Hobden, Stephen, *International Relations and Historical Sociology* (London: Routledge, 1998).

Hobsbawn, E.J., *Nations and Nationalism Since 1870* (Cambridge: Cambridge University Press, 1990).

Hobsbawn, Eric, *On History* (London: Wedenfeld and Nicolson, 1997).

Hoffman, Piofr, 'Death Time and History: Division II of Being and Time' in Guignon, Charles (ed.), *The Cambridge Companion to Heidegger* (Cambridge University Press, 1993).

Holsti, K.J., *International Politics. A Framework for Analysis* (Englewood Cliffs, N.J.: Prentice Hall, 1967).

Hosti, K.J., 'Mirror, Mirror on the Wall, which are the Fairest Theories of All?', *International Studies Quarterly* Volume 33 (1989).
Holzapfel, Tamara, 'Latin America Literature' in Knippers Black (ed.), *Latin America. Its Promise and its Problems* (Boulder Colo: Westview, 1995).
Hugueney, Clodoaldo, 'Brazilian Foreign Policy at the Beginning of the Twenty-First Century' in Álvaro De Vasconcelos & Helio Jaguaribe (eds.), *The European Union, Mercosul and the New World Order* (London: Frank Cass, 2003)
Hurrel, Andrew, 'Explaining the Resurgence of Regionalism in World Politics', *Review of International Studies*, 21:4 (1995).
Hurrel, Andrew, 'Security in Latin America', *International Affairs* 74:3 (1998): pp. 529–549.
Huymans, Jef. and James Der Derian, 'The Unbearable Lightness of Theory' in Neumann, Iver. B. and Waever, Ole (eds), *The Future of International Relations, Masters in the Making* (London: Routledge, 1997).
Infante, Maria Teresa, Interview at the Ministry for External Relations, November, Santiago, 2000.
Insulza, José Miguel, *Ensayos sobre política exterior de Chile* (Santiago: Editorial Las Andes, 1998).
Inayatullah, Naeem & Blaney, David, 'Knowing Encounters. Beyond Parochialism in International Relations' in Lapid, Yosef & Kratochwil, Fredrich (eds), *The Return of Culture and Identity in IR Theory*. (Boulder, Colo: Lynne Rienner Publishers, 1996).
Ireland, Gordon*, Boundaries and Possessions and Conflicts in South America* (Cambridge, Mass.: Harward University Press, 1988).
Irigoin Barrenne, Jeanette, 'La Evolución del Papel del Congreso en los Acuerdos Internacionales' in Sánchez & Pereira (eds), *150 Anos de Política Exterior Chilena* (Santiago: Editorial Universitaria Santiago de Chile, 1977).
Jahn, Beate, *The Cultural Construction of International Relations* (Basingstoke: Palgrave, 2000).
Jara, Joan, *Victor, An Unfinished Song* (London: Jonathan Cape, 1983).
Jelin, Elizabeth, 'Los Movimientos Sociales y los Actores Culturales en el Escenario Regional. El Caso del MERCOSUR' in De Sierra, Jerónimo, *Los Rostros del MERCOSUR* (Buenos Aires: CLACSO, 2001).
Jenkins, Keith*, Re Thinking History* (London: Routledge, 1991).
Jenkins, Keith, *On What is History* (London: Routledge, 1995).
Jocelyn-Holt Letelier, Alfredo, *El Chile perplejo. Del Avanzar sin Transar Al Transar sin Parar* (Santiago: Editorial Planeta, 1999).
Joignant, Alfredo & Menendez, Amparo, '*De la "Democracia de los Acuerdos" a las dilemas de la polis. Transición incomplete o ciudadanía pendiente?*' in Menéndez, Amparo (ed.). *La Caja de Pandora* (Santiago: Planeta, 1999).
Jung, C.G., *Memories, Dreams, Reflections* (London: Fontana Press, 1995).
Katzman, Martin T., 'Translating Brazil's Economic Potential into International Influence' in Selcher, Wayne A., *Brazil in the International System: The Rise of a Middle Power* (Boulder: Westview, 1981).

Kaufman Purcell, Susan, 'The New U.S–Brazil Relationship' in Kaufman Purcell, Susan & Roett, Riordan (eds), *Brazil Under Cardoso* (Boulder: Lynne Rienner, 1997).
Kemp, Anthony, *The Estrangement of the Past. A Study in the Origins of Modern Historical Consciousness* (New York; London: Oxford University Press, 1991).
Keohane, Robert (ed.), *Neorealism and its Critics* (New York: Columbia University Press, 1986).
Keohane, Robert, *International Institutions and State Power* (Boulder, Colo: Westview, 1989).
Klein, Melanie, *The Pscho-Analysis of Children* (London: The Hogarth Press and the Institute of Psychoanalysis, 1973).
Klom, Andy, 'Mercosur and Brazil: a European Perspective', *International Affairs* 79:2 (2003): pp. 351–368.
Knight, Thomas J., *Latin America Comes of Age* (London: The Scarecrow Press, 1979).
Koonings, Kess, 'Shadows of Violence and Political Transition in Brazil: From Military Rule to Democratic Governance' in Koonings, Kees & Kruijt, Dirk (eds), *Societies of Fear. The Legacy of Civil War, Violence and Terror in Latin America* (London: Zed Books, 1999).
Kornbluh, Peter, *The Pinochet File. A Declassified Dossier on Atrocity and Accountability* (New York: 2003).
Kratochwil, Friedrick, 'Is the Ship of Culture at Sea or Returning' in Lapid, Yosef & Kratochwil, Fredrich (eds), *The Return of Culture and Identity in IR Theory* (Boulder, Colo.: Lynne Rienner Publishers, 1996).
Lacan, Jacques, *Ecrits A Selection* (London: Tavistock Publications, 1977).
Lacan, Jacques (Introduction by David Macey), *The Four Fundamental Concepts of Psycho-analysis* (London: Vintage, 1998).
Lambourne, Alan C., 'Theory and Politics in World Politics', *International Relations Quarterly* 41:2 (1997): pp. 187–214.
Lapid, Yosef, 'The Third Debate: On the Prospects of International Theory in a Post-Positivist Era', *International Studies Quarterly* 33:3 (1989): pp. 235–254.
Lapid, Yosef & Kratochwil, Fredrich (eds), *The Return of Culture and Identity in IR Theory* (Boulder, Colo: Lynne Rienner Publishers, 1996).
Larrain, Jorge, *Ideology and Cultural Identity, Modernity of the Third World Presence* (Cambridge, UK; Cambridge, MA.: Polity Press, 1994).
Lecaros, Luis Melo, 'Trayectoria del Ministro de Relaciones Exteriores y las Problemas en la conducción de la diplomacia Chilena' in Sánchez, Walter G. & Pereira L. (eds), *150 Anos de Política Exterior Chilena* (Santiago: Editorial Universitaria Santiago de Chile, 1977).
Lechner, Norbert, *Nuestros Miedos in Chile Entre la II Cumbre y la detención de Pinochet* (Santiago FLACSO Chile, 1998).
Lechner, Nobert & Guell, Pedro, 'Chile: La política de la memoria' in Menéndez, Amparo (ed.), *La Caja de Pandora* (Santiago: Planeta, 1999).
Lemair, Anika, *Jacques Lacan* (London: Routledge and Kegan, 1977).

Levinas, Emmanuel, *Totality and Infinity* (Pittsburgh, Pennsylvania: Duquesne University Press, 1969).
Levinas, Emmanuel, *Of the God that comes to Mind* (Stanford, California: Stanford University Press, 1998).
Levine, Robert M. & Crocitti, John J. (eds), The *Brazil Reader: History, Culture, Politics* (Durham: Duke University Press, 1999).
Lewis, Daniel K., *The History of Argentina* (New York, Macmillan, 2001).
Liebman, Seymour B., *Exploring the Latin American Mind* (Chicago: Nelson Hall, 1976).
Linklater, Andrew, *Beyond Realism and Marxism. Critical Theory and International Relations* (Basingstoke: Macmillan, 1990).
Linklater, Andrew, 'Neo Realism in Theory and Practice' in Booth, Ken & Smith Steve (ed.), *International Relations Today* (Cambridge: Polity Press, 1995).
Lira, Elizabeth & Loveman, Brian, *Las ardientes cenizas de olvido* (Santiago: Lom Ediciones, 2000).
Little, Walter, 'International Conflict in Latin America', *International Affairs* 63 (1986–87): pp. 589–601.
Loveman, Brian, *The Legacy of Hispanic Capitalism* (New York: Oxford University Press, 1988).
Lowental, D., *The Past is a Foreign Country* (Cambridge, UK; Cambridge, New York: Cambridge University Press, 1985).
Lynch, John, 'The Origins of Spanish American Independence' in Bethell, Leslie, *The Cambridge History of Latin America* Vol 4 (Cambridge: Cambridge University Press, 1986).
Lyotard, Jean-Francios, *Lyotard Reader*, in Benjamin, Andrew (ed.), (Oxford: Blackwell, 1989).
Lyotard, Jean-Francois, *Political Writings* (Minneapolis: Regents of University of Minnesota, 1993).
MacIntyre, Alastair, *After Virtue* (London: Duckworth, 1999).
Machiavelli, Niccolo, *The Prince*, introduction, translation and notes by Paul Sonnino (New Jersey: Humanities Press, 1996).
Manfred, Wilfred & Infante, Maria Teresa, 'La política exterior chilena en los anos 90: el gobierno de Presidente Aylwin y algunas proyecciones', *Estudios Sociales* 75 (1993).
Mares, David R., *Violent Peace, Militarised Interstate Bargaining in Latin America* (New York: Columbia University Press, 2001).
Mares, David R., 'Foreign Policy in Argentina, Brazil and Chile: The Burden of the Past, the Hope for the Future', *Latin American Research Review* 29:1 (1994).
Martin, Gerald, *Journey Through the Labyrinth. Latin American Fiction in the Twentieth Century* (New York: Verso, 1989).
Martinez Sotomayor, Carlos, 'Presencia de la educación y la cultura en las relaciones internacionales de Chile', *Estudios Internacionales* 59 (1982).
Martinez Sotomayor, Carlos, *Reflexiones y testimonias políticas* (Santiago: Corporación de Investigación para de Desarrollo, 1987).

Mazlish, Bruce, 'Group Psychology and the Problems of Contemporary History' in Cocks, Geoffrey & Crosby, Travis L., *Readings in the Method of Psychology, Psychoanalysis and History* (New Haven: Yale University Press, 1987).

McCann, Frank D., 'Brazilian Foreign Relations in the Twentieth Century' in Selcher, Wayne A., *Brazil in the International System: The Rise of a Middle Power* (Boulder: Westview, 1981).

Mecham, Michael, 'Mercosur: A Failing Development Project?', *International Affairs* 79:2 (2003): pp. 369–387.

Meneses C. Emilio, *Coping with Decline: Chilean Foreign Policy during the Twentieth Century* (University of Oxford, 1988). Doctoral Thesis.

Mifsud, Tony, 'Human Rights and Dictatorship. The Case of Chile' in Rupesinghe, K. and Rubio C. (eds), *The Culture of Violence* (New York: United Nations University Press, 1994).

Milet, Paz, *La política exterior chilena en el 97:los desafíos en la reinserción en Chile 1997. Analysis y Opiniones* (Santiago: Flacso, 1998).

Miller, David, *On Nationality* (Oxford: Clarendon Press, 1995).

Miranda, Carlos, 'Un comentario sobre la imagen internacional de chile', *Revista de Ciencia Política* VII: 2 (1985): pp. 189–193.

Moneta, Carlos J. & Rolf Wichmann, 'Brazil and the Southern Cone' in Selcher, Wayne A., *Brazil in the International System: The Rise of a Middle Power* (Boulder: Westview, 1981).

Moniz Bandeira, Luiz Alberto, 'Brasil, Estados Unidos y los Procesos de Integración', *Nueva Sociedad* 186 (2003): pp. 142–157.

Moran, Dermot, *Introduction to Phenomenology* (London; New York: Routledge, 2000).

Morande Lavin, José & Duran, Roberto, 'Percepciones en la política exterior chilena: Un estudio sobre lideres de opinión publica', *Revista Diplomacia* 26 (1993).

Morgenthau, Hans J., *Scientific Man vs Power Politics*. (Chicago: Chicago UP, 1946).

Morgenthau, Hans J., *Politics in the Twentieth Century*, abridged edition (Chicago: University of Chicago Press, 1971).

Morgenthau Hans J., *Politics Among Nations. The Struggle for Power and Peace* (New York; London: McGraw-Hill, 1985/1993).

Morgenthau, Hans J., 'A Realist Theory of International Relations' in Vasquez, John A. (ed.), *Classics of International Relations* (London: Prentice Hall, 1990).

Morris, Michael (ed.), *Great Power Relation in Argentina, Chile and Antarctica*, (Basingstoke: Macmillan, 1990).

Morse, Richard M., 'The Multiverse of Latin America Identity 1920–1970' in Bethell, Leslie (ed.), *The Cambridge History of Latin America* Vol. 10 (Cambridge: Cambridge University Press, 1995).

Moulian, Tomas, *Chile Actual* (Santiago: Lom Arcis, 1997).

Muñoz, Heraldo, *Las Relaciones del Gobierno Militar Chileno* (Santiago: Prospel-Cerc, 1986).

Munoz, Heraldo, 'Chile's External Relations under the Military Government' in Valenzuela and Venezuela (eds), *Military Rule in Chile* (Baltimore; London: Johns Hopkins University Press, 1986).
Munoz, Heraldo (ed.), *Chile: Política exterior para la democracia* (Santiago: Pehuén Editores, 1989).
Munoz, Heraldo, 'La agenda futura de la política exterior de Chile' in Muñoz, Heraldo (ed.), *Chile: Política exterior para la democracia* (Santiago: Pehuén Editores, 1989).
Muñoz, Heraldo, 'Política exterior de Chile en el ano del plebiscito' in Muñoz, Heraldo (ed.), *A la espera de una nueva etapa. Anuario de políticas exteriores latinoamericanos 1988–1989* (Santiago: Prospel, 1990).
Muñoz, Heraldo, 'The Dominant Themes in Latin American Foreign Policy' in Munoz, Heraldo & Tulchin, Joseph (eds), *Latin America in World Politics* (Boulder, Colo: Westview, 1996).
Muñoz, Heraldo, 'Good-bye U.S.A' in Tulchin, Joseph S. and Ralph H. Espach (eds), *Latin America in the New International System* (Boulder: Lynne Rienner, 2001).
Muñoz, Heraldo & Asenjo, Daniel, 'Chile: él ultimo ano del régimen del general Pinochet' in Muñoz, Heraldo (ed.), *A la espera de una nueva etapa. Anuario de políticas exteriores latinoamericanos 1988–1989* (Santiago: Prospel, 1990).
Muñoz, Heraldo & Tulchin, Joseph (eds), *Latin America in World Politics* (Boulder, Westview, 1996).
Nagel, Thomas, *The View from Nowhere* (New York; Oxford: Oxford University Press, 1986).
Namier, Lewis, 'History and Political Culture' in Stern, Fritz (ed.), *Varieties of History From Voltaire to the Present* (New York: Vintage, 1972).
Nardin, Terry & Mapel, David R. (eds), *Traditions of International Ethics* (Cambridge: Cambridge University Press, 1992).
Nef, Jorge, 'Contradicciones en el "Modelo Chileno"' in Menéndez, Amparo (ed.), *La Caja de Pandora* (Santiago: Planeta, 1999).
Neruda, Pablo, *Antología Poética* (Madrid: Alianza Editorial, 1986).
Neufeld, Mark, 'Reflexivity and International Relations Theory' in Turenne Sjolander, Claire and Cox, Wayne S. (eds), *Beyond Positivism. Critical Reflections on International Relations* (Boulder, Colo.: Lynne Rienner Publishers, 1994).
Neufeld, Mark, *The Restructuring of International Relations Theory* (New York: Cambridge University Press, 1995).
Neumann, Iver B and Waever, Ole (eds), *The Future of International Relations, Masters in the Making* (London: Routledge, 1997).
Nicolson, Sir Harold, *Diplomacy* (New York: Oxford University Press, 1969).
Nietzsche, Friedrich, *The Genealogy of Morals* (New York: Vintage, 1964).
Nietzsche, Friedrich, *Beyond Good and Evil* (Harmondsworth: Penguin, 1990).
Nolte, Nolte, *El Juicio de la Historia Espectros del Pasado en América Latina in Chile Entre la II Cumbre y la Detención de Pinochet* (Santiago: Flasco Chile, 1998).

Norden, Deborah & Russell, Roberto, *The United States and Argentina in a Changing World* (London: Routledge, 2002).
Onega, Susana & Garcia Landa, José Ángel (eds), *Narratology* (New York; London: Longman, 1996).
Oppenheim, Lois Hecht, *Politics in Chile. Democracy, Authoritarianism, and the Search for Development* (Boulder, Colo: Westview Press, 1999).
Orrego Vicuña, Francisco, *La Participación de Chile en el Sistema Internacional* (Santiago: Editorial Nacional Gabriela Mistral, 1974).
Orrego Vicuña, Francisco, 'Trayectoria y orientaciones de la política exterior de Chile', *Seguridad Nacional*, Santiago (1976): pp. 73–82.
Orrego Vicuña, Francisco (ed.), *Los Estudios Internaciones en Latín América* (Santiago: Editorial Universitaria, 1981).
Orega Vicuña, Francisco, *Chile las Modernizaciones Pendientes y su Incidencia en las Relaciones Internacionales para el Siglo XXI* (Santiago: Consejo Chileno Para Las Relaciones Internacionales, 1993).
Orrego Vicúña, Francisco, 'La modernización de la política exterior de Chile' in *Societas: Boletín de la Academia chilena de ciencias sociales, políticas y morales*, 2–3 (1993).
Orrego Vicuña, Francisco, *Testimonio de la Sociedad Chilena en su Transición Hacia un Nuevo Siglo* (Santiago: Academia Chilena de Ciencias Sociales Políticas y Morales. Santiago: Instituto de Chile, 2000).
Piava, Paulo & Gazel, Ricardo, 'Mercosur: Past, Present, and Future', *Nova Economia Belo Horizonte* 13:2 (2003): pp. 115–136.
Pang, Eul-Soo, *The International Political Economy of Transformation in Argentina, Brazil and Chile* (Basingstoke: Palgrave Macmillan, 2002).
Parish, Randall. R., Jr. (2000), *Stability with Hegemony: Brazil, Argentina, and Southern Cone Integration.* NAFTA–MERCOSUR Working Paper Series No 3. The University of Albuquerque, New Mexico.
Parkinson, Fred, 'South America, the Great Powers and the Global System' in Morris, Michael (ed.), *Great Power Relations in Argentina, Chile and Antarctica*, (Basingstoke: Macmillan, 1990).
Paiva, Paulo & Gazel, Ricarda, 'Mercosur: past, present, and future' *Nova Economia Belo Horizonte* 13:2 (2003): pp. 115–136.
Paul, Robert A., 'Freud's Anthropology: A Reading of the "Cultural Books"' in Neu, Jerome (ed.), *The Cambridge Companion to Freud* (Cambridge: Cambridge University Press, 1991).
Peck, F. Taylor, 'Conflict and Challenge: The Transition to Power Politics 1860–1870' in Eugene Davis, John J. Finan & Taylor Peck, *Latin American Diplomatic History* (Baton Rouge: Louisiana State University Press, 1977).
Pendle, George, *A History of Latin America* (Harmondsworth: Penguin, 1964).
Pereira Larrain, Teresa, 'La Consolidación Territorial con las Países Limítrofes', in Sánchez, Walter G. & Pereira, L. (eds), *150 Anos de Política Exterior Chilena* (Santiago: Editorial Universitaria Santiago de Chile, 1977).

Perus, Francoise, 'Modernity, Postmodernity and Novelistic Form in Latin America' in Chanady (ed.), 1994.
Philips, Nicola, 'Integration and Subregionalism in the Americas', *International Affairs* 79:2 (2003): pp. 257–279.
Pike, Frederik, *Chile and the United States* (New York: University of Notre Dame Press, 1983).
Pinochet de la Barra, 'La Antártica Chilena y sus Implicancias Diplomáticas' in Sánchez, Walter G. & Pereira, L. (eds), *150 Anos de Política Exterior Chilena* (Santiago: Editorial Universitaria Santiago de Chile, 1977).
Pinochet de la Barra, 'Chile y sus vecinos' in Muñoz, Heraldo (ed.), *Chile: Política exterior para la democracia* (Santiago: Pehuén Editores, 1989).
Pittman, Howard T., 'Geopolitics and Foreign Policy in Argentina, Brazil and Chile' in Ferris, Elizabeth G. & Lincoln, Jennie K. (eds), *Latin American Foreign Policies. Global and Regional Dimensions* (Boulder. Colo.: Westview Press, 1981).
Podilla Ballestreros, Elias, *La Memoria y el Olvido. Detenidos Desaparecidos en Chile* (Santiago: Ediciones Orígenes, 1994).
Portales C. Carlos & Valdes, Juan Gabriel, 'El futuro de las relaciones chilenos-norteamericanos' in Muñoz, Heraldo (ed.), *Chile: Política Exterior Para la Democracia* (Santiago: Puhúen Editores, 1989).
Portales Cifuentes, Carlos, 'Una Agenda Chile–Brasil para los Noventa in Rojas' in José Garrido & Alamos Varas Pilar (eds), *Relaciones Chile–Brasil en la Década de los noventa* (Santiago:Instituto de Estudios Internacionales, 1992).
Porter, Tony, 'Postmodern Political Realism and International Relations Theory's Third Debate' in Turenne Sjolander, Claire and Cox, Wayne S. (eds), *Beyond Positivism. Critical Reflections on International Relations* (Boulder, Colo.: Lynne Rienner Publishers, 1994).
Puga Cappa, Alvero, 'El pensamiento nacionalista del Gobierno de Chile', *Seguridad Nacional*, Santiago (1976).
Puryear, Jeffrey, *Thinking Politics: Intellectuals in Democracy in Chile* (Baltimore, Maryland; London: Johns Hopkins University Press, 1994).
Quezada, A. Gonzalo, 'Hacia un esquema de los estudios en política exterior de Chile' in *Revista de Ciencia Política* VII: 2 (1985).
Radcliff, Sarah and Westwood, Sallie, *Remaking the Nation. Place, Identity and Politics in Latin America* (London; New York: Routledge, 1996).
Ramos, Joseph & Ulloa Urrutia, Alfil, 'El Tratado de Libre Comercio entre Chile y Estados Unidos', *Estudios Internacionales* 141 (2003): pp. 45–68.
Rapoport, Maria, *El Laberinto Argentino* (Buenos Aires: Editorial Universitaria de Buenos Aires, 1997).
Ray, James Lee, 'International Relations in Latin America, Conflict and Cooperation' in Knippers Black (ed.), *Latin America. Its Promise and its Promise* (Boulder, Colo.: Westview, 1991).

Rayas Arevena, Francisco, *Chile y Argentina: hacia una política de complementación binacional y subregional* in *La política exterior chilena en el 97: los desafíos en la reinserción in Chile 1997 Análisis y Opiniones* (Santiago: Flacso, 1998).

Reid, Anna, 'Disintegration, dismemberment and discovery of identities and histories: Searching the "gaps" for depositories of alternative memories in the narratives of Diamela Eltit and Carmen Boullosa' in *Bulletin of Latin American Research* 17:1 (1998).

Renan, Ernest, *What is a Nation* in Bhabha, Homi K., 'Dissemination: time, narrative, and the margins of the modern nation' in Bhabha, Homi K. (ed.), *Nation and Narration* (London: Routledge, 1990).

Ricoeur, Paul (edited and translated by Thompson, John B.), *Hermeneutics and the Human Sciences* (Cambridge: Cambridge University Press, 1981).

Ricouer, Paul, 'The Time of Narrating (Erzahlzeit) and Narrated Time (Erzahlle Zeit)' Onega, Susana & Garcia Landa, Jose Angel (eds), *Narratology* (New York; London: Longman, 1996).

Rimoldi de Ladman, Eve, 'Los Gobiernos Constitucionales de Argentina 1983–1998 Similitudes y Diferencias de su Política Exterior' in Rimoldi de Ladman, Eve (ed.), *Política Exterior y Tratados Argentina Chile Mercosur* (Buenos Aires: Ciudad Argentina, 1999).

Rippy, Fred J., *Latin America* (Ann Arbor: The University of Michigan, 1958).

Roa, Armando, *Chile y Estados Unidos: sentido histórico de los pueblos* (Santiago: Dolmen, 1997).

Robben, Antonius, 'The Fear of Indifference: Combatants' Anxieties about Political Identity of Civilians during Argentina's Dirty War' in Koonings, Kees & Kruijt, Dirk (eds), *Societies of Fear. The Legacy of Civil War, Violence and Terror in Latin America* (London: Zed Books, 1999).

Robinson, William I. 'Global Crisis and Latin America', *Bulletin of Latin American Research* 23:2 (2004): pp. 135–153.

Roett, Riordan (ed.), *Mercosur Regional Integration, World Markets* (Boulder, Colo: Lynne Rienner Publishers, 1999).

Rojas Aravena, Francisco, *Construyendo un nuevo perfil externo: Democracia, modernización, pluralismo en Construyendo un nuevo perfil externo: Democracia, modernizacion, pluralismo. La política exterior chilena Enero 1993–Marzo 1994* (Santiago: FLACSO, 1994).

Rojas Aravena, Francisco, 'Chile: Cambio Política e Inserción Internacional 1964–1997', *Estudios Internacionales* 119–120 (1997).

Rojas Aravena, Francisco, *Chile–Peru: revisando las agendas con una mirada de futuro in Chile: entre la II cumbre y la detención de Pinochet* (Santiago: Flacso, 1998).

Rojas Aravena, Francisco, 'Transition in Civil-Military Relations in Chile Contributions in a New Internacional Framework' in Domínguez, Jorge I. (ed.), *International Security and Democracy: Latin America and the Caribbean in the Post-Cold War Era* (Pittsburgh: University of Pittsburgh Press, 1998).

Rojas, Sánchez & Fontaine, Talavera, 'Debate Sobre La Posición de las FF.AA Frente al Gobierno Militar', *Estudios Públicos*, 91 (2003), pp. 301–310.
Rojas, Mix, 'Noción de América Latina' in *Araucania de Chile* 47/48 (1990).
Roniger, Lius & Sznajder, Mario, *The Legacy of Human Rights Violations in Latin America* (Oxford: Open University Press, 1999).
Rorty, Richard, 'Wittgenstein, Heidegger and the Reification of Language' in Guignon, Charles (ed.), *The Cambridge Companion to Heidegger* (Cambridge: Cambridge University Press, 1993).
Rosenhau, James N., *Global Voices. Dialogues in International Relations* (Boulder, Colo: Westview Press, 1993).
Roudinesco, E., *Jacques Lacan: An Outline of the Life and History of a System of Thought* (Oxford: Polity Press, 1997).
Rouquie, Alain & Suffern, Stephen, 'The Military in Latin American Politics Since 1930' in Bethell, Leslie (ed), *The Cambridge History of Latin America* Vol. 6 (Cambridge: Cambridge University Press, 1994).
Ruggie, John Gerard, *Constructing the World Polity* (London; New York: Routledge, 1988).
Rupert, Mark, 'Alienation, Capitalism and the Inter-State System: Towards a Marxian/ Gramscian Critique' in Gill, Stephen (ed.), *Gramsci Historical Materialism and International Relations* (Cambridge; New York: Cambridge University, 1993).
Russell, Roberto & Tokatlian, Juan Gabriel, 'From Antagonistic Autonomy to Relational Autonomy: A Theoretical Reflection from the Southern Cone', *Latin American Politics and Society* 45:1 (2003): pp. 1–24.
Russell, Bertrand, *History of Western Philosophy* (London: Routledge, 1946).
Saccone, María Alejandra, 'Aspectos políticos-diplomáticos de una nueva prioridad de la política exterior argentina: el Mercosur' in CIRIR (eds), *La Política Exterior del Gobierno de Menem. Seguimiento y reflexiones al promediar su mandato* (Rosario: Ediciones CIRIO, 1994).
Sadler, Ted, 'The Postmodernist Politicization of Nietzsche' in Patton, Paul (ed.), *Nietzsche, Feminism and Political Theory* (London; New York: Routledge, 1993).
Safford, Frank, 'Politics, Ideology and Society in Post Independence Spanish America' in Bethell, Leslie (ed.), *The Cambridge History of Latin America* Vol. III (Cambridge: Cambridge University Press, 1985).
Salamovich, Sofia, 'Learning to Recover: The Psychological Effects of Repression' in Angell and Pollack (eds), *The Legacy of Dictatorship: Political, Economic and Social Change in Pinochet's Chile* (The Institute of Latin American Studies. Liverpool: University of Liverpool, 1993).
Sallum Jr. Brasilio, 'The Changing Role of the State: New Patterns of State-Society Relations in Brazil at the End of the Twentieth Century' in D'Alva Kinzo, Maria & Dunkerley, James (eds), *Brazil Since 1985. Economy, Politics and Society* (London: University of London, 2003).

Sánchez, Walter G., 'Las Tendencias Sobresalientes de la Política Exterior Chilena' in Sánchez, Walter G. & Pereira, L. (eds), *150 Anos de Política Exterior Chilena* (Santiago: Editorial Universitaria Santiago de Chile, 1977).

Sánchez, Walter G. & Pereira, L. (eds), *150 Anos de Política Exterior Chilena* (Santiago: Editorial Universitaria Santiago de Chile, 1977).

Scollon, Ron and Scollon Wong, Suzanne, *Intercultural Communication* (Oxford, UK; Cambridge, Mass.; Blackwell Publishers, 1995).

Sehlinger, Peter J, 'Las Armas Diplomáticas de Inversionistas Internacionales Durante la Guerra del Pacifico' in Sánchez, Walter G. & Pereira, L. (eds), *150 Anos de Política Exterior Chilena* (Santiago: Editorial Universitaria Santiago de Chile, 1977).

Sepúlveda Almarza, Alberto, 'Problemas Para el Desarrollo de las Estudios Sobre Relaciones Internacionales en Chile' in Orrego Vicuña, Francisco (ed.), *Los Estudios Internaciones en Latín América* (Santiago: Instituto de Estudios Internacionales de la University de Chile, Editorial Universitaria, 1981).

Shapiro, Samuel, *Cultural Factors in Inter-American Relations* (University Notre Press, 1966).

Shaw, Carolyn M, 'Limits to Hegemonic Influence in the Organization of American States', *Latin American Politics & Society* 45:3 (2003): pp. 59–92.

Shotter, John, *Cultural Politics of Everyday Life* (Buckingham: Open University Press, 1993).

Silva Espejo, Rene, 'La Prensa en la Política Exterior Chilena y en la Configuración de la imagen Internacional del País' in Sánchez, Walter G. & Pereira, L. (eds), *150 Anos de Política Exterior Chilena* (Santiago: Editorial Universitaria Santiago de Chile, 1977).

Silva, Eduardo, *The State and Capital in Chile. Business Elites, Technocrats and Market Economics* (Boulder, Colo.: Westview Press, 1996).

Silva, Eduardo, 'Capital and the Lagos Presidency: Business as Usual', *Bulletin of Latin American Research*, 21:3 (2002): pp. 339–357.

Silva, Patricio, 'Intellectuals, Technocrats and the Social Change in Chile: Past, Present and Future Perspectives' in Angell and Pollack (eds), *The Legacy of Dictatorship: Political, Economic and Social Change in Pinochet's Chile* (The Institute of Latin American Studies. Liverpool: University of Liverpool, 1993).

Silva, Patricio, 'Doing Politics in a Depoliticised Society: Social Change and Political Deactivation in Chile', *Bulletin of Latin American Studies* 23:1 (2004): pp. 30–42.

Skidmore, Thomas E. (ed.), *The Politics of Military Rule* (Oxford: Oxford University Press, 1988).

Skidmore, Thomas. E., 'Studying the History of Latin America, A Case of Hemispheric Convergence', *Latin American Research Review* 33: 1 (1998).

Smith, Anthony. D., *The Nation Invented, Imagined, Reconstructed* (Reno: University of Nevada, 1991).

Smith, Hazel, *European Union Foreign Policy and Central America* (New York: St Martin's Press, 1995).

Smith, Peter H., 'Strategic Options for Latin America in Tulchin, Joseph S. & Espach, Ralph H. (eds), *Latin America in the New International System* (Boulder: Lynne Rienner, 2001).

Smith, Peter H., *Democracy in Latin America* (Oxford; Oxford University Press, 2005).

Smith, Steve, 'Paradigm Dominance in International Relations: The Developments of International Relations as a Science', *Millennium Journal of International Studies* 16:2 (1987): pp. 109–206.

Smith, Joseph, *History of Brazil, 1500–2000* (London: Pearson Education, 2002).

Soares de Lima, Maria Regina, 'Brazil's Response to the New Regionalism in Chile' in Mace, Gordon & Therien, Jean Philippe (eds), *Foreign Policy and Regionalism in the Americas* (Boulder, Colo: Lynne Rienner Publishers, 1996).

Sommer, Dorris, 'Irresistible Romance: the Foundational Fictions of Latin America' in Bhabha, Homi K. (ed), *Nation and Narration* (London: Routledge, 1990).

Sommer, Dorris., 'Love and Country in Latin America: An allegorical Speculation' in Ringrose, M. & Lerner, A. (eds), *Reimagining the Nation* (Buckingham: Millennium Publishing Group, 1993).

Sotomayor Valazquez, Arturo C, 'Civil-Military Affairs and Security Institutions in the Southern Cone: The Sources of Argentine–Brazilian Nuclear Cooperation', *Latin American Politics and Society* 46:4 (2004): pp. 29–60.

Steves, Franklin, *Regional Integration and Democratic Consolidation in the Southern Cone*, Essex Papers in Politics and Government (2000).

Sung Kwak, Joe, *Determinants of Chilean Foreign Policy*, Ph.D Thesis for the University of Liverpool, 1996.

Tapia, Gabriel Gaspar, 'Desafíos y Dilemas de Seguridad en América Latina en la post Guerra Fría', *Estudios Internacionales* 141 (2003): pp. 23–44.

Taylor, Charles, 'Engaged Agency and Background in Heidegger', in Guignon, Charles (ed.), *The Cambridge Companion to Heidegger* (Cambridge University Press, 1993).

Tedesco, Laura, *Democracy in Argentina. Hope and Disillusion* (London: Frank Cass Publishers, 1999).

Tedesco, Laura, 'Democracy in Latin America: Issues of Governance in the Southern Cone', *Bulletin of Latin American Studies*, 23:1 (2004): pp. 30–42.

Toro, A. Horacio, 'Seguridad Nacional y Política Exterior en los Objetivos Nacionales' in Sánchez, Walter G. & Pereira, L. (eds), *150 Anos de Política Exterior Chilena* (Santiago: Editorial Universitaria Santiago de Chile, 1977).

Tulchin, Joseph S., 'Continuity and Change in Argentine Foreign Policy in Munoz, Heraldo & Tulchin, Joseph (eds), *Latin America in World Politics* (Boulder, Colo.: Westview, 1996).

Tulchin, Joseph S. & Espach, Ralph H., 'Latin America in the New International System: A Call for Strategic Thinking' in Tulchin, Joseph S. & Espach, Ralph H, (eds), *Latin America in the New International System* (Boulder, Colo.: Lynne Rienner, 2001).

Turenne Sjolander, Claire and Cox, Wayne S. (eds), *Beyond Positivism. Critical Reflections on International Relations* (Boulder, Colo.: Lynne Rienner Publishers, 1994).

United Nations, *Desarrollo Humano. Las Paradojas de la Modernización* (New York: United Nations, 1998).

United Nations, *Desarrollo Humano. Nosotros los Chilenos Un Desafió Cultural* (New York United Nations, 2002).

Valdivia Ortiz de Zárate, Verónica, 'Estatismo y Neoliberalismo: Un Contrapunto Militar Chile 1973–1979', *Historia Santiago* 34 (2001): pp. 167–226.

Valenzuela, Arturo, *The Breakdown of Democratic Regimes. Chile* (Baltimore; London: Johns Hopkins University Press, 1978).

Valenzuela, Arturo, 'Party Politics and the Crisis of Presidentialism in Chile' in Diamond, Larry, Linz, Juan J. & Lipset, Martin Seymour (eds), *Democracy in Developing Countries* (Boulder, Colo.: Lynne Reinner, 1984).

Valenzuela, Arturo (eds), *The Failure of Parliamentary Democracy* (Baltimore; London: Johns Hopkins University Press, 1994).

Vals Pereira, Lia, 'Towards the Common Market of the South: Mercosur's Origins, Evolution and Challenges' in Roett, Riordan (ed.), *Mercosur Regional Integration, World Markets* (Boulder, Colo: Lynne Rienner Publishers, 1999).

Van Klaveren, Alberto, 'El análisis de la política exterior latinoamericana: perspectivas teóricas' in Munoz, Heraldo & Tulchin, Joseph (eds), *Entre la autonomía y la subordinación. Política exterior de los países latinoamericanos* (Santiago: Grupo Editor Latinamericos, 1984).

Van Klaveren, Alberto, 'Chile: la política exterior de la transición', *América Latina Internacional* 1:2 (1994).

Van Klaveren, Alberto, 'Understanding Latin American Foreign Policies' in Munoz, Herlado & Tulchin, Joseph (eds), *Latin America in World Politics* (Boulder, Colo: Westview, 1996).

Van Klaveren, Alberto, *Hacia un regionalismo abierto in Estudio Internacionales* (Santiago: Instituto de Estudios Internacionales de la Universidad de Chile, 1997).

Van Klaveren, Alberto, 'Inserción internacional de Chile' in Toloza, Cristian & Lahera, Eugenio (eds), *Chile en los noventa* (Santiago: Dolmen Ediciones, 1998).

Van Klaveren, Alberto, interview. The Ministry of External Affairs. Santiago November, 2000.

Vasquez, John A., 'Colouring it Morgenthau: New Evidence for an Old Thesis on Quantitive International Politics' in Vasquez, John A. (ed.), *Classics of International Relations* (London: Prentice Hall, 1990).

Véliz, Claudio, 'Nacionalismo, Globalizaciones y la Sociedad Chilena', *Estudios Internacionales* 127–128 (1999): pp. 35–53.

Vera Castillo, Jorge, 'Política Exterior Chilena y MERCOSUR: Hacia una Seguridad Subregional con Medidias de Confianza Mutua (2000–2010)', *Estudios Internacionales* 126 (1999).

Verdugo, Patricia, *Chile, Pinochet and the Caravan of Death* (Miami: North–South Centre Press, 2001).

Vial Correa, Gonzalo, *Histórica de Chile (1981–1973)* Vol. II (Santiago: Editorial Santilliana, Santiago, 1981).

Vial Correa, Gonzalo, *Historia de Chile. Educación Media* (Santiago: Santillana, 1994).

Vidal, Hernán, *Política Cultural de la Memoria Histórica, Derechos Humanos y Discursos Cultural en Chile* (Santiago: Mosquito Editores, 1997).

Villalobos R. Sergio, 'La Situación Internacional y la Independencia e Identidad Nacional' in Sánchez, Walter G. & Pereira, L. (eds), *150 Anos de Política Exterior Chilena* (Santiago: Editorial Universitaria Santiago de Chile, 1977).

Villalobos, Sergio, *Historia del Pueblo Chileno* (Santiago: Editorial Universitaria, 1999).

Waddell, D.A.G., 'International Politics and Latin American Independence' in Bethell, Leslie, *The Cambridge History of Latin America* Vol. III (Cambridge: Cambridge University Press, 1985).

Walker, R.B.J., *Explorations in Peace and Justice: New Perspectives on World Order* (Boulder, Colo.: Lynne Rienner, 1988).

Walker, R.B.J., 'The *Prince* and "The "Pauper": Tradition, Modernity, and Practice in the Theory of International Relations' in Der Derian, James & Shapiro, Michael J. (eds), *International/Intertextual Relations. Post Modern Readings of World Politics*, Lexington, Mass.: Lexington Books, 1989.

Walz, Kenneth, *Theory of International Politics* (New York: McGraw-Hill, 1979).

Waltz, Kenneth N., 'Anarchic Orders and Balances of Power' in Keohane, Robert (ed.), *Neorealism and its Critics* (New York: Columbia University Press, 1986).

Waltz, Kenneth. N., 'Law and Theories' in Keohane, Robert (ed), *Neorealism and its Critics* (New York: Columbia University Press, 1986).

Waltz, Kenneth N., 'Political Structures' in Keohane, Robert (ed.), *Neorealism and its Critics* (New York: Columbia University Press, 1986).

Weber, Samuel, 'Mass Mediauras; or, Art, Aura and Media in the work in the work of Walter Benjamin' in Ferris, David S. (ed.), *Walter Benjamin, Theoretical Questions* (Stanford: Stanford University Press, 1996).

Weigel, Sigrid, *Body and Image Space. Re-Reading Walter Benjamin* (London, New York: Routledge, 1996).

Weeks, Gregory, 'The "Lessons" of Dictatorship: Political Learning and the Dictatorship in Chile', *Bulletin of Latin American Research* 21:3 (2002): pp. 396–412.

Whelan, James R., *Out of the Ashes* (Washington: Regney Gateway, 1989).

Whitaker, Arthur P., *The United States and the Southern Cone* (Cambridge, Mass.: Harvard University Press, 1976).

White, Hayden, 'The Value of Narrativity in the Representation of Reality' in Onega, Susana & Garcia Landa, Jose Angel (eds), *Narratology* (New York; London: Longman, 1996).

Whitehead, Laurence, 'The European Union and the Americas' in Bulmer-Thomas, Victor & Dunkerley, James (eds), *The United States and Latin America: The New Agenda* (London: Institute of Latin American Affairs, 1999).
Wight, Martin, 'The Balance of Power' in Butterfield, Herbert & Wight, Martin (eds.), *Diplomatic Investigations. Essays in the Theory of International Politics* (London: George Allen and Unwin Ltd., 1966).
Wight, Martin, *Power Politics* (Harmondsworth, Penguin, 1979).
Wilde, Alexander, 'Irruptions of Memory: Expressive Politics in Chile's Transition to Democracy', *Journal of Latin American Studies* 31:2 (1999): pp. 473–500.
Wilhelmy, Manfred, 'Hacia un Análisis de la Política Exterior Chilena Contemperaría', *Estudios Internacionales* 48 (1979).
Wilhelmy, Manfred, 'Politics, Bureaucracy and Foreign Policy in Chile' in Orrego Vicuña, Francisco (ed.), *Los Estudios Internacionales en Latín América* (Santiago: Instituto de Estudios Internacionales de la Universidad de Chile. Santiago: Editorial Universitaria, 1981).
Wilhelmy, Manfred, 'Las decisiones de política exterior en Chile' in Russell, Roberto (ed.), *Política exterior y la toma de decisiones en América Latina* (Santiago: Grupo Editor Latinoamericano, 1990).
Wilhelmy, Wilfred, 'Las objetivos de la política exterior latinoamericana', *Estudios Internacionales* 94 (1991).
Wilhelmy, Manfred & Fuentes, Cristián, 'De la reinserción a la diplomacia para el desarrollo: política exterior de Chile 1992–1994' in Van Klaveren, Alberto, *América Latina en el mundo* (Santiago, Propel Editorial los Andes, 1997).
Wilhelmy, Manfred & Infante, Maria Teresa, 'La Política Exterior Chilena en los Anos 90: El Gobierno del Presidente Aylwin y Algunas Proyecciones', *Estudios Sociales* 75:1 (1993).
Wilhelmy, Manfred & Lazo, Rosa Maria, 'La Política Multilateral de Chile en Asia-Pacifico', *Estudios Internacionales* 117 (1997): pp. 3–35.
Williams, Colin H., *Called Unto Liberty* (Clevedon: Multilingual Matters, 1994).
Williamson, Edwin, *The Penguin History of Latin America* (London: Penguin, 1992).
Wittgenstein, Ludwig, *Culture and Value*, translated by Peter Winch (Chicago: The University of Chicago Press, 1980).
Wolin, Richard, *Walter Benjamin. An Aesthetic Redemption* (New York: Columbia University Press, 1982).
Young, Robert, *Intercultural Communication. Pragmatics, Genealogy, Deconstruction* (Clevedon: Multilingual Matters, 1996).
Zea, Leopoldo, *The Latin American Mind* (Norman, Okla: University of Oklahoma Press, 1963).
Zea, Leopoldo, *Latin America and the World* (Norman, Okla.: University of Oklahoma, 1969).
Zelinsky, Wilbur, *The Shifting Symbolic Foundations of American Nationalism* (Chapel Hill: North Carolina Press, 1988).

Zizek, Slavoj, *Looking Awry. An Introduction to Jacques Lacan through Popular Culture* (Cambridge, Mass; London: Massachusetts Institute of Technology, 1991).

Zizek, Slavoj, *Tarrying with the Negative. Kant, Hegel and the Critique of Ideology* (Durham: Duke University Press, 1993).

Zizek, Slavoj, 'Fantasy as a political category' in Elizabeth and Edmond Wright (eds), *The Zizek Reader* (Oxford, UK; Malden, MA.: Blackwell Publishers, 1999).

Index

Note: Numbers in brackets preceded by *n* refer to footnotes. Bold page numbers indicate maps.

ABC countries 1, 22, 33-4, 49-50, 127-30
   see also Argentina; Brazil; Chile
ABC, El Tratado de (1915) 50
africanization 4
Alberti, Juan Bautista 49
Alfonsín, Raúl 22, 57, 58, 59, 86, 119
Allende government 41, 101-2(*n*2), 113, 120, 123
   overthrow of 101, 108
Altamirano, Carlos 101(*n*2)
Alwyn government 111-12, 116-17
Ancon, Treaty of (1883) 101
Andean Pact 111
Angola 83
anti-Americanism 120-1, 130
anti-communism 82, 83, 104, 109, 116
Araucanian War 107
Aravena, Chile-Peru 124
Arendt, Hannah 29(*n*31), 40
Argentina 5, 19, **46**, 47-71, **100**, 127
   and Brazil 6, 9, 14, 15-16, 47, 49-50, 57, 59-62, 70-1, 129
      democratization and 93
      future of 97, 99
      history of relations 78, 79, 85-7, 95-6
      Iguaçu Declaration (1985) 86
      Mercosur issues 88, 88(*n*45), 89-90, 132, 133
   Buenos Aires 50, 53, 86
      province 48-9
   and Chile 7, 9, 14, 48, 49-50, 56-7, 62, 65, 118-20, 124-5
   and Cuba 65, 68
   democracy in 8, 10, 15, 16, 48, 57-60
   development in 24, 49
   dirty war in 30, 39, 59
   economy of 50, 51, 54-5
      crises in 55
         hyperinflation 47, 63
      exports 6, 54-5, 68
      internal market 13
      trade relations 58
      wages 54
   elite of 32-3, 51, 70
   and Falklands/Malvinas *see* Falklands/Malvinas
   gauchos in 32, 49
   geography of 47, 49(*n*1)
   global ambition of 47, 52
   history of 48-52
   human rights in 55, 57
   immigration in 50
   indigenous peoples of 32, 49
   and Mercosur 1-2, 20, 34, 47, 60-2, 66-71, 129, 132
   military rule of 48, 52, 54-7, 133-4
      legacy 43, 57, 58-9, 63, 127-8, 134
   national identity in 10-11, 14, 27, 48, 50, 52-4
      and dictatorship 58-9
      exceptionalism 48, 53, 59
      historical legacy 30, 42, 43-4, 63, 127-8, 134
      and political violence 38-9, 42
   national security of 14
   and NATO 15, 65
   Patagonia 49
   Peronist era 52
   political violence in 38-9
   realist foreign policy in 22-3, 63-5, 66, 70
   regionalism in 47-8, 65-6
   unemployment/poverty in 13
   and US 7, 10-11, 14-16, 47-8, 51-2, 56
      anti-Americanism 79, 130
      policy shift towards 62-3, 65-8, 129
Arica 9, 40, 108, 117
armed forces 7
   -civilian relations 22
   see also military rule
Asia 5, 129

see also China; India; Japan
Asuncion, Treaty of (1991) 12
autonomy 10-11, 63-4, 70, 83, 95-6, 128
Aylwin government 11, 104, 119

Bachelet, Michelle 125($n64$)
Barriero, Major 57
Bauman, Zymunt 42
Beagle channel dispute 118-19
Beirsteker, Thomas J. 27($n26$)
Bello, Andres 106-7
Benjamin, Walter 30, 36
Bessone, Gen Diaz 39
Bielsa, Rafael 68, 99
Bolivar, Simon 14, 108
Bolivia 7, 8-9, 38, **46**, 49, **72**, 96, **100**, 101, 117-18, 125
Bonifácio, José 77
border disputes 7, 8-9
Borges, Jorge Luis 51, 53
Branco, Castelo 80, 81
Brazil **72**, 73-99, 127
   and Argentina see under Argentina
   autonomy of 83, 95-6, 98-9
   and Chile 9, 123, 124
   and Cuba 96
   democratization in 8, 16, 23-4, 43, 92-3
   development in 74-5, 81, 93, 94, 98
   economy of 12, 73
      crises in 84-5, 93
      growth in 74-5, 81, 93, 98
      internal market 13
      international trade 79, 84-5, 94-5, 96-9, 129-30
   and EU 90, 99
   Foreign Ministry (*Itamaraty*) 6, 12, 43, 75, 78, 84, 85, 97
      influence of 92-3, 94-5, 98, 128
   and FTAA 87-9, 95, 97
   geography of 76, 78
   global ambition of 5, 6-7, 59, 73, 96-7
   history of 76-81
      colonial 73-4, 76-7
   human rights in 82-3
   Lula's policies 94-7
   and Mercosur 1-2, 16, 69-71, 86-92, 97-9, 123, 129, 131, 132
   military rule in 75, 80-1
      legacy of 93, 128

   national identity 10, 27, 43, 48, 75, 80, 83
   national security of 14, 80-1, 83-4
   people of 73
      racial mix 77
   poverty/inequality in 79-80
   realist foreign relations in 85, 87-8
   regional ambition of 1, 5-7, 17, 19-20, 24, 65, 74, 85-92, 123, 128-9, 133
      diplomacy in 95-6, 98-9
      hidden agenda for 92-3
   and UN 73, 79
   and US 7, 12, 15, 17, 19-20, 59, 73, 74-5, 86, 91, 93
      aid 81, 82
      autonomy and 95-6, 98-9, 128-31
      history of relations 77-9, 81-5
      Itamaraty and 94-5, 98
   and Venezuela 96
Britain 51, 52, 55-6, 65, 69
   and Brazil 73, 74, 76, 78-9
Buenos Aires 50, 53, 86
   province 48-9
Bull, Hedley 20($n3$)
Bush, George Sr 66
Bush, George W. 67, 87, 96, 125, 133

Caldas, Ricardo Wahrendroft 92-3, 98($n78$)
Calvo Clause 108
Cammack, Paul 91
Campos del Hielos 119
Canada 5
Cancun talks 61, 97, 129
Cardoso, Fernando Henrique 13, 80($n17$), 85, 89, 94, 98
Caribbean 4
Carranza, Mario 91
Carribean 128
Carter, Jimmy 56, 82, 128
Castro, Fidel 96
Cavallo, Domingo Felipe 23, 64
Central America 3, 56, 128
CEPAL 92
Chakrabarti Pasic, Sujata 24
Chavez, Hugo 15, 16, 68, 74, 96, 130
'Chicago Boys' 102
Chile 5, 19, **100**, 101-25, 127
   Allende government see Allende government

and Argentina 7, 9, 14, 48, 49-50, 56-7, 62, 65, 118-20, 124-5
armed forces of 39-42
and Bolivia 7, 8-9, 38, 101, 117-18, 125
border disputes 101, 117, 118-19, 125
and Brazil 9, 86, 123, 124
Concertación 23, 24(*n*14), 103
copper industry in 115, 117
democratization in 8, 11-12, 16, 30, 62, 102, 104, 111-14, 119
diplomacy of 106-7
economy of
    foreign investment 115
    growth/ development in 11-12, 13, 24, 102, 103-4, 112, 114-15
    international trade 11-12, 103, 115, 121-4
        bilateral agreements 1, 117, 122, 124, 129
        global 6
        and NAFTA 14, 121, 122, 129
    under military rule 102
and Europe 116-17
exceptionalism in 13-14, 107-8, 109-11, 113
geography of 13-14, 101
history of 48, 105-9
human rights in 62, 103, 114
illegal immigration in 9
and Mercosur 1, 13, 16, 20, 105, 118, 119-20, 122, 125, 129, 132
military rule in 9, 11, 40-2, 101-3, 111, 133-4
    legacy of 43, 57, 62, 102, 104, 127-8, 134
military spending in 111-12
national identity in 10, 14, 23, 27, 48, 125
    and historical legacy 30, 40-2, 43-4, 105, 107, 110-11, 127-8, 134
    and policy making 105-6, 107-9, 124
    and political violence 39-42
national security of 101
and Peru 7, 8-9, 117, 125
poverty in 13
realist policies in 23, 103
regionalism of 122-4
secret police of (DINA) 40(*n*68)

and UN 17, 116
and US 7, 14-15, 105, 108, 116, 120-2, 124, 129, 130
    as Pacific rival 109
China
    and Argentina 68
    and Brazil 5, 83, 90, 97
    and Chile 124
Cisneros, Andrés 65
Clinton, Bill 60, 85, 116, 120
coalition of the willing 17
Cold War 56, 84, 104-5, 116, 128
    US foreign relations in 4
Collor de Mello government 58, 58(*n*32), 85
Colombia 15, 17, 95, 132
colonialism 14
copper 115, 117
Correa, C. 85
Correa, Enrique 112
Costa Rica 17, 95
Cuba 15, 65, 68, 96
culture 9-10, 24, 37-9, 44

Da Motta Veiga, Pedro 15
da Silva, Lula 5, 16, 34, 68, 87, 89-90, 93, 98, 123, 124, 130
    effects of policies of 94-7
Dasein 29, 29(*nn*31, 32)
de Lima, Soares 15
de los Andes, San Martin 48
de Rosas, Juan Miguel 48-9
de San Martin, José 14
democratization 7-9, 16, 127, 133-4
    and foreign policy 22
    see also under individual countries
destiny, notions of 44
development 11, 12-13, 24
Di Tella, Guido 23, 44, 64, 67
Diamint, Rut 22(*n*10)
DINA 40(*n*68)
diplomacy 93, 94, 95-6, 97, 106-7, 128
Dominican Republic 17
Drago Doctrine 51, 70
Drago, Luis María 51

ECLAC (Economic Commission for Latin American Co-operation) 102
Ecuador 117

El Salvador 17, 56
empiricism 26
Errázuriz Correa, Hernán Felipe 120
Escudé, Carlos 9
Europe 51, 52, 53, 84, 105
European Union (EU) 2, 7, 105
   and Brazil 90, 99
   and Mercosur 4-5, 68, 90, 99, 129, 130, 132
exceptionalism 10, 13-14, 33, 48, 53, 59, 66, 70, 92

Falklands/Malvinas 8, 38, 39, **46**, 47, 55-6, 57, 69
Fermandios, Joaquín 112
Fernández, Alberto 67
Fernández, Aníbal 67
Fernández, Joaquin 120-1
Figari, Guillermo Miguel 52
Figueiredo regime 86, 95
First World War 50, 79
Fontana, Andrés 9
foreign policy formation 2, 127-34
   and democratization 22, 127-8
   and national identity 9-11, 42, 44-5
Foucault, Michel 26(*n*23), 36-8
free trade/market 87-8, 93, 102, 121-2, 129
Free-trade Area of the Americas *see* FTAA
Frei Montalva, Eduardo 11, 115, 120, 121, 123, 134
Frondizi, Arturo 53
FTAA (Free-trade Area of the Americas) 5, 61, 62, 74, 87-9, 91, 95, 97, 125
Fuentes, Cristian 111
Fujimori government 117

G77 82, 85
Galtieri regime 56, 59
Garreton, M.A. 115
GATT 84, 95
gauchos 32, 49
Gazmuri, Cristián 41
Geertz, Clifford 30-1, 42
Geisel regime 82, 83, 93
George, Jim 26
Germany 51, 82
Giddens, Anthony 31-2
Gilpin, Robert 9-10
Gomez Mera, Laura 61

Goulart government 80, 81, 98
Gramscian School 36-8
Great Depression 52
Group of 77 (G77) 82, 85
Guerro Yoachim, Christián 109
Gulf War (1991) 65, 69

Hamilton, Paul 34
Harking Bill (1976) 82-3
Heidegger, Martin 26, 28-9, 30
Heine, Jorge 104
hemispheric free-trade area 2, 6, 12, 14
Hirst, Monica 4, 8, 116
historical narrative 34-6, 39-44
Hobden, Stephen 21-2(*n*9)
Hosti, K.J. 25
Hugueney, Clodoaldo 89
human rights 8, 55, 57, 82-3, 128, 133
Hurrel, Andrew 86
hyperinflation 47, 63

Iguaçu Declaration (1985) 86
immigration 9, 50
import substitution model 16
India 131
   and Brazil 5, 85, 97, 99
Infante, Maria Teresa 114
Insulsa, José Miguel 44, 105, 110, 117, 124
intellectual property rights 84
international relations 2-3, 9-10, 17, 20-9, 134
   historical narrative in 30-1, 34-6
   moral basis of 51
   realism/neorealism in *see* realism/neorealism
   universalism/localism in 24-9
intervention
   military 8
   unilateral 3-4
Iraq War (2003) 3, 17, 120, 124
Italy 51

Japan 84, 90
Jara, Victor 40

Keohane, Robert 20, 20(*n*3)
Kirchner government 16, 67-8, 69, 87, 89-90, 124
Klom, Andy 90, 92, 94

Index

Lagos, Gustavo 103, 111
Lagos, Ricardo 62, 116, 120, 123
Laguna del Desierto 119
Lapper, Richard 68
Latin America
  autonomy in 63-4
  civilian-military relations in 113
  colonial period 76-7
  democratization in 92
  elite-local relations in 32-3
  interventionism in 102
  regional identity in 53, 108, 110-11, 123-4
  regionalism in 89-90
  security of 83-4
  trade of 4
  US and *see under* United States
  see also ABC countries; Southern Cone; *and see individual countries*
League of Nations 79
Letelier, Orlando 114
Lima Convention (1993) 117
Locke, John 26
Lowental, David 31
Lula *see* Da Silva, Lula
Lyotard, Jean-Francois 35, 53

McCann, Frank D. 77
Machiavellian politics 20($n3$)
Madrid, Treaty of (1750) 74, 76
Malvinas *see* Falklands/Malvinas
manifest destiny 66($n60$)
Martinez de Hoz, José 54, 55
Marxism 26, 36-7, 39
  see also anti-communism
Medici regime 80, 82
Menem, Carlos 7, 10, 15, 39, 58($n32$), 60, 63, 69, 134
  and realism 22-3, 24, 27, 33
  and US 64, 65, 66, 67, 129
Mercosur 1-2, 6-8, 13-14, 16-17, 118, 127
  and Argentina *see under* Argentina
  and Brazil *see under* Brazil
  and Chile *see under* Chile
  Common External Tariff 61($n40$), 129
  crises in 61-2
  and EU 4-5, 68, 90, 99, 129, 130, 132
  and FTAA 87-9
  politicization of 68-9, 132-3
  and US 19-20, 34, 61, 87, 89-90, 96, 130
Mexico
  and NAFTA 5
  and US 3, 131
Middle East 4, 38, 83, 97
military rule 23, 127
  human rights abuses in 8
  legacy 43
  and national identity 38-42
  see also under individual countries
military tutelage 92, 104, 111-12
Miller, David 14
Mitre, Pres 49
Molina Doctrine 41
Monroe Doctrine 51, 77-8
Morgenthau, Hans J. 20-1($n3$), 25, 44
Moro, Battle of 40
Morse, Richard M. 33
Munoz, Heraldo 123
Munroe Doctrine (1823) 3

NAFTA (North American Free-trade Area) 5, 95, 116, 121, 122
Nagel, Thomas 28
nationalism/national identity 9-11, 31-4
  and disparate cultures 32
  exceptionalism 10, 13-14, 33
  and historical narrative 34-6
  and political violence 38-45
  see also under individual countries
NATO 15
natural resources 3, 115, 117
neorealism *see* realism/neorealism
Neufeld, Mark 25
Nicaragua 17, 56, 67
9/11
  post- 36($n59$), 61, 94
    US foreign relations 3-4
Nixon, Richard 82, 131
non-intervention 51
non-proliferation agreements 9
Norden, Deborah L. 62-3
Noriega, Roger 67
nuclear issues 9, 82

OAS (Organization of American States) 124
oil 3
open regionalism 5

Orrego Vicuña, Fransisco 41

Pacific, War of (1871-3) 9, 49, 101, 108, 109, 117
Panama 17
Papal Treaties (1984) 118-19
Paraguay **46**, 49, 78, 86, 132
    and Mercosur 1
Parish, Randall 89
Patagonia 49
Paz y Amistad, Tratado de (1984) 62
peripheral realism 3
Peru 7, 8-9, 49, **72**, 95, **100**, 117, 125
Perus, Francois 32
Philips, Nicola 91
Pike, Frederick B. 109
Pinochet, Augusto 11, 13, 23, 40-2, 55(*n*22), 103, 113-14, 116, 120
    arrest of 103, 107, 107(*n*19), 114
police, secret 40(*n*68), 114
Portugal 5, 76
post-colonialism 27, 32
power 36-8
    maximizer, state as 20, 22-3, 25, 28
    soft/hard 36
Prebisch, Paul 102

Quadros government 81

rational actor, state as 20, 23, 25, 28
Reagan, Ronald 56, 85, 128
realism/neorealism 3, 9, 17, 20-4, 34
    agency problem 25
    English School 20-1(*n*3)
    four tenets of 20-1
    inclusivity/localism in 24-9
    objectivity in 28
    peripheral 3, 24, 63-5, 83(*n*27)
    perspective school 23
    reductionism in 21
    scientific method in 20(*n*3), 21, 26
realismo periférico 3, 24, 63-5
regime change, in US foreign policy 3-4
regionalism 5, 7-8, 13-15
Ricouer, Paul 26, 27
Rio Branco (Brazilian foreign minister) 78, 78(*n*10)
Rio de Janeiro 76, 77, 78
River Plate region 96

Robinson, William I. 13
Rojas Sánchez, Gonzalo 41
Rolls Royce 69
Roosevelt Corollary (1904) 3
Rosas 78
Ruggie, John Gerard 27-8
Russell, Roberto 62-3

Sanchez, Walter G. 110
Sarmiento, Domingo Faustino 32, 49, 52-3
Sarney, José 86, 92
Second World War 79
security, national 9, 24
    see also under specific countries
Silva, Costa e 81
Silva, Patricio 112
Smith, Peter H. 92
Smith, Steve 25
Soares de Lima, Maria Regina 83
Sotomayor, Arturo C. 58
South Africa 97
South-South regionalism 5, 123, 132
Southern Cone 1, 85-92, 127, 133
    and Asia 5, 115
    Brazil's dominance of 7, 19-20, 59, 95-6
    colonial period 14
    democratization in 7-9, 22, 43, 75, 92-3
    economic development in 11, 12-13, 115, 134
    economic foreign policy in 11-13
    EU relations with 4-5
    foreign investment in 5
    inter-state conflict in 7
    internal/external politics in 24
    and Iraq War 3, 17
    national identity in 9-11, 14
        and political violence 38-45
    regionalism in 5-6, 13-15, 31-4, 89-90
    and US 2, 3-4, 14-17, 96, 115, 116, 130
    see also ABC countries; *and see individual countries*
Soviet Union 4, 84
Spain 5, 90
    as colonial power 14, 48, 76, 77, 107(*n*19)

Tacna 108, 117, 123
tariffs 102, 122, 129
Taylor, Charles 29

'thick present' 30-1, 42
Third World 66, 93, 96-7, 123
'Third Worldism' 63, 81-2
Tierra del Fuego 7, 47, 49, 62
trade
    Asia-Latin America 5
    and development 16-17
    EU-Mercosur 4-5, 68-9
    free 4-5
        see also hemispheric free-trade area
    global 12
    intra-regional 1, 6
    sanctions 84-5
    South-South 5
    US-Latin America 2, 4
    see also Mercosur; *and see under*
        specific countries
trade unions 54
Triple Alliance, War of (1864-70) 49, 78
Tulchin, Joseph S. 22, 53, 54, 59, 66,
    66(*n*61)

unemployment 102
unilateral intervention 3-4
United Nations (UN) 15, 65, 82
    Security Council 3, 17, 116, 120, 124
    Brazil and 73, 79
United States 114
    and ABC countries 50
    foreign aid from 82-3
    hegemony of 1, 2, 7, 12, 128-9
        limits of 3, 10-11, 17, 116
    and Iraq War 120
    and Mercosur 19-20, 34, 61, 87, 89-90,
        96, 130
    relations with Latin America 2, 19-20,
        33-4, 51, 56, 59, 60, 96, 128, 131-2
    activities in Central America 56
    trade 5, 7, 61
    unilateral intervention of 3-4
    and War on Terror 4, 36(*n*59)
    see also under individual countries
Uruguay **46**, 49, 78
    and Mercosur 1

Valdivia Ortiz de Zárate, Verónica 41
van Klaveren, Alberto 106(*n*15), 113, 119,
    121
Varas, Pilar Alamos 109, 110
Vasquez, John A. 20-1
Vatican 118-19
Venezuela 15, 16, 51, 68, 86, 96, 124, 125,
    130, 131, 133
Vicuna, Orrego 109, 110-11
Videla regime 54, 59

Wahrendroft Caldas, Ricardo 92-3, 98(*n*78)
Walker, R.B.J. 37-8
Waltz, Kenneth 21
War on Terror 3, 4
Warren, Christopher 82
water issues 3
Westinghouse 82
White, Hayden 35
Wight, Martin 20(*n*3)
Wilde, Alexander 24(*n*14)
Wilhelmy, Manfred 111, 114
Williamson, Edwin 52
WTO (World Trade Organization) 61, 97

Yrigoyen, Hipólito 51
Yrigoyenismo 51